JUNIOR
LISTENING EXPERT

A Theme-Based Listening Course for Young EFL Learners

Level **1**

JUNIOR
LISTENING EXPERT

Level 1

Series Editor	Dong-sook Kim
Project Editors	Yu-jin Lee, Hyun-joo Lee, Ji-hee Lee
Contributing Writers	Patrick Ferraro, Rebecca Cant, Susan Kim
Illustrators	Kyung-ho Jung, Eun-jung Shin
Design	Hoon-jung Ahn, Ji-young Ki, Hye-jung Yoon, Min-shin Ju
Editorial Designer	Jong-hee Kim
Sale	Ki-young Han, Kyung-koo Lee, In-gyu Park, Cheol-gyo Jeong, Nam-jun Kim, Woo-hyun Lee
Marketers	Hye-sun Park, Kyung-jin Nam, Ji-won Lee, Yeo-jin Kim
ISBN	979-11-253-4044-7
Photo Credits	www.fotolia.com
	www.dreamstime.com
	www.istockphoto.com

INTRODUCTION

Junior Listening Expert is a four-level listening series for EFL learners, particularly older elementary school students and junior high school students. Systematically designed to improve listening skills, its audio material is offered in a variety of formats, covering a wide-range of topics.

Features

Theme-Based Units

Every level contains twelve units, each covering a lively topic such as food, lifestyle, sports, IT, or social issues. A variety of listening formats expose students not only to everyday dialogues, but also to more advanced informative material.

Systematic Design

Each unit is composed of five closely related sections that allow students to develop their listening skills step-by-step. As students pass through each of the five sections, they have the opportunity to evaluate their progress and build confidence in their listening abilities.

A Variety of Question Types

A variety of question types are provided, including identifying the main idea, finding specific details, and making inferences. These serve to familiarize students with the standard types of listening test formats.

A Focus on Critical Thinking

Students are not only exposed to social issues through the listening material, but are also encouraged to think about these issues and form their own opinions.

Format

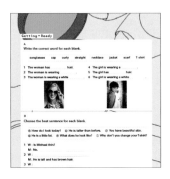

Getting Ready

This section utilizes a quiz to introduce the key vocabulary words and expressions that will appear in the unit. It is designed to facilitate easier understanding for students preparing to tackle challenging topics in English.

Listening Start

In this section, students have the chance to check their listening comprehension and master key expressions by answering questions and taking dictation. This prepares them for the Listening Practice and Listening Challenge sections.

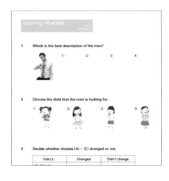

Listening Practice

Students are given the opportunity to practice a variety of listening question types in this section. It enables them to develop the different listening skills required for each question type.

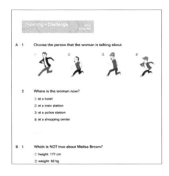

Listening Challenge

This section presents students with two long listening passages and a pair of checkup questions for each passage. This section challenges students to understand a higher level of English and upgrade their listening skills.

Critical Thinking

This section encourages students to think about a social issue related to the unit's topic. After listening to different opinions about an issue, students develop their own opinion, which they then express in a speaking activity.

Vocabulary List

This section provides easy access to key vocabulary. It contains the new vocabulary words from each unit.

Dictation

This section focuses on helping students improve the accuracy of their listening skills by requiring them to take dictation.

Table of **Contents**

UNIT 01   Appearance   8

UNIT 02   School Life   14

UNIT 03   Transportation & Location   20

UNIT 04   Seasons & Weather   26

UNIT 05   Family   32

UNIT 06   Friends   38

UNIT 07   Music   44

UNIT 08   Holidays   50

UNIT 09   Shopping   56

UNIT 10   Advice   62

UNIT 11   Boys & Girls   68

UNIT 12   Jobs   74

           Vocabulary List   80

           Dictation   87

01 Appearance

Getting ★ Ready

A

Write the correct word for each blank.

| sunglasses | cap | curly | straight | necklace | jacket | scarf | T-shirt |

1 The woman has _____ hair.
2 The woman is wearing _____.
3 The woman is wearing a white _____.

4 The girl is wearing a _____.
5 The girl has _____ hair.
6 The girl is wearing a white _____.

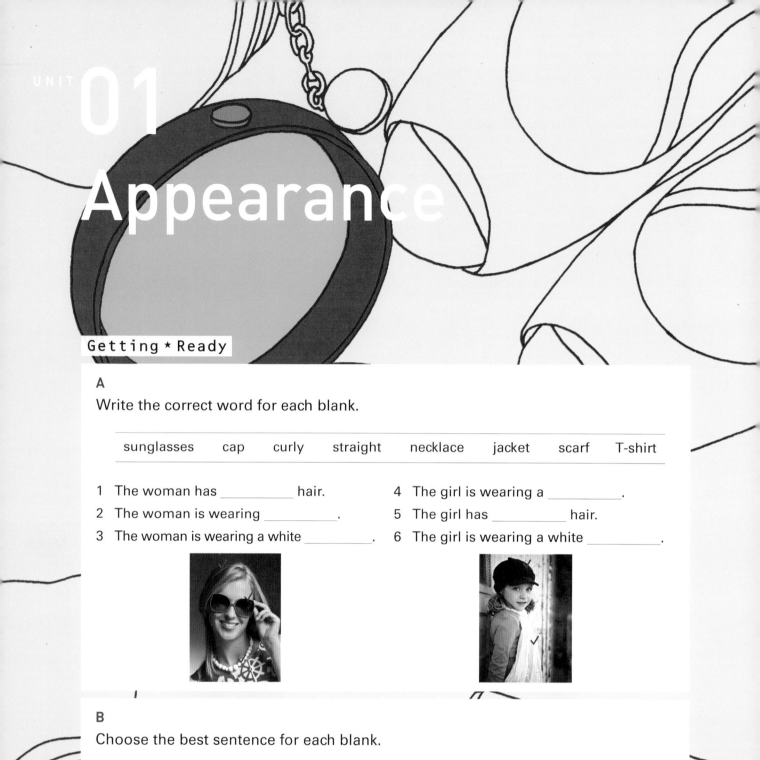

B

Choose the best sentence for each blank.

ⓐ How do I look today?   ⓑ He is taller than before.   ⓒ You have beautiful skin.
ⓓ He is a little fat.   ⓔ What does he look like?   ⓕ Why don't you change your T-shirt?

1 W : Is Michael thin?
   M : No. _____

2 W : _____
   M : He is tall and has brown hair.

3 W : _____
   M : You look great.

1   Choose Julia in the picture.

+ Listen again and fill in the blanks.

M: Mom, _____ _____ this picture of my classmates.

W: Oh, is your friend Julia in the picture?

M: Yes. She's _____ _____.

W: You mean the girl with a hair band?

M: No, she's Nancy. Julia is wearing a necklace.

W: Oh, I found her. She's _____ _____.

2   Which part of Angelina's face does the boy like most?

① eyes

② skin

③ mouth

④ lips

+ Listen again and fill in the blanks.

M: Angelina is _____ _____ _____. She has beautiful big blue eyes. I _____ her eyes _____. She also has very beautiful skin. She has a wide mouth, and her lips are _____ _____. Some people don't like her lips, but I like them.

1   Which is the best description of the man?

① ② ③ ④

2   Choose the child that the man is looking for.

①    ②   ③   ④

3   Decide whether each choice changed or not.

Vicky's...	Changed	Didn't change
(A) Weight		
(B) Height		
(C) Hairstyle		

4   What will the man probably do next?

① Change his T-shirt

② Put on a brown jacket

③ Go shopping with the woman

④ Wait for the woman to change her clothes

5   Choose the correct picture for each person.

(1) Kate: _____   (2) Rachel: _____   (3) Sarah: _____

6   Choose Danny in the picture.

7   Why does the man choose Scarlett as the main actress?

① She acts well.

② She is not too tall.

③ She has a nice voice.

④ She is very beautiful.

8   Which is NOT true about Cathy?

① She is Tina's cousin.

② She has many friends.

③ She is quite tall.

④ She has long blond hair.

A - 1   Choose the person that the woman is talking about.

①    ②    ③    ④

2   Where is the woman now?

① at a hotel

② at a train station

③ at a police station

④ at a shopping center

B - 1   Which is NOT true about Melisa Brown?

① height: 177 cm

② weight: 56 kg

③ eyes: brown

④ hair: long and red

2   Why did Melisa Brown stop working as a model?

① She hurt her leg.

② She felt tired.

③ She wanted to study.

④ She was interested in another job.

 Critical ★ Thinking

Makeup

1 Check [✓] if each person is for or against men wearing makeup.

	For	Against
(1) May	☐	☐
(2) Chris	☐	☐
(3) Kelly	☐	☐

2 Match each person with their opinion.

(1) May ·   · ⓐ Men can put on makeup if they want to.

(2) Chris ·   · ⓑ Men look better without makeup.

(3) Kelly ·   · ⓒ Men look better when they wear makeup.

What do you think?

1

Check [✓] if you have the same opinion. You can add your own opinion in the blank.

☐ Men who wear makeup look nicer.

☐ Makeup is a way for men to express themselves.

☐ I don't like to see men wearing makeup.

☐ Makeup is for women only. When men wear makeup, it is not natural.

_____

2

Talk about the following questions with your partner.

· Have you ever seen a man wearing makeup? What did you think?

· If your brother wanted to wear makeup, what would you say?

School Life

Getting ★ Ready

A

Match each word with the correct definition.

1 to arrive too late for something · · ⓐ talent
2 to get points in a sport · · ⓑ miss
3 the conditions that people live or work in · · ⓒ score
4 an ability to do something well · · ⓓ research
5 to study something carefully to get new information · · ⓔ environment

B

Choose the best sentence for each blank.

> ⓐ How's your life at school? ⓑ This is not my day. ⓒ Which subject do you like?
> ⓓ Hand it in by next Friday. ⓔ Why were you absent from school? ⓕ Is there any
> homework for tomorrow?

1 W: _____
   M: English is my favorite.
2 W: When is the due date?
   M: _____
3 W: _____
   M: I was very sick.

1   Choose each person's favorite subject.

(1) David: _____

(2) Nicole: _____

① history   ② science   ③ music   ④ English

+ Listen again
and fill
in the blanks.

W: What is your _____ _____, David? Science?

M: No, I like history. You know, my history teacher is so pretty.

W: I _____ _____, too, but I don't like history. There is too much homework.

M: Then, _____ _____ do you like, Nicole?

W: My favorite subject is music.

2   Why was the boy late for school?

① He was sick.

② He woke up late.

③ He took the wrong bus.

④ He missed the school bus.

+ Listen again
and fill
in the blanks.

W: John, I didn't see you _____ _____.

M: Well... I arrived at around 10 o'clock, Ms. Johnson.

W: Did you _____ _____ late?

M: No. I was late because I met my old friend at the bus stop.

W: What happened?

M: I thought we talked for just a moment. But twenty minutes passed.

W: So you _____ _____ _____ _____?

M: Yes. I'm sorry.

1 Check [✓] how each person feels about his or her school life.

	Happy	Unhappy
(1) Emma		
(2) Bill		
(3) Debbie		

2 What is the relationship between the speakers?

① student – student

② teacher – student

③ parent – teacher

④ school bus driver – student

3 Why does Kate feel bad?

① Her school is too far away.

② She had a fight with her classmate.

③ There are too many things to study.

④ Some subjects are difficult to understand.

4 Choose a school event that each person enjoyed most.

(1) Michael: _____   (2) Helen: _____

5 What day is it today?

	① Mon	② Tue	③ Wed	④ Thu
1	Music	French	Math	French
2	History	Science	Art	History
3	French	English	Music	Math
4				

6 Why did John call Anna?

① To ask about homework

② To borrow an English dictionary

③ To make a plan to do homework together

④ To tell her why he was absent from school

7 What will the boy probably do next?

① Study at home

② Go to the hospital

③ Prepare for school

④ Take online classes

8 Choose the wrong information about the homework.

Today's homework

① Type: group work

② Topic: one part of the human body

③ Product: three-page report

④ Due date: tomorrow

A - 1   Why did the boy nearly miss the school bus?

① He forgot the bus number.

② He got up too late.

③ He waited at the wrong bus stop.

④ He didn't know the correct bus schedule.

2   Check [✓] how the boy feels about each of the following.

	Good	Bad
(1) Teacher		
(2) Classmates		
(3) Gym		

B - 1   Choose what happened to the boy in each class.

(1) English class: _____   (2) Science class: _____

2   Which best describes the boy's situation?

① The walls have ears.

② When it rains, it pours.

③ The early bird catches the worm.

④ There is a time for everything in life.

 Critical ★ Thinking

Homeschooling

1 Check [✓] if each person is for or against homeschooling.

	For	Against
(1) Tony	☐	☐
(2) Julia	☐	☐
(3) Darren	☐	☐

2 Match each person with their opinion.

(1) Tony •   • ⓐ Students learn social skills in schools.

(2) Julia •   • ⓑ Home is a better learning environment.

(3) Darren •   • ⓒ Each student can learn what they need to learn by getting homeschooled.

What do you think?

1

Check [✓] if you have the same opinion. You can add your own opinion in the blank.

☐ Children should learn how to get along with others at school.

☐ Teachers know more about their subjects, so they can teach better than parents.

☐ When children get homeschooled, they can focus on their talents.

_____

2

Talk about the following questions with your partner.

• Have you ever met any people who are homeschooled?

• If your parents wanted to homeschool you, would you like it?

Transportation & Location

Getting ★ Ready

A

Fill in each blank with the correct word or expression.

1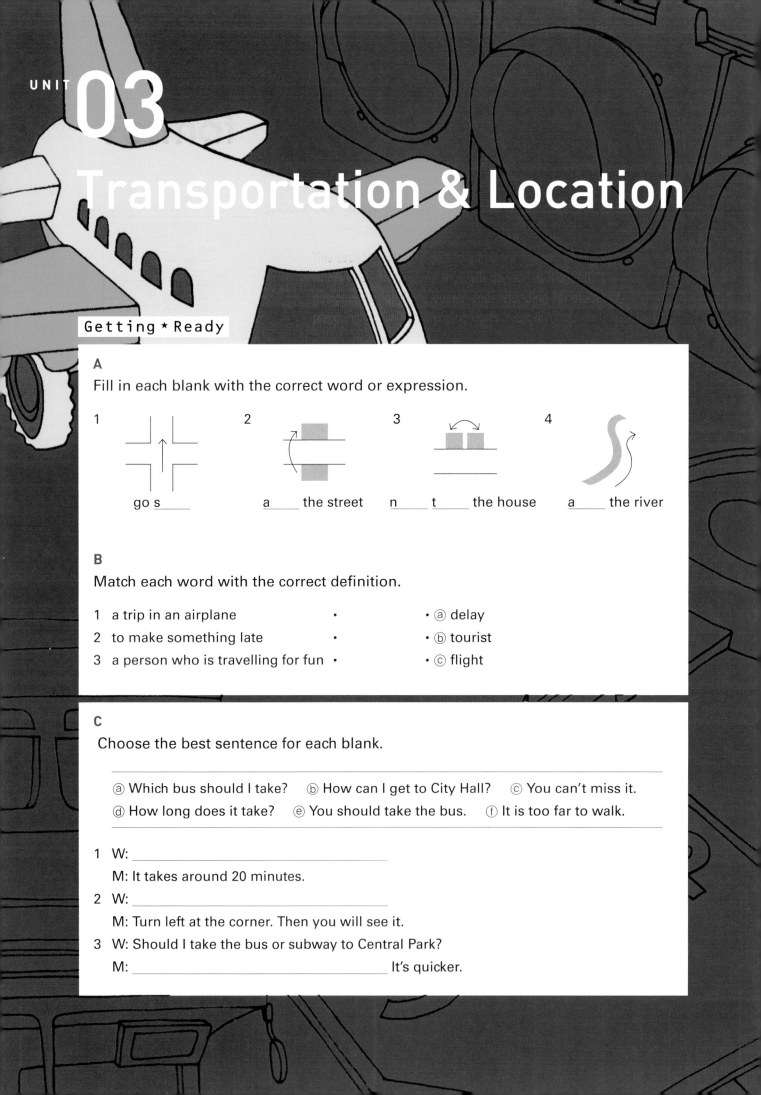

go s_____

2

a____ the street

3

n___ t____ the house

4

a____ the river

B

Match each word with the correct definition.

1   a trip in an airplane   •   • ⓐ delay
2   to make something late   •   • ⓑ tourist
3   a person who is travelling for fun •   • ⓒ flight

C

Choose the best sentence for each blank.

ⓐ Which bus should I take?   ⓑ How can I get to City Hall?   ⓒ You can't miss it.
ⓓ How long does it take?   ⓔ You should take the bus.   ⓕ It is too far to walk.

1 W: _____
   M: It takes around 20 minutes.
2 W: _____
   M: Turn left at the corner. Then you will see it.
3 W: Should I take the bus or subway to Central Park?
   M: _____ It's quicker.

1   Choose the Guggenheim Museum on the map.

+ Listen again
and fill
in the blanks.

W: _____ _____ . Do you know where the Guggenheim

    Museum is?

M: Yes. Go straight one block and _____ _____ at the corner.

W: Turn right at the corner?

M: That's right. Then you will see it _____ _____ _____ .

W: I see. Thank you.

2   How will the man get to Central Park?

① by bus

② by taxi

③ by subway

④ by bicycle

+ Listen again
and fill
in the blanks.

W: Where are you going?

M: _____ _____ _____ Central Park to meet Lena. But

    I'm late.

W: Oh, you should hurry.

M: Do you think the subway is _____ _____ the bus?

W: No. You have to change subway lines. _____ _____

    _____ .

M: Okay. Thank you.

1 Where can you hear this kind of announcement?

① in an airplane   ② at the airport

③ in a travel agency   ④ in a subway train

2 Which bus will the man take?

① number 13   ② number 15

③ number 24   ④ number 30

3 Choose Star Café on the map.

22

4 How did the woman get to each place?

| ⓐ by bus | ⓑ by taxi | ⓒ by subway | ⓓ on foot |

 ▶  ▶

Big Ben   (1) _____   Tower Bridge   (2) _____   Piccadilly Circus

5   When will the train arrive at the station?

① 10:30   ② 11:00

③ 11:30   ④ 13:00

6   What will they probably do next?

① Take a taxi

② Wait for the next bus

③ Go to the train station

④ Go to the theater on foot

7   Choose the wrong information.

① to the Louvre Museum

② take no. 24 bus

　　　└▶ ③ the stop next to the library

④ takes 30 minutes

8   Choose Times Square station on the map.

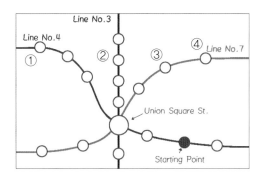

A - 1   What is the relationship between the speakers?

① hotel staff – guest

② travel guide – tourist

③ taxi driver – passenger

④ flight attendant – passenger

2   Where will the woman go tomorrow?

① Tokyo Hotel

② Tokyo Tower

③ Disney Land

④ Shibuya

B - 1   Why is the man going to take the subway?

① He is late for the concert.

② The subway station is nearby.

③ It is cheaper than taking the bus.

④ He feels sick when he takes the bus.

2   Choose Carnegie Hall on the map.

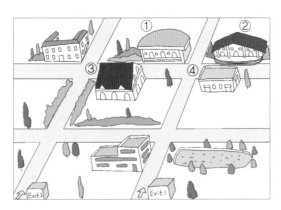

Manners in the Subway

1 How does the man feel now?

① sad

② angry

③ bored

④ worried

2 Choose two pictures showing what happened to the man.

①  ②  ③  ④

What do you think?

1

Which is NOT good manners on the subway? You can add your own opinion in the blank.

- ☐ Talking on the phone
- ☐ Listening to music loudly
- ☐ Having food or drinks
- ☐ Watching TV or videos without earphones

_____

2

Talk about the following questions with your partner.

- If you checked any of the things above, what are your reasons?
- What do you do when you see people with bad manners on the subway?

Seasons & Weather

Getting ★ Ready

A

Choose the correct word to best describe each picture.

ⓐ dry ⓑ sunny ⓒ storm ⓓ shower ⓔ lightning ⓕ cloudy

1 _____ 2 _____ 3 _____ 4 _____

B

Choose the best sentence for each blank.

ⓐ It's hot throughout the year. ⓑ What will the weather be like tomorrow? ⓒ Is there only one season? ⓓ We have four seasons. ⓔ It will be snowing a lot. ⓕ When will it clear up?

1 M: _____
   W: Not until this Friday.
2 M: How's the weather in Indonesia?
   W: _____
3 M: _____
   W: It's going to rain.

1   When are they going to the amusement park?

① Thursday

② Friday

③ Saturday

④ Sunday

+ Listen again and fill in the blanks.

W: _____ _____ to an amusement park this Thursday.

M: I heard it's going to be cloudy and rainy in the afternoon.

W: When will it _____ _____?

M: Well, not until this Friday.

W: Is it going to be sunny _____ _____ _____?

M: No, but it won't rain.

W: Then, _____ _____ go this Saturday?

M: Okay.

2   Choose each person's favorite season.

(1) Jacky: _____   (2) Paul: _____   (3) Nora: _____

+ Listen again and fill in the blanks.

W1: I'm Jacky. I love hot weather because I can _____ _____ in the hot sun.

M: I'm Paul. I like snow. Skiing and snowboarding are my _____ _____.

W2: I'm Nora. I love warm weather. I like to _____ _____ _____ and see lots of beautiful flowers.

1   Choose today's weather for New York and Seattle.

(1) New York: _____   (2) Seattle: _____

①   ②   ③   ④

2   How does the man feel now?

① happy

② nervous

③ excited

④ disappointed

3   Choose each country's best season for travel.

ⓐ spring	ⓑ summer	ⓒ fall	ⓓ winter

(1) Greece: _____   (2) England: _____

4   What will they probably do next?

① Go home

② Buy an umbrella

③ Go to a café

④ Take a walk

5   Choose tomorrow's weather for each city.

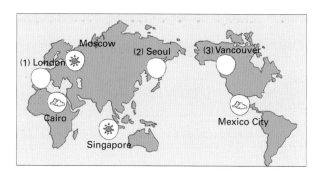 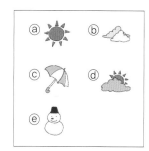

6   Choose the right order of the weather.

① sunny → cloudy → rainy

② rainy → snowy → cloudy

③ sunny → rainy → snowy

④ snowy → sunny → cloudy

7   Which are two signs that it will rain soon?

①    ②    ③    ④

8   What's the weather like in December in Indonesia?

① hot and dry

② hot and rainy

③ cold and dry

④ cold and rainy

A - 1 What is the man mainly talking about?

① What causes lightning

② When lightning happens

③ Why lightning is dangerous

④ How to act when there's lightning

2 Who is doing something wrong?

B - 1 What are they planning to do for their father's birthday?

① Go to a nice restaurant

② Go shopping with their dad

③ Throw a garden party

④ Make a birthday cake

2 How will the weather be on Saturday?

① sunny

② rainy

③ windy

④ cloudy

 Critical ★ Thinking

Four Seasons

1   Check [✓] whether each person likes or doesn't like having four seasons.

	Likes	Doesn't like
(1) Marina	☐	☐
(2) Seyoon	☐	☐
(3) Yuki	☐	☐

2   Choose each person's opinion.

(1) Marina: _____   (2) Seyoon: _____   (3) Yuki: _____

ⓐ I like to buy nice clothes every season.

ⓑ I can enjoy different sports each season.

ⓒ It's good to enjoy the changes in each season.

ⓓ I have to spend money on clothes for each season.

What do you think?

1

Check [✓] if you have the same opinion. You can add your own opinion in the blank.

☐   It's hard to live in a country where it's hot or cold all the time.

☐   Having only one kind of weather is good because I can save money on clothes.

☐   I don't like having four seasons because I catch colds when the seasons change.

2

Talk about the following questions with your partner.

· Do you have four seasons in your country?

· How many seasons do you want to have? Why?

UNIT 05
Family

Getting ★ Ready

A

Match each word with the correct definition.

1 sad because you are alone   •   • ⓐ share

2 to use something with other people   •   • ⓑ income

3 money that you get from doing work   •   • ⓒ successful

4 your sister's husband or your wife's brother •   • ⓓ lonely

5 making a lot of money and doing well •   • ⓔ brother-in-law

B

Choose the best sentence for each blank.

> ⓐ I'm an only child.   ⓑ I have a large family.   ⓒ Do you like having many sisters?
> ⓓ Did you feel lonely in France?   ⓔ I take after both of them.   ⓕ He is one year
> older than you.

1 M: _____
    W: Yes, I missed my family a lot.

2 M: How many brothers and sisters do you have?
    W: I don't have any. _____

3 M: Who do you look like, your father or mother?
    W: _____

1 Choose the correct family tree.

①
Grandfather — Grandmother

Father — Mother

Older brother — Me — Younger brother

②
Grandmother

Father — Mother

Older sister — Me — Younger brother

③
Grandfather

Father — Mother

Older brother — Me — Younger sister

④
Grandfather — Grandmother

Father — Mother

Older sister — Me — Younger brother

+ Listen again
and fill
in the blanks.

W: Ted, _____ _____ _____ are in your family?

M: I have a big family. I'm living with my grandparents and my parents.

W: _____ _____ _____ brothers or sisters?

M: Yes. I have one older sister and one _____ _____.

2 What's the main reason the woman likes her brother-in-law?

① He is good-looking.

② He is humorous.

③ He gives her pocket money.

④ He is nice to her sister.

+ Listen again
and fill
in the blanks.

M: Did your big sister _____ _____?

W: Yes. She got married last year.

M: Do you like your brother-in-law?

W: Yes, I do. He often gives me pocket money.

M: (laughing) So _____ _____ you like him!

W: The main reason is that he's so funny. He always _____

_____ _____.

1 Choose which face is John's.

2 How old is the woman?

① 16 　　　　　 ② 17 　　　　　 ③ 18 　　　　　 ④ 19

3 According to Dan, what are two bad points of having a big family?

① His house is noisy.

② His parents care only about his sisters.

③ He can never use the computer alone.

④ He had to wear old clothes from his brothers.

4 What present are they going to buy?

①  ② ③  ④

5   Choose the right hobby for each person.

(1) Father: _____   (2) Mother: _____   (3) Brother: _____   (4) Me: _____

ⓐ Cooking   ⓑ Rollerblading   ⓒ Playing the piano

ⓓ Watching movies   ⓔ Skiing   ⓕ Hiking in the mountains

6   Check [✓] T for true or F for false.

	T	F
(1) Angelina Jolie's father is an actor.	☐	☐
(2) Angelina Jolie has an older brother.	☐	☐
(3) Angelina Jolie's uncle was famous in the 1970s.	☐	☐

7   Match each person with his or her wish.

(1) Linda •   • ⓐ   I'd like to have a younger sister.

(2) Jenny •   • ⓑ   I'd like to have an older sister.

(3) Tom •   • ⓒ   I'd like to have an older brother.

8   What are May and Cathy's full names now?

(1) May   ⓐ May Pitt   ⓑ May Smith

(2) Cathy   ⓐ Cathy Jones   ⓑ Cathy Stevens

A - 1   What is the topic of the movie?

① The power of love

② The importance of family

③ The role of a father in a family

④ The importance of a happy family for children

2   Check [✓] T for true or F for false.   T   F

(1) The movie is about a successful careerman's dream.   ☐   ☐

(2) The man is married in real life.   ☐   ☐

(3) The man enjoyed his life in the dream.   ☐   ☐

B - 1   Choose the thing that the man does NOT say he missed.

① Talking with his family

② His family's large apartment

③ His mom's cooking

④ His father's attention

2   Which best describes the situation?

① Rome was not built in a day.

② Better late than never.

③ No news is good news.

④ There's no place like home.

DINK

1 Which couple is a DINK couple?

①
We both have jobs, and we have one son.

Kate & Steve

②
Only my husband has a job. We don't have any plans to have a kid.

Jessi & Mark

③
We both have jobs. We don't want to have children.

Emily & Alex

2 Choose each person's opinion.

(1) Paul: _____   (2) Jill: _____

ⓐ You will be happy when you see your children grow up.

ⓑ If you have children, you won't feel lonely.

ⓒ Without children, you can have fun in your life.

What do you think?

1

Check [✓] if you have the same opinion. You can add your own opinion in the blank.

☐ It's okay not to have kids if you don't want to.

☐ You can enjoy your life more without kids.

☐ Think about when you are old and sick. You'll need children to take care of you.

_____

2

Talk about the following questions with your partner.

• Have you seen any DINK couples around you?

• Do you want to have children in the future? Why or why not?

UNIT 06 Friends

A

Choose the correct word for each definition.

ⓐ chat   ⓑ helpful   ⓒ interest   ⓓ whole   ⓔ shy   ⓕ worried   ⓖ brave

1   not afraid of difficult or dangerous things: _____
2   to talk to someone on the Internet: _____
3   uncomfortable and nervous about speaking to other people: _____
4   feeling unhappy because you are thinking about a problem: _____
5   something that you enjoy doing or learning about: _____

B

Choose the best sentence for each blank.

ⓐ We had a big fight.   ⓑ She is good at science.   ⓒ What is your best friend like?
ⓓ Why don't you call him?   ⓔ We have many things in common.   ⓕ She makes me laugh a lot.

1   W: _____
    M: He is gentle and humorous.
2   W: Do you often see Angela these days?
    M: No. _____
3   W: Is Bill your best friend?
    M: Yes. _____

1 Which is NOT true about Jenny?

① She is from Korea.

② She loves to take trips.

③ She likes Johnny Depp.

④ She likes to talk with new people.

+ Listen again
and fill
in the blanks.

M: Who is your _____ _____?

W: My best friend is Jenny. She comes from Korea.

M: _____ is she _____?

W: She is shy but humorous. She likes to travel to new places in her

_____ _____.

M: I see. What do you do when you see her?

W: We're big fans of Johnny Depp. So we usually _____

_____ _____.

2 Choose the kind of friend that each person wants to have.

(1) Roy: _____   (2) Sue: _____   (3) Tim: _____

ⓐ   ⓑ   ⓒ

+ Listen again
and fill
in the blanks.

M1: I'm Roy. I want my friend to live _____ _____

_____. Then, we could easily spend time together.

W: I'm Sue. I want my friend to _____ _____ _____

science. Then, he or she could help me study.

M2: I'm Tim. I want my friend to like sports. It _____ _____

_____ to go to the gym together.

1   How does the man feel now?

① tired

② sorry

③ angry

④ happy

2   Check [✓] the correct information about each person.

	Jack	Steve
(1) likes comic books		
(2) is a school basketball player		
(3) is popular among girls		

3   What will the woman do today?

① Make travel plans

② Go to the hospital

③ Meet an online friend

④ Talk with her friend online

4   What is the man mainly talking about?

① Ways to be a good friend

② The importance of friends

③ Tips for making new friends

④ The importance of joining clubs

5   Why is the man angry with Catherine?

　① She didn't come on time.

　② She didn't wait for him.

　③ She saw the movie with another friend.

　④ She wanted to see a different movie.

6   Choose each person in the picture.

(1) Gina: _____　　　(2) Kelly: _____　　　(3) Rachel: _____

7   What is the reason that Nick has NOT seen Billy?

　① Nick was very busy.

　② Nick had a fight with Billy.

　③ Nick moved to North Carolina.

　④ Billy goes to school in a different city.

8   What is the man's problem?

　① His friend tells lies.

　② His friend copies him.

　③ He doesn't have time to meet his friend.

　④ He doesn't like his friend's fashion choices.

A - 1 What can you do on the website?

① Make new friends

② Join clubs with friends

③ Chat with classmates

④ Find old friends from childhood

2 Which is NOT true about the website?

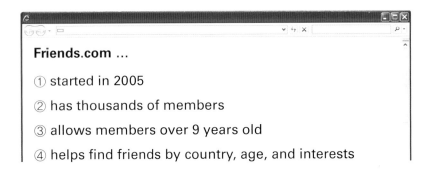

Friends.com ...

① started in 2005

② has thousands of members

③ allows members over 9 years old

④ helps find friends by country, age, and interests

B - 1 What did Sarah and her friend want to do on the first day of their trip?

(1) Sarah: _____   (2) Her friend: _____

   ⓐ      ⓑ      ⓒ

2 What is Sarah's advice for Ricky?

① Travel alone.

② Change the travel schedule.

③ Discuss the schedule with his friend.

④ Collect more information about Spain.

 Critical ★ Thinking

The Number of Friends

1 Check [✓] T for true or F for false.

	T	F
(1) She has only a few close friends.	☐	☐
(2) She usually talks to her parents about her problems.	☐	☐
(3) She thinks she needs more friends.	☐	☐

2 According to her father, what are two good points of having many friends?

① He can learn a lot from them.

② He can have better social skills.

③ He can get help from them.

④ He can have more fun with them.

What do you think?

1

Check [✓] if you have the same opinion. You can add your own opinion in the blank.

☐ I want many friends so that I never feel lonely.

☐ When I really need some help, only a few close friends will help me.

☐ I can learn different things from different friends. So I want many friends.

_____

2

Talk about the following questions with your partner.

• How many friends do you have?

• Do you think you need more friends than that? Why or why not?

Music

Getting ★ Ready

A

Choose the correct word for each blank.

1 Types of music _____s   2 Kinds of _____s

   pop   jazz   flute   cello

      rock   violin

> ⓐ genre
> ⓑ audition
> ⓒ orchestra
> ⓓ instrument

B

Match each word with the correct definition.

1 to make someone feel happy •   • ⓐ please

2 a very successful song or movie •   • ⓑ noise

3 a loud or unpleasant sound •   • ⓒ hit

C

Choose the best sentence for each blank.

> ⓐ I want to join the orchestra. ⓑ I'm a big fan of his. ⓒ Why didn't you enjoy the concert? ⓓ What song are you going to sing? ⓔ Do you listen to music when you study? ⓕ I'm going to play the cello.

1 W: What are you going to play?

 M: _____

2 W: Are you going to Usher's concert?

 M: Yes, _____

3 W: _____

 M: Yes. It helps me focus on studying.

1   How does the man feel now?

① sad

② tired

③ excited

④ worried

+ Listen again
and fill
in the blanks.

M: I'm going to go to Usher's concert tomorrow. I'm _____ _____ _____ _____ his. I bought all of his CDs and I can sing all of his songs. I can't believe that I'm going to see him tomorrow. I don't think I'll _____ _____ _____ sleep tonight!

2   What will they do on Thursday?

① Take a music lesson

② Go to the orchestra audition

③ Go to an orchestra's concert

④ Look for new orchestra members

+ Listen again
and fill
in the blanks.

W: Daniel, look at this! The school orchestra is looking for new members.

M: Oh, I want to _____ _____ _____ and play the flute again. Are you interested?

W: Yes. I don't _____ _____ _____ very well, but I want to try.

M: That's a good idea. You can _____ _____ _____ in the orchestra.

W: The auditions are this Thursday. Let's go together.

M: _____ _____.

1   Which instrument will the man play?

    ①    ②    ③    ④

2   Check [✓] T for true or F for false about Yuhki Kuramoto.   T   F

    (1) He majored in music in college.   ☐   ☐

    (2) His first album was made in 1986.   ☐   ☐

    (3) The woman likes *Lake Louise* most among his songs.   ☐   ☐

3   Which best describes the situation?

    ① Easy come, easy go.

    ② No news is good news.

    ③ Rome was not built in a day.

    ④ Don't judge a book by its cover.

4   Check [✓] how the man felt about the concert.

	Good	Bad
(1) Singer's voice		
(2) Singer's stage manners		
(3) Concert hall		

5 Choose the wrong information about the concert.

The Smith Family's Spring Concert

① Welcome to our jazz concert.

② Location: Denver High School hall

③ Time: Friday, May 20th, at 7 p.m.

④ Dress code: Formal clothes

6 Where is the conversation taking place?

① at a song contest

② at a music lesson

③ at a classical concert

④ in an instrument store

7 What is the woman's job?

① a singer   ② a dancer   ③ a radio DJ   ④ a music teacher

8 Which of the following is NOT true about the graph below?

〈The Kinds of Music Teens Enjoy Most〉

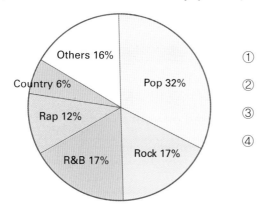

Others 16%

Country 6%

Rap 12%

R&B 17%

Rock 17%

Pop 32%

①

②

③

④

A - 1 What is the relationship between the speakers?

① singer – fan

② teacher – student

③ teacher – parent

④ reporter – pianist

2 Why does the man choose Grand Academy?

① Its teachers are more famous.

② It is cheaper.

③ It is closer.

④ Its programs are better.

B - 1 What is the woman mainly talking about?

① Music for a good night's sleep

② Why you should listen to music

③ Ways of choosing good music

④ Tips for reducing stress with music

2 Choose all of the woman's advice.

ⓐ Take a walk with music.

ⓑ Use headphones or earphones.

ⓒ Listen to music for more than 30 minutes.

ⓓ Choose different music based on your mood.

ⓔ Get into a comfortable position while listening to music.

 Critical ★ Thinking

Listening to Music

1 **What is Steve mainly talking about?**

① Is music helpful for studying?

② How can you focus on studying?

③ Why is it good to listen to music?

④ How does our brain work while listening to music?

2 **Choose each person's opinion.**

(1) Steve: _____   (2) Steve's mother: _____

ⓐ Our brain can only focus on one thing at a time.

ⓑ We aren't bothered by outside noise when we listen to music.

ⓒ If we study with music, we usually pay more attention to the music.

What do you think?

1

Check [✓] if you have the same opinion. You can add your own opinion in the blank.

☐ I can study for a longer time when listening to music.

☐ When I listen to music, I don't hear the noise around me.

☐ When I study with music, I usually start to sing along to the song.

2

Talk about the following questions with your partner.

• Do you listen to music when you study?

• Do you think it is possible to focus on two different things at the same time?

08 Holidays

A

Choose the correct word for each definition.

ⓐ relax   ⓑ servant   ⓒ turkey   ⓓ international

ⓔ meaningful   ⓕ relative   ⓖ celebrate

---

1 important or useful: _____

2 relating to more than one country: _____

3 a member of the same family: _____

4 a large bird that looks like a chicken: _____

5 to stop worrying about things and spend time resting: _____

B

Choose the best sentence for each blank.

ⓐ Are you making something for Thanksgiving?   ⓑ It's on the second Sunday of June.   ⓒ What are you doing during your vacation?   ⓓ How was your Christmas?   ⓔ I heard you're planning to visit France for a vacation.   ⓕ Is today a special holiday?

---

1 M: _____

    W: Yes. It's Independence Day.

2 M: _____

    W: I'm going camping near Stanley Park.

3 M: _____

    W: No, I'm not. I'm staying home.

1 Which food will they make for Thanksgiving?

(1) Cindy: _____   (2) Jake: _____

① ② ③ ④

+ Listen again
and fill
in the blanks.

M: Cindy, are you _____ _____ for Thanksgiving?

W: Yes. I'm going to cook yams.

M: What are they?

W: They're _____ _____ _____ sweet potato. They are

really yummy.

M: I see. _____ _____ the turkey?

W: My parents will cook it. How about you, Jake?

M: I'm going to try _____ _____ _____ _____.

W: Wow! Good luck.

2 What are they going to do in the evening?

① Join a parade

② Go to a party

③ Watch fireworks

④ Watch TV at home

+ Listen again
and fill
in the blanks.

W: Look, there's a parade. Is today a _____ _____ in America?

M: Yes. Today is American Independence Day.

W: Oh, I see.

M: Are you _____ _____ this evening?

W: Not really. I was going to stay home and watch TV.

M: There'll be _____ _____ downtown tonight. Let's go and

watch them together.

W: Sure. That _____ _____!

1   Choose the picture that shows Songkran.

①    ②    ③    ④

2   Circle the date they are going camping.

JUNE

SUN	MON	TUE	WED	THU	FRI	SAT
	1	2	3	4	5	6
7	8	9	10	11	12	13
14	15	16	17	18	19	20
21	22	23	24	25	26	27

3   Why will the woman NOT go traveling?

① She is in the hospital.

② She has a lot of work to do.

③ Her friend is sick.

④ She doesn't have enough money.

4   Choose the things that Chinese people do each day.

(1) The day before New Year's Day: _____

(2) New Year's Day: _____

ⓐ Visit their relatives   ⓑ Have a party with friends

ⓒ Cook food   ⓓ Watch fireworks

ⓔ Clean their houses

5   Which book is the man going to buy?

① a comic book

② a TV guide

③ a cook book

④ a travel guidebook

6   What is Joe going to do during the vacation?

①    ②    ③    ④

7   Choose the presents that Tom and Mary want.

(1) Tom: _____

(2) Mary: _____

> ⓐ a cellphone
>
> ⓑ an MP3 player
>
> ⓒ a sweater
>
> ⓓ a coat

8   Write T for true or F for false about Edinburgh Festival Fringe.

(1) It's the oldest arts festival in the world.   _____

(2) Famous stars will attend it.   _____

(3) It's held for about three weeks in July.   _____

A - 1 Which is NOT mentioned about Boxing Day?

① Where it started

② When it is

③ Why it's called "Boxing Day"

④ What people buy on that day

2 Choose all the things that people will do on Boxing Day.

① Go shopping

② Give gifts to workers   ·

③ Have a party with neighbors

④ Say thanks to their parents

B - 1 Circle the date of Mother's Day and Father's Day on the calendar.

MAY						
SUN	MON	TUE	WED	THU	FRI	SAT
					1	2
3	4	5	6	7	8	9
10	11	12	13	14	15	16
17	18	19	20	21	22	23
24	25	26	27	28	29	30
31						

JUNE						
SUN	MON	TUE	WED	THU	FRI	SAT
	1	2	3	4	5	6
7	8	9	10	11	12	13
14	15	16	17	18	19	20
21	22	23	24	25	26	27
28	29	30				

2 Which flower do people give to their mothers on Mother's Day?

①    ②   ③   ④

Critical ★ Thinking

Spending Holidays

1   What are they mainly talking about?

① How the Christmas holidays started

② What they will do next Christmas holidays

③ What the true meaning of the Christmas holidays is

④ How we should spend our Christmas holidays

2   Choose the thing that Tim did during the Christmas holidays.

During the holidays,

I _____ .

ⓐ watched TV   ⓑ ate holiday food   ⓒ studied

ⓓ worked part-time   ⓔ helped poor people

What do you think?

1

Check [✓] if you have the same opinion. You can add your own opinion in the blank.

☐ Holidays are a time for going to new places and doing new things.

☐ We should spend time with our families on holidays.

☐ If I don't take a rest, I feel tired after the holidays.

_____

2

Talk about the following questions with your partner.

· What do you usually do during the holidays?

· What is the best way to spend the holidays?

Shopping

A

Match each word with the correct definition.

1 someone who likes shopping too much • • ⓐ order
2 to ask for something to be sent • • ⓑ product
3 something that is made to be sold • • ⓒ simple
4 basic, without unnecessary things • • ⓓ exchange
5 to give something and recieve something different • • ⓔ shopaholic

B

Choose the best sentence for each blank.

ⓐ Are you looking for something?   ⓑ Why don't you buy a miniskirt later?   ⓒ This pink one sells best.   ⓓ How would you like to pay?   ⓔ What do you think about this jacket?   ⓕ It's on sale.

1 M: Which one is the most popular?
 W: _____

2 M: _____
 W: I want to buy some shoes for my brother.

3 M: _____
 W: By credit card.

1   Which camera will the woman buy?

①    ②    ③    ④

+ Listen again
and fill
in the blanks.

M: Hello. _____ _____ _____ _____?

W: Yes. I'm looking for a digital camera.

M: Here are some different _____ _____ digital cameras.

W: Which ones are popular?

M: This pink one and that silver one sell best.

W: I like the silver color, but it's _____ _____.

M: The pink camera is easier to carry around.

W: Okay. _____ _____ _____.

57

2   How much money will the man pay?

① $40

② $50

③ $70

④ $80

+ Listen again
and fill
in the blanks.

W: Are you _____ _____ something?

M: Yes. I want to buy some shoes for my girlfriend.

W: _____ _____ these?

M: I think my girlfriend will like them. _____ _____ are they?

W: They're $40.

M: Wow. That's expensive.

W: They were $80, but they're _____ _____ now.

M: Really? Then I'll take them.

1 Put all the things they will buy in the shopping cart.

> ⓐ yogurt
>
> ⓑ milk
>
> ⓒ orange juice
>
> ⓓ tomato juice
>
> ⓔ ice cream

2 What will they probably do next?

①  ②  ③  ④

3 How much money did the man pay in total?

① $5

② $6

③ $11

④ $12

4 What is the man mainly talking about?

① The best places to shop

② Clothes shopping tips

③ Where to buy cheap clothes

④ Good points of shopping with friends

5   Why did the woman call?

     ① To get her money back

     ② To order a skirt

     ③ To complain about bad service

     ④ To exchange the skirt she bought

6   Write the floor each person will go to.

     (1) Tom   I want to buy shoes for my father.   _____ floor

     (2) Harry   I need sunglasses for the summer.   _____ floor

     (3) Sally   I'd like to try on pretty skirts.   _____ floor

7   Which dress is the woman going to buy?

8   Write T for true or F for false about *Mark's*.

     (1) *Mark's* sells items for boys.   _____

     (2) *Mark's* has both online and offline stores.   _____

     (3) There will be a spring sale from this Sunday.   _____

A - 1   Choose all the items the man buys.

2   How much money is he going to pay?

① $1,300

② $1,400

③ $1,500

④ $1,600

B - 1   Where will the woman go shopping?

① IFC Mall

② Harbor City

③ Pacific Place

④ Times Square

2   Which is NOT true?

① There are over 700 stores in Harbor City.

② Pacific Place is bigger than Harbor City.

③ There are many good places to eat in Pacific Place.

④ Times Square is popular with young people.

Shopaholic

1 **What is the man's job?**

① teacher   ② counselor

③ shop owner   ④ home shopping host

2 **Choose all the man's advice.**

> You should _____.

ⓐ try not to use credit cards   ⓑ shop with a friend

ⓒ find new hobbies   ⓓ do not watch home shopping channels

ⓔ think carefully before buying things

What do you think?

1

These are some tips for shopaholics. Which ideas do you think are good? You can add your own opinion in the blank.

☐ Make a "No Shopping Day" for yourself.

☐ Take only a little cash when going shopping.

☐ Write a spending diary to control your buying.

☐ Make a shopping list before going shopping.

_____

2

Talk about the following questions with your partner.

• How often do you shop in a month?

• What can you do to be a smart shopper?

Advice

Getting ★ Ready

A

Match each word with the correct definition.

1 to go to a place regularly   •   • ⓐ cheat
2 almost the same, but not exactly   •   • ⓑ similar
3 to break the rules for a better grade   •   • ⓒ attend

B

Choose the one that does NOT fit in the blank.

1 lose _____   2 make _____

ⓐ interest / ⓑ advice / ⓒ weight   ⓐ a lie / ⓑ a friend / ⓒ some cookies

C

Choose the best sentence for each blank.

ⓐ Why don't you set a schedule for using the computer?   ⓑ How did you solve the problem?   ⓒ I think you'll lose interest after a short time.   ⓓ I have only a year to prepare for the entrance exam.   ⓔ What's the matter?   ⓕ I'm shorter than most other students.

1 W: _____
   M: Okay. I should try that.
2 W: _____
   M: I'm worried because I didn't study enough.
3 W: Why don't you allow me to attend the academy?
   M: _____

1 What is the man's problem?

① He had a fight with his friend.

② His new high school is too far away.

③ It is difficult for him to study many subjects.

④ He doesn't know anyone at his new school.

+ Listen again
and fill
in the blanks.

W: Tomorrow is your first day of high school. _____ _____ _____ _____ ?

M: I'm nervous.

W: Why? What's the matter?

M: My friends all went to different schools. I won't know anyone.

W: Oh, _____ _____. You'll make a lot of new friends soon.

2 What present will the woman give her boyfriend?

①   ②  ③  ④

+ Listen again
and fill
in the blanks.

W: _____ _____ is Valentine's Day. I need something for my boyfriend.

M: How about Christina Aguilera's new CD? He likes her songs.

W: Well, _____ _____ he already has it. And I want something more special.

M: Then, _____ _____ _____ make him some cookies yourself? It's not very difficult.

W: That's a good idea.

1 Match each person with his or her wish.

(1) Jane •   • ⓐ I want to become taller.

(2) Tom •   • ⓑ I want to buy some new clothes.

(3) Susan •   • ⓒ I'd like to get better grades.

2 What is the woman's advice?

① Say sorry to Jack first.

② Make a new best friend.

③ Talk with Jack about the matter.

④ Explain to the other friends that Jack told lies.

3 What is the man's problem?

① He lost his concert ticket.

② The concert is too expensive for him.

③ His parents don't like Hilary Duff.

④ His friends don't want to go to the concert with him.

4 What will the woman probably do next?

5   How did the man's family solve the problem?

① By buying one more computer

② By using the computers at the library

③ By using the computer only on weekends

④ By making a schedule for using the computer

6   How does the woman feel now?

① angry

② bored

③ happy

④ worried

7   Check [✓] T for true or F for false.   T   F

(1) The man's mother doesn't want him to attend a dance academy.   ☐   ☐

(2) The man took swimming classes for about two months.   ☐   ☐

(3) The man will join a free dance club.   ☐   ☐

8   Which of the following is NOT true about the graph below?

⟨The People that Teenagers Talk to about Their Problems⟩

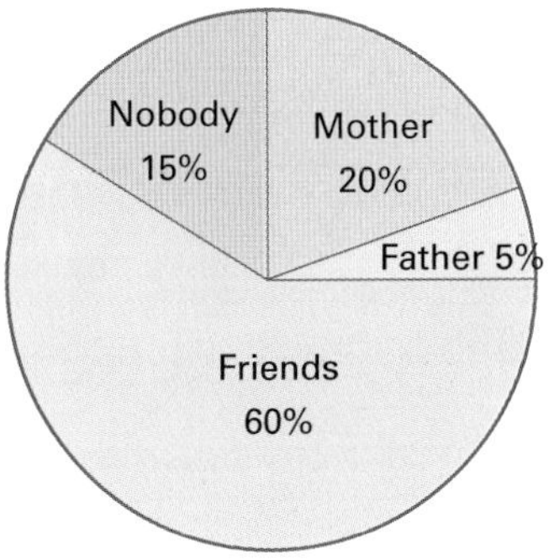

Nobody 15%
Mother 20%
Father 5%
Friends 60%

①
②
③
④

A - 1   What does the woman want to be in the future?

① a painter

② a teacher

③ a musician

④ a travel guide

2   Choose the best advice for the woman.

① Better late than never.

② All roads lead to Rome.

③ Two heads are better than one.

④ Where there's smoke, there's fire.

B - 1   What is the woman's problem?

① She had a big fight with her boyfriend.

② She doesn't want to go shopping with Amy.

③ Amy and her boyfriend don't like each other.

④ She made two different plans for the same day.

2   What is the woman going to do on Saturday?

①    ②    ③    ④

 Critical ★ Thinking

Girlfriend's Advice

1 Check [✓] T for true or F for false.   T   F

(1) Chris doesn't think that he is fat.   ☐   ☐

(2) Chris is on a diet.   ☐   ☐

(3) Chris is worried that his girlfriend doesn't love him.   ☐   ☐

2 Match each person with their opinion.

(1) Anne: _____   (2) Alex: _____

ⓐ Chris' girlfriend should love him just as he is.

ⓑ Chris should ask his girlfriend to help him lose weight.

ⓒ If Chris loves his girlfriend, he should try to lose weight.

What do you think?

1

Check [✓] if you have the same opinion. You can add your own opinion in the blank.

☐ Chris should follow his girlfriend's advice.

☐ Though she is Chris' girlfriend, it is rude of her to talk about his weight.

☐ If Chris' girlfriend wants him to lose weight, she doesn't really love him.

2

Talk about the following questions with your partner.

• Imagine you are Chris. In this situation, what would you do?

• If your boyfriend/girlfriend gave you advice about something personal, would you follow it?

UNIT 11
Boys & Girls

Getting ✶ Ready

A

Choose the correct word for each definition.

ⓐ cosmetics   ⓑ average   ⓒ upset   ⓓ mind

ⓔ envy   ⓕ present   ⓖ homemaker

1   happening or existing now: _____

2   unhappy or angry: _____

3   something that you put on your face, such as lotion: _____

4   to want something that somebody else has: _____

5   a person who takes care of his or her own house: _____

B

Choose the best sentence for each blank.

ⓐ I wish I were a girl.   ⓑ Start by making small talk.   ⓒ Why don't you tell her your feelings?   ⓓ Do you miss your first love?   ⓔ I don't think she was my type.   ⓕ My girlfriend acts too nice to other boys.

1   W: How was your blind date?

   M: Not so good. _____

2   W: Do you like being a boy?

   M: No. _____

3   W: _____

   M: Yes. I will never forget her.

1   Circle the result of each blind date.

(1)

Alice: Good / Bad

(2)

Jim: Good / Bad

+ Listen again and fill in the blanks.

W: I'm Alice. When I first saw him, I didn't think he was _____ _____. But when we talked, I thought he was very kind. We're going to _____ _____ _____ this Sunday.

M: I'm Jim. I saw a movie and had dinner with a pretty girl today. But she wouldn't _____ _____ anything. I don't want to see her again.

2   What does the man want to be in the future?

① a cook

② a painter

③ an engineer

④ a househusband

+ Listen again and fill in the blanks.

W: What do you want to be when you _____ _____?

M: Well, when I was young, I wanted to be a painter.

W: Did you _____ _____ _____?

M: Yes. Now I want to be a homemaker like my mom.

W: Really? That's interesting.

M: I just _____ _____ and cleaning.

69

1 What is the man going to buy?

①  ②   ③  ④

2 Why is the woman angry at the man?

① He is too busy.

② He doesn't call her often.

③ He doesn't express his love.

④ He didn't remember her birthday.

3 Check [✓] whether each person likes or doesn't like being a boy.

	Likes	Doesn't like
(1) Sam	☐	☐
(2) Bill	☐	☐
(3) Jack	☐	☐

4 What is the topic of the talk?

① A healthy diet is important.

② Most actresses are too thin.

③ All people are beautiful in some way.

④ Boys don't know normal girls' weight.

5 Who has the same opinion as the woman?

① Girls don't forget their first love.   Iris

② Only my present love is important.   Helen

③ Girls don't forget their last love.   Tina

6 How does the man feel now?

① angry

② happy

③ worried

④ nervous

7 Choose the correct text message that the man will send.

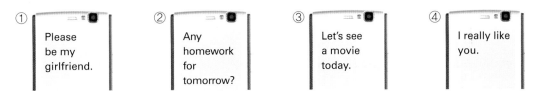

① Please be my girlfriend.

② Any homework for tomorrow?

③ Let's see a movie today.

④ I really like you.

8 Write T for true or F for false about the book, *Understanding*.

(1) It is Johnny Gray's first book. _____

(2) It is about why men and women are different. _____

(3) It will be sold starting October 20th. _____

A - 1   What kind of program is it?

① a talk show

② a quiz show

③ a newscast

④ a dating show

2   What is the answer to the quiz question?

①    ②    ③   ④

B - 1   Why did the woman have a fight with her boyfriend?

① He told a lie to her.

② He has another girlfriend.

③ He didn't keep a promise.

④ He was friendly to other girls.

2   What is the woman going to give her boyfriend?

① a comic book

② a bag

③ a photo album

④ a wallet

 Critical ★ Thinking

Friendship

1 What are they arguing about?

① What is true friendship?

② What do boys want from girls?

③ Can boys and girls be just friends?

④ Why is trust important for a couple?

2 Why does Amy want to meet Jason tomorrow?

① To give him a birthday present

② To get advice about her boyfriend

③ To say she won't see him anymore

④ To buy things for a birthday party together

What do you think?

1

Check [✓] if you have the same opinion about friendship between boys and girls. You can add your own opinion in the blank.

☐ I know a boy and a girl who have a true friendship.

☐ It is impossible, because one of them might love the other someday.

☐ Friends are just friends. It doesn't matter if they are a boy and a girl.

2

Talk about the following questions with your partner.

• Imagine you are Amy. What would you do in this situation?

• Have you ever had the same problem with your boyfriend or girlfriend?

Jobs

Getting ★ Ready

A

Match each word with the correct definition.

1 to get something ready   •   • ⓐ owner

2 a person who has something   •   • ⓑ customer

3 to give someone drinks or food   •   • ⓒ host

4 a person who buys things or services   •   • ⓓ prepare

5 a person who introduces a television show •   • ⓔ serve

B

Choose the best sentence for each blank.

ⓐ What do you do?   ⓑ I'm good at writing.   ⓒ I wanted to do something to help animals.   ⓓ Are you interested in cooking?   ⓔ What would you like to do in the future?   ⓕ Do you have any experience?

---

1 W: _____

   M: I would like to be a news reporter.

2 W: _____

   M: I am a flight attendant.

3 W: Why did you become an animal doctor?

   M: _____

1 Choose the job that the man is introducing.

①  ②  ③  ④

+ Listen again and fill in the blanks.

M: Do you know what a sommelier does? A sommelier _____ _____ a restaurant. He or she knows a lot about wine. He or she helps customers _____ _____ _____ _____ for their food. He or she also chooses and buys _____ _____ for the restaurant.

2 What is the woman's job?

① a firefighter

② a police officer

③ a bank clerk

④ a travel writer

+ Listen again and fill in the blanks.

W: Harry! _____ _____ _____ _____.

M: Lisa! It's great to see you again.

W: Do you still work at the fire station in Chicago?

M: Yes. _____ _____ _____ _____? I heard that you work at a bank.

W: I did. But I changed my job. Now I _____ _____ a travel writer.

M: That's nice.

1   Choose each person's job.

(1) Nancy: _____   (2) Rebecca: _____   (3) Maria: _____

2   What is the main reason the woman wants to open a restaurant?

① She likes cooking.

② She wants to make a lot of money.

③ She wants to have a lot of free time.

④ Her parents run a very famous restaurant.

3   What is the man's advice?

① Join a singing club.

② Spend more time singing.

③ Sing often in front of people.

④ Have many different experiences.

4   Why did the man call the woman?

① To order Chinese food

② To get a job at the restaurant

③ To sign up for a cooking class

④ To make a reservation for dinner

5   Choose the man's opinion about his job.

(1) What he likes: _____   (2) What he dislikes: _____

ⓐ Can drink various kinds of coffee   ⓑ Makes a lot of money

ⓒ Spends a lot of time standing   ⓓ Meets many different people

ⓔ Gets headaches because of the strong smell

6   When is the man unhappy with his job?

① When he cannot cure animals

② When animals behave badly

③ When he meets rude customers

④ When he has to work for long hours

7   What is the woman mainly talking about?

① How to bungee-jump safely

② What a bungee jumpmaster does

③ The difficulties of being a bungee jumpmaster

④ The qualities that a bungee jumpmaster needs

8   Choose the jobs in the order the man had them.

_____ → _____ → _____

ⓐ movie director   ⓑ actor

ⓒ sales clerk   ⓓ basketball player

A - 1   What is the relationship between the speakers?

① actor – movie director

② reporter – fashion designer

③ customer – shop owner

④ fashion model – photographer

2   Why was it difficult for the man to prepare his work?

① He was in a bad condition.

② He didn't have enough money.

③ He couldn't learn Asian alphabets easily.

④ He worked with people from all over the world.

B - 1   Who is the right person for the advertisement?

① I have an idea for a new TV program!

② I want to become a home shopping host!

③ I work for a home shopping company!

④ I bought a product from Victory Home Shopping!

Julie   Helen   Marie   Sally

2   According to the advertisement, which is NOT true?

① The winner will get a lot of money.

② Only women can apply.

③ Only those under the age of 40 can apply.

④ An email should be sent before March 12th.

Critical ★ Thinking

A Star's Life

1 Check [✓] T for true or F for false.

	T	F
(1) He practices dancing every day.	☐	☐
(2) One of his friends became a famous singer.	☐	☐
(3) He likes Justin Timberlake most.	☐	☐

2 Choose the man's two opinions about stars.

① They can make money easily.

② They can travel all around the world.

③ They can get expensive clothes for free.

④ They have many famous friends.

What do you think?

1

These days, many teenagers want to become stars. Check [✓] if you have the same opinion. You can add your own opinion in the blank.

☐ It is natural because stars are very popular and earn a lot of money.

☐ Teenagers should first think about whether they have enough talent.

☐ It's a worrying trend because teenagers don't know about the difficulties of stars' lives.

2

Talk about the following questions with your partner.

• Have you ever thought about being a star?

• What do you think your life would be like if you were a star?

Vocabulary ★ List

classmate
jeans
mean
hair band
necklace
find
favorite
actress
most
skin
wide
quite
thick
tie
put on
attention
look for
brown
skirt
white
blouse
take A to B
information center
change
a lot
thin
these days
a little
fat
grow
centimeter
hairstyle
pants
instead
wait
jacket

clothes
curly
straight
lose
stress
worried
slowly
member
famous
rock group
singer
sunglasses
handsome
guy
scarf
play
too
main
actor
a bit
act
voice
blind date
cousin
kind
funny
blond
type
police station
train station
cap
handbag
fashion
model
weigh
kilogram
become
appear

show
exciting
last year
break
off work
again
hurt
tired
be interested in
another
job
uncomfortable
makeup
different
natural
take care of
appearance
rule
live
freely
put on makeup
without

favorite
subject
science
history
homework
arrive
around
wake up
late
bus stop
happen
for a moment
pass

miss
sick
wrong
get up
early
a lot of
hate
have fun
interesting
learn
try
activity
everything
seem
hard
difficult
check
exam
result
sometimes
bring
textbook
forget
prepare
parent
fight
know
helpful
later
life
far away
classmate
understand
sports day
score
goal
soccer
win

field trip

remember

art gallery

wonderful

stay up all night

math

French

be absent from

have a cold

anyway

research

dictionary

borrow

plan

together

online

point

get ready

hospital

project

list

part

human

report

hand in

product

due date

almost

leave

on time

make a mistake

strict

at first

actually

friendly

disappointed

gym

correct

cell phone

take away

get back

drop

bottle

terrible

wall

pour

catch

worm

teach

homeschooling

according to

each

talent

poor

environment

smoke

alcohol

get along with

important

social

skill

homeschool

UNIT 03

museum

straight

block

turn

corner

hurry

subway

quick

line

pilot

plane

take off

head

international

airport

enjoy

flight

announcement

travel agency

across

street

try to-v

lost

post office

police station

next to

hear

bell

ring

circus

musical

on foot

delay

heavy snow

any

problem

ticket

theater

too ~ to-v

far

pay

library

near

a lot

need

change

stop

before

place

visit

popular

among

tourist

go shopping

store

along

staff

guest

guide

driver

passenger

flight attendant

hall

carsick

out of

exit

concert

nearby

cheap

upset

rude

loudly

turn down

volume

choice

manner

teenage

hamburger

smell

act

sad

angry

bored

worried

amusement park
cloudy
rainy
clear up
not until
sunny
weekend
hot
weather
sun
snow
ski
snowboard
warm
go on a picnic
flower
wait for
call
be busy v-ing
travel
have a good time
enjoy oneself
ask
outdoor
sure
news
nervous
excited
disappointed
country
Greece
England
spring
summer
stay
during
perfect
winter

set
fall
should
umbrella
shower
believe
take a walk
stop
strong
storm
gray
resort
on the way to
clear
soon
also
bird
fly
low
surprising
sign
way
fish
jump
spider
funny
still
throughout
dry
April
end
October
November
March
lightning
first
dangerous
hold
stand
under

safe
inside
get out
cause
happen
act
birthday
restaurant
throw a garden party
heavy
watch
clothes
cost
spend

grandparent
grandfather
grandmother
get married
brother-in-law
often
pocket money
main
reason
always
laugh
good-looking
humorous
show
picture
take after
both
tell
handsome
face
introduce
plus
perfect

twin
wear
noisy
sometimes
quiet
care about
never
alone
present
already
shopping mall
various
hobby
hike
mountain
movie
action movie
rollerblade
prize
contest
cook
delicious
food
Academy Award
actor
producer
uncle
share
only child
cute
husband
family name
same
usually
tradition
follow
successful
single
one day
wake up

wife	matter	age	album
careerman	forget	chat	hit
anymore	explain	childhood	among
in the end	miss	allow	major in
find out	tired	careful	fat
finally	have ~ in common	for example	ugly
realize	comic book	whole	stage
power	basketball	schedule	appearance
importance	popular	advice	surprised
role	plan	discuss	voice
real	online	collect	easy
apartment	until	worried	judge
lonely	make the first move	ask	cover
miss	friendly	a few	so-so
have a cold	helpful	enough	sweet
at that time	join	social skill	do one's best
take care of	club		please
attention	interest		jazz
describe	tip	UNIT 07	hold
situation	fight		casual
build	understand	fan	location
double	on time	believe	dress code
income	thin	sleep	formal
kid	brave	tonight	introduce
in other words	even	orchestra	actually
couple	bungee-jump	look for	conversation
choose	department store	flute	take place
grow up	close	interested	classical
	move	cello	heavily
UNIT 06	college	audition	guess
	call	practice	listener
shy	reason	test	low
humorous	city	ready	lively
fan	the other day	yet	cheer up
take a trip	lesson	nervous	pop music
easily	as well	instrument	genre
spend	lie	violin	percent
be good at	copy	instead	rap music
gym	choice	pianist	country music
date	website	science	improve
		record	

university
prepare
had better
attend
academy
far
future
relationship
stress
relax
comfortable
position
lie down
floor
take a walk
reduce
headphone
earphone
more than
based on
mood
focus on
noise
research
newspaper
according to
brain
at once
possible
bother
outside
pay attention to

UNIT 08

Thanksgiving
yam
sweet potato
yummy
turkey

bake
pumpkin
pie
parade
holiday
Independence Day
stay
firework
downtown
festival
throw
stranger
bring
bicycle
camp
vacation
hospital
New Year's Day
clean
relative
knife
bookstore
guidebook
beach
attend
present
cellphone
expensive
sweater
coat
international
art
hold
star
weekday
past
servant
master
put
box

gift
worker
popular
sale
neighbor
carnation
celebrate
traditionally
rose
these days
instead
calendar
relax
part-time
meaningful
take a rest

UNIT 09

digital camera
silver
sell
carry
off
yogurt
instead
later
wedding
take a break
cap
on sale
cheap
hat
in total
sense
style
item
look at
try on
put on

place
point
order
miniskirt
exchange
get money back
size
complain
floor
brand-name
event
pair
dress
simple
ribbon
recommend
teenage
pants
product
be famous for
quality
offline
anytime
laptop
speaker
mouse
credit card
add
tiring
restaurant
theater
meal
result
shopaholic
nervous
control
hobby
follow
counselor
owner

host
channel
carefully

UNIT 10

nervous
anyone
soon
fight
subject
Valentine's Day
already
cookie
grade
most
wish
tell a lie
calm down
maybe
make a mistake
matter
explain
ticket
lose
ready
trip
worried
puppy
look after
keep
in that case
search for
probably
terrible
similar
solve
set a schedule
library
weekend

cheat
bored
attend
academy
allow
interest
stop
give up
free
teenager
museum
Rome
painting
amazing
decide
artist
enter
somewhat
prepare
entrance exam
painter
musician
travel guide
road
lead
smoke
promise
forget
instead
lose weight
fat
follow
healthy
disagree
accept
be on a diet

UNIT 11

type

pay
blind date
grow up
painter
mind
homemaker
cook
clean
engineer
househusband
clothes
cute
upset
often
these days
reason
October
express
be interested in
a variety of
envy
care about
weight
average
actress
healthy
diet
normal
miss
part
past
quite
surprising
present
try on
almost
blouse
department store
believe
feeling

small talk
text message
finally
title
difference
explain
relationship
a couple of
question
correct
point
glass
bottle
fruit
cosmetics
newscast
act
other
comic book
romantic
photo album
lie
keep a promise
friendly
wallet
not ~ anymore
in my opinion
happen
between A and B
trust
argue
friendship

UNIT 12

sommelier
wine
customer
choose
fire station

85

bank	cure	star
writer	behave	earn
firefighter	badly	amazing
police officer	rude	wonderful
bank clerk	bungee jumpmaster	for free
prepare	certain	
information	quality	
photographer	bungee jumping	
look after	dangerous	
serve	safely	
open	training	
own	brave	
be interested in	bungee-jump	
main	difficulty	
owner	used to-v	
run	basketball	
be good at	player	
shy	movie director	
in front of	audition	
practice	sales clerk	
whenever	magazine	
anymore	design	
experience	letter	
Chinese	Asian	
I'm afraid (that)	language	
order	Japanese	
sign up for	learn	
make a reservation	reporter	
barista	photographer	
coffeehouse	condition	
cool	alphabet	
taste	home shopping	
hard	host	
all day long	project	
various	chance	
headache	task	
strong	winner	
animal	apply	
perfect	advertisement	
sometimes	lucky	

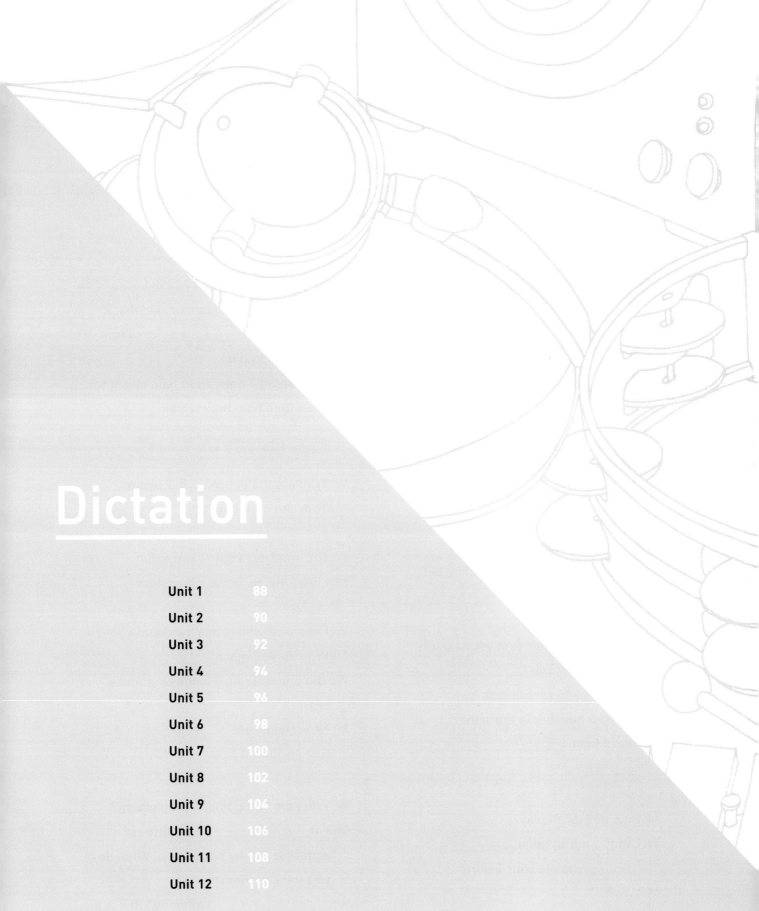

Dictation

Unit 1	88
Unit 2	90
Unit 3	92
Unit 4	94
Unit 5	96
Unit 6	98
Unit 7	100
Unit 8	102
Unit 9	104
Unit 10	106
Unit 11	108
Unit 12	110

UNIT 01 Appearance

Listening * Practice
Answers p. 2

1

W: ① He has _____ _____.

② He is sitting on the chair.

③ He is _____ _____ _____.

④ He is putting on glasses.

2

M: Attention, please! We're _____ _____ a child. Her name is Tiffany and she is _____ _____ _____. She has short brown hair. She is wearing a blue skirt and _____ _____ _____. If you find her, please take her to the information center. Thank you.

3

W: Oh, my god! You're Tom, aren't you?

M: Vicky? _____ _____ _____ _____! You've changed a lot.

W: Have I? (*laughs*) I was very thin, but these days I am _____ _____ _____.

M: But you look great. And you're much taller than before.

W: Yes. I grew 10 centimeters.

M: But your hairstyle is the same.

W: That's right. I _____ _____ _____.

4

M: How do I look today?

W: Umm… not so good. _____ _____ _____ change your T-shirt?

M: Why?

W: I don't think a black T-shirt looks good with your brown pants.

M: Really? Then, I'll go and _____ _____ _____. I'll wear a white shirt instead.

W: Okay. I'll wait here.

5

W1: I'm Kate. I have very curly hair. But I don't like it. I want to _____ _____ _____.

W2: I'm Rachel. These days, I'm losing too much hair. My doctor said that it is _____ _____ _____. I'm worried about it.

W3: I'm Sarah. I have short hair. I want to have long hair, but my hair _____ _____ _____.

6

W: Who are the people in this picture?

M: They are members of _____ _____ _____ _____.

W: Oh, are they? I didn't know that.

M: I like Tony. He is the singer. He's _____ _____.

W: I see. And who is this handsome guy?

M: Who do you mean?

W: The one wearing a white shirt and a scarf.

M: He is Danny. He _____ _____ _____.

7

W: What are you doing, Mr. Spielberg?

M: I'm _____ _____ pictures of actresses for my next movie. What do you think of them?

W: _____ _____ Katherine? She is a great actress.

M: But isn't she too tall? You know, the main actor is _____ _____ _____.

W: Oh, right. Then, what about Scarlett?

M: Good idea. She's _____ _____ Katherine.

8

(*Telephone rings.*)

M: Hello?

W: Hi, this is Tina.

M: Hi, Tina. _____ _____?

W: How about a blind date this Sunday?

M: That sounds good! Who is the girl?

W: She is my cousin, Cathy.

M: _____ _____ _____?

W: She is kind and funny. She has many friends.

M: Great. What does she look like?

W: She's _____ _____ _____, but she is very cute. She has long blond hair.

M: I think she's my type!

Listening ★ Challenge Answers p. 2

A [1-2]

(*Telephone rings.*)

M: Hello, this is the _____ _____. How can I help you?

W: My name is Leanne Parker. A man just _____ _____ _____ at the Boston train station!

M: Did you see him? What did he _____ _____?

W: He was short. And... he was wearing a brown jacket.

M: Anything else?

W: Hmm... oh, he was _____ _____

_____ _____.

M: Okay, and could you tell me about your bag?

W: It is a big white handbag.

M: All right. Please wait at the train station. We will be there _____ _____ _____.

B [1-2]

W: My name is Melisa Brown. I'm a 21-year-old _____ _____. I am 177 centimeters tall, and I weigh 60 kilograms. I _____ _____ _____ and long red hair. I became a model when I was 16 years old. I appeared in many famous fashion shows. It was _____ _____. But last year I broke my leg. So I had a year off work. Now I want to work again.

89

Critical ★ Thinking Answers p. 2

W1: I'm May. I feel uncomfortable when I see men who _____ _____. Men and women are different. Men look nicer when they look natural.

M: I'm Chris. These days, men also want to _____ _____ _____ their appearance. Makeup helps men look better.

W2: I'm Kelly. _____ _____ _____ _____ that men cannot wear makeup? No, there isn't. I think all people should _____ _____.

UNIT 02 School Life

1

W1: I'm Emma. To go to school, I must

_____ _____ _____. I must also

do a lot of homework. I hate school.

M: I'm Bill. At school, I can play with my

friends. I have _____ _____

_____ _____ there.

W2: I'm Debbie. It is very interesting to

_____ _____ _____ in school.

And I can try many fun activities.

2

M: How's your life at school? _____

_____ _____?

W: I think so, Mr. Robinson.

M: Good. You seem to study hard.

W: I'm trying to. But I feel that some

subjects are difficult.

M: _____ _____. I checked your exam

results, and you're doing well.

W: Thank you.

M: But sometimes you don't _____

_____ _____. Don't forget to

prepare everything for class.

W: Okay, sir.

3

M: How's it going, Kate?

W: Not good.

M: _____ _____? Did you have a

fight with your friend?

W: I have to study too many subjects, so

_____ _____ _____.

M: Do you have a lot of homework, too?

W: Yes. I don't know why we must

_____ _____ _____ _____.

M: Cheer up! They'll be helpful later in life.

4

W: Michael, when was the best time in

your school life?

M: Last sports day. I _____ _____

_____ for my soccer team, and we

won!

W: Right! You were great.

M: Thanks. _____ _____ _____,

Helen?

W: I liked the field trip most.

M: Do you mean when we went to Rose

Lake?

W: No. Do you remember the art gallery in

Seattle? I _____ _____ _____

by Picasso there.

5

W: _____ _____ _____.

M: I stayed up all night doing math homework.

W: What? We have one more day to do

math homework.

M: No, we don't. Math is _____ _____

_____ today.

W: What are you talking about? Today's

first class is French.

M: Really? Oh, no. I thought _____

_____ _____.

W: That's too bad. Don't forget that we

have English homework today.

6

(*Telephone rings.*)

W: Hello.

M: Hi, Anna. This is John.

W: John! Why were you _____ _____

school today?

M: I had a cold, but I feel better now.

W: Then, will you come to school tomorrow?

M: I will. Anyway, is there _____ _____ for tomorrow?

W: Yes, you should research about John F. Kennedy.

M: Anything else?

W: That's all. And _____ _____ _____ for English class.

M: Okay. Thanks.

7

M: Mom, do I have to go to school today?

W: Are you _____ _____?

M: No, I just don't want to go.

W: Are you kidding?

M: I can study at home by _____ _____ _____. Why should I study at school?

W: I understand your point. But studying isn't everything. You can learn many other things at school.

M: But Mom...

W: _____ _____ _____ _____, now!

8

M: Attention, students! This homework is a _____ _____. Make groups of four members and give me a list of members by tomorrow. Your project is to choose one part of the _____ _____ and research it. You should write a three-page report. Please _____ _____ _____ by next Friday.

A [1-2]

W: How was your first day at your new school?

M: Great. But I almost _____ _____ _____ _____.

W: Why? You left home on time.

M: But I made a mistake. It comes at 7:10, not at 7:15.

W: Really? I'll _____ _____ _____ earlier, then. So, how was your school?

M: My teacher Ms. Sullivan _____ _____ at first, but she's actually very friendly.

W: Good. How about your classmates?

M: There are _____ _____ _____ in my class, so I'm happy.

W: (laughing) Good for you.

M: But I _____ _____ _____ the school gym. It's too old.

B [1-2]

M: Emily, I'm having a bad day!

W: _____ _____?

M: In my English class, my teacher saw me using my cell phone. So he _____ _____ _____.

W: Did you get it back after class?

M: No, I can get it back _____ _____.

W: That's too bad.

M: Also, in science class, I _____ _____ _____, and it broke.

W: How terrible!

M: That's not all. I have a history test in the afternoon, but I can't find my notebook.

W: That's too bad.

91

M: This is not my day.

M1: I'm Tony. Some people teach their
    children _____ _____ . So, their
    children don't go to school. I think this
    homeschooling is a good idea. Parents
    can choose _____ _____ _____
    according to each child's talent.

W: I'm Julia. Many schools have poor
   learning environments. Also, children
   can _____ _____ or drinking
   alcohol because of friends. Therefore,
   I think homeschooling is better for
   children.

M2: I'm Darren. In school, children can learn
    how to _____ _____ _____
    other people. Homeschooling can't
    teach this important thing.

92

UNIT 03 Transportation & Location

Listening ★ Practice   Answers p. 3

1
M: Good afternoon. I'm James Parker, the
   pilot of this plane. We just _____
   _____ and are heading for Hong Kong
   International Airport. It takes about
   _____ _____ . Today's weather
   is fine. So, please _____ _____
   _____ with us. Thank you.

2
M: Excuse me. _____ _____ _____
   _____ to Jurong Bird Park here?

W: No. The bus stop is just over there,
   across the street.

M: Oh, I see. Do you know which bus
   should I take?

W: I think _____ _____ _____
   _____.

M: Number thirty?

W: No, number thirteen.

M: Okay, thanks.

3
(Telephone rings.)

W: Thank you for calling Star Café.

M: Hello, I'm trying to get there now, but
   _____ _____ .

W: What can you see around you?

M: Well, there is a post office on my left.

W: Then, go straight one block and
   _____ _____ .

M: Okay.

W: Then you will see the police station. The
   café is _____ _____ it.

4
W: Today was my first day in London. In the
   morning, I _____ _____ _____
   to Big Ben. It was very tall, and I heard
   the bell ring. Then I _____ _____
   _____ to Tower Bridge. It was
   beautiful. After that, I went to Piccadilly
   Circus _____ _____ and saw a
   famous musical.

5
M: Attention, please! The train from Boston
   is delayed _____ _____ heavy
   snow. It was going to arrive at 11:00,
   but it will _____ _____ _____
   _____ . Sorry for any problems. Thank

you for your understanding.

6

W: Michael! I'm sorry, _____ _____.

M: Oh, Lisa! The bus just left.

W: I'm really sorry! When will the next bus come?

M: _____ _____ _____ _____.
   Why were you late?

W: I went to the train station to buy tickets. It took a long time.

M: I see. Let's take a taxi. The theater is

_____ _____ _____ _____.

W: Okay. I will pay!

7

W: Henry, do you know _____ _____
   _____ _____ the Louvre Museum?

M: Yes. You can get there on the number 24 bus.

W: Where is the _____ _____?

M: It's across from the library.

W: Oh, so it's quite near. _____ _____
   _____ _____ _____?

M: It takes about thirty minutes.

W: I see. Thanks a lot.

8

W: Excuse me. Does this line go to Times Square?

M: No. You need to _____ _____
   _____.

W: Oh, really? Which line do I need to take?

M: Let me see. You have to _____
   _____ _____ _____ from Union Square station.

W: Union Square station? I see.

M: Times Square is just _____ _____
   from Union Square station.

Listening · Challenge Answers p. 3

A [1-2]

M: Good morning. _____ _____,
   ma'am?

W: To Tokyo Hotel, please. How long will it take?

M: About 15 minutes. _____ _____
   _____ _____?

W: I'm from Canada.

M: I see. Have you ever been here before?

W: No. Are there any _____ _____
   _____ _____?

M: What about Tokyo Tower or Disney Land? They are popular places for tourists.

W: I see. And where can I go shopping?

M: Shibuya is a good shopping place. There are many stores _____ _____
   _____.

W: Thank you. I'll go shopping there tomorrow.

B [1-2]

M: Helen, do you know how I can get to Carnegie Hall?

W: Yes. You are going to _____ _____
   _____, aren't you?

M: That's right. I don't like buses because I
   _____ _____.

W: I know. Anyway, do you know 57th Street station?

M: Yes, I do.

W: Okay. There, you should _____
   _____ _____ exit number 1.

M: Exit number 1?

W: Yes. Then, go straight for two blocks

and turn left. You will see the hall _____ _____ _____. You can't miss it.

W: Dave, is something wrong? You look upset.

M: I met some rude people _____ _____ _____.

W: What happened?

M: Well, a girl was listening to music very loudly.

W: Why didn't you ask her to _____ _____ _____ _____?

M: I did, but she said no. She said that it was her choice.

W: She really _____ _____ _____.

M: That's not all.

W: What else?

M: A teenage boy got on the subway and started to eat a hamburger. It _____ _____.

W: Oh, dear.

M: I can't understand why they _____ _____ _____. They should learn better manners.

UNIT 04 Seasons & Weather

1

(Telephone rings.)

W: Hello.

M: Hello, Mom. It's me.

W: John! I _____ _____ _____ your call.

M: Sorry, Mom. I was busy traveling.

W: So _____ _____ _____ in New York?

M: It was cloudy yesterday, but it has _____ _____ now.

W: That's good. Are you having a good time?

M: I'm _____ _____. So, how's Seattle?

W: It's snowing a lot.

2

M: What will the weather be like tomorrow, Sandy?

W: Why do you ask?

M: I'm going to _____ _____ _____.

W: Wait. Did you say it's tomorrow?

M: Yeah, is there some problem?

W: I heard _____ _____ _____ _____.

M: Oh, no! Are you sure?

W: Yes. It's going to rain all day.

M: That's bad news! I don't want to _____ _____ _____ _____ in the rain.

W: That's too bad.

3

M: I've traveled to many countries. My _____ _____ are Greece and England. Greece is nice in the spring. In the summer, it's _____ _____ _____ _____ there. In England, the sun stays up till 10 o'clock in the evening during summer. So it's the perfect time to travel there. _____ _____ _____, the sun sets too early.

4

M: Oh, _____ _____. I should buy an

umbrella.

W: Just wait a while. I think it's just a shower.

M: Really?

W: Believe me. The weather in London

_____ _____ _____ in a day.

M: Then why don't we wait in that café

over there?

W: Okay. Let's go to Hyde Park and _____

_____ _____ when the rain stops.

M: Great.

5

M: Let's look at the weather _____

_____ _____ for tomorrow. There'll

be strong storms in London. Singapore

will be very _____ _____ _____.

In Seoul, it'll be gray and a little cold.

And it will be _____ _____

_____ in Vancouver.

6

W: I went to _____ _____ _____

yesterday. On the way to the resort,

the weather was _____ _____

_____. But when we arrived, it

started to rain. I thought I wouldn't be

able to ski. But soon, the rain changed

to snow. Skiing _____ _____

_____ was cold, but also very nice.

7

W: Look at that bird. It's _____ _____

_____.

M: Is that surprising?

W: When a bird flies low, it's a sign that it

will _____ _____.

M: Really? Are there any other ways to

know when it will rain?

W: Yes. Fish jump out of the water, and

spiders come into houses.

M: That's funny. Still, I don't believe it.

W: Let's _____ _____ _____ then.

8

M: _____ _____ _____, right?

W: Yes, I am.

M: How's the weather there?

W: It's hot _____ _____ _____.

M: So is there only one season?

W: Well, we have a dry season and a rainy

season.

M: When are they?

W: Dry season starts _____ _____

and ends around October, and rainy

season is from _____ _____

_____.

M: I see.

95

Listening * Challenge   Answers p. 4

A [1-2]

M: Let's learn what we should do when

_____ _____. First, it's dangerous

to hold an umbrella or stand under a

tree. It's safe to be in a low place. If

there's a tall building, _____ _____.

If you are in a car, stay in it to be safe.

But if you are in the water, you should

_____ _____.

B [1-2]

W: Next Wednesday is Dad's birthday.

_____ _____ _____ _____?

M: How about going to a nice restaurant

together?

W: Well... I don't think he'd like that. _____
_____ throwing a garden party?

M: That's a good idea. But we should check the weather on the Internet first.

W: Let's see. It's going to rain with _____ _____ next Wednesday.

M: That's not good. What will the weather be like this weekend?

W: It'll be _____ _____ _____.

M: Okay. If it doesn't rain, let's do it this Saturday.

W: Great!

Critical ★ Thinking   Answers p. 4

W1: I'm Marina. I think it's good to have four seasons. I _____ _____ the changes in each of the seasons.

M: I'm Seyoon. Because we _____ _____ _____, we have to buy many clothes. It costs a lot of money to buy them.

W2: I'm Yuki. I like sports a lot. I like having four seasons because I can _____ _____ _____ during each season.

UNIT 05 Family

Listening ★ Practice   Answers p. 4

1

M: My name is John. _____ _____ _____ _____ a picture of my family. You can see my father, my mother and me. I _____ _____ both of my parents. I have my father's nose and

mouth. And I have my mother's eyes. People tell me _____ _____.

2

W: Tony. Do you know the boy _____ _____ Jack?

M: Oh, he's my brother, Chuck.

W: He's very handsome. Can you _____ _____ _____ _____?

M: (laughing) He's much younger than you. Plus he has a girlfriend.

W: Oh, boy.

M: I have an _____ _____, too.

W: Really? How old is he?

M: He's nineteen. He's one year _____ _____ _____.

W: Perfect!

3

W: _____ _____ brothers and sisters do you have, Dan?

M: I have two older brothers and _____ _____ _____.

W: Wow. You have a large family. Do you like having many brothers and sisters?

M: Well, not always. _____ _____ _____ _____, I had to wear old clothes from my brothers.

W: That's too bad.

M: And the house is noisy. Sometimes I want to be _____ _____ _____ _____.

4

W: Jack, Mom's birthday is tomorrow. What should we buy her _____ _____ _____?

M: Why don't we buy her a scarf?

W: She already has so many.

M: Then, _____ _____ _____?

Summer is almost here.

W: That's a good idea. She _____

_____ _____.

M: Let's go to the shopping mall now to buy them.

W: Okay.

5

W: My family members have various hobbies. My father _____ _____ in the mountains every weekend. My mother likes to _____ _____. She loves action movies. My brother loves rollerblading. He _____ _____ _____ _____ in a rollerblading contest. I enjoy cooking. I like to make delicious food for my family.

6

M: Do you know that Angelina Jolie's _____ _____ are famous like her? Her father, Jon Voight, won an Academy Award for Best Actor. Her older brother, James Haven, _____ _____ an actor and producer. Her uncle, Chip Taylor, was a famous singer _____

_____ _____.

7

W1: I'm Linda. I only have brothers. I want to _____ _____ with an older sister.

W2: I'm Jenny. My friend Lily has an older brother. He _____ _____ _____ so much. I'd like to have a brother like him.

M: I'm Tom. I'm _____ _____ _____.

I want to have a cute younger sister.

8

M: May, is your _____ _____

_____ Pitt?

W: Yes.

M: That's the same family name as yours.

W: In America, each woman usually uses her husband's family name.

M: What was your family name before _____ _____ _____?

W: It was Smith.

M: How about Cathy? Cathy's family name is Stevens, but _____ _____ is Jones.

W: Using the husband's family name is a tradition. But some women _____

_____ _____.

Listening ∗ Challenge Answers p. 4

A [1-2]

W: Yesterday, I saw _____ _____

_____. In the movie, a man lives a successful single life. One day, everything changes. He _____

_____ and has a wife and children. He's not a successful careerman anymore. But he enjoys his new life. In the end, he _____ _____ that his family life was just his dream. He finally realizes that family is _____ _____

_____ _____ in life.

B [1-2]

W: _____ _____! How was your life in France?

M: Well, I lived alone in a small apartment.

W: So, did you _____ _____?

M: Yes. I missed talking with my family. I also missed my mom's food.

97

W: I heard you _____ _____ there, too.

M: Yes. I had a bad cold.

W: That's too bad!

M: At that time, I really missed being taken care of by _____ _____.

W: So, are you having fun with your family now?

M: Of course! I'm _____ _____ _____ _____ at home. I love my family!

Critical★Thinking Answers p. 4

M: Jill, what does "DINK" mean?

W: It means "_____ _____ _____ _____." In other words, it's a working couple without kids.

M: So, they both work but don't _____ _____ _____ _____?

W: Yes. Think about the money people spend on their kids. Without kids, couples can _____ _____ _____ _____ their hobbies.

M: Even so, I think they'll feel lonely without children.

W: I don't think so, Paul. DINK couples can have fun with all their friends. Why should they _____ _____ _____ _____?

UNIT 06 Friends

Listening ★ Practice Answers p. 5

1

M: Mom, what's the date today?

W: It's May 11th.

M: Oh, my god!

W: _____ _____ _____?

M: Yesterday was Helen's birthday.

W: She is one of your best friends. How could you _____ _____ _____?

M: I thought today was May 10th. What should I do?

W: Give _____ _____ _____ _____. And explain why you missed her birthday.

M: Okay.

2

M: My name is Jack. My _____ _____ is Steve. We have many things in common. We both like comic books and computer games. Also, we are _____ _____ at our school. He is handsome and kind, so he is _____ _____ with girls. But I'm not.

3

M: You _____ _____ _____. What's up?

W: I have a great plan for today.

M: _____ _____ _____?

W: I'm going to meet Julie. She is my friend on the Internet.

M: Oh, is this your first time to meet her?

W: Yes. We _____ _____ _____ last month, but she was sick then.

M: I see. Have a good time!

4

M: Do you want to make many new friends at your new school? Then, _____ _____ _____ until other people talk to you. You should make the first move. And smile! It makes you look friendly. It's also helpful to _____ _____ _____. You can meet people with the same interests.

5

M: Mom, I'm home.

W: You came home too early. Didn't you _____ _____ _____ _____ with Catherine?

M: Yeah, I planned to. But we _____ _____ _____ _____.

W: What happened?

M: We were going to meet at 3, but she was _____ _____ _____.

W: Oh, no! I understand why you are angry with her.

6

W: When I went to France, I made _____ _____ _____. Gina is good at making funny faces. She made me laugh a lot. Kelly is very pretty, but she has short hair and _____ _____ _____. Rachel is very short and thin, but she is brave. She even _____ _____!

7

W: Nick, I saw Billy last Saturday.

M: Billy? Where?

W: _____ _____ _____ at the department store.

M: Oh, I really miss him. I haven't seen him _____ _____ _____ _____.

W: Really? I thought you and Billy were close friends.

M: We were. But he _____ _____ North Carolina last year. He got into a

college there.

W: Then, _____ _____ _____ call him?

M: I will.

8

M: I like my friend Matt, but we _____ _____ _____ _____. When I do something, he does the same thing. The other day, I bought a shirt. The next day, he was _____ _____ _____ _____. When I started swimming lessons, he joined the swimming class _____ _____.

Listening • Challenge Answers p. 5

A [1-2]

M: Do you want to _____ _____ from all over the world? If so, *Friends.com* is _____ _____ _____ on the Internet. This website opened in 2005. Now we have thousands of members from over 150 countries. Anyone _____ _____ _____ can become a member of this site. After you join us, you can find new friends easily _____ _____, age, and interests. Join now and be our friend.

B [1-2]

W: You look excited, Ricky.

M: I'm _____ _____ _____ with my friend. We're going to Spain!

W: Great! But you should _____ _____ _____. When I travelled with my friend, we had many problems.

M: What were the problems, Sarah?

99

W: _____ _____ _____ _____ ,

    for example, I wanted to go shopping

    and she wanted to go skiing. So, I spent

    the whole day fighting with her.

M: So _____ _____ _____ _____ ?

W: Before you travel, talk about the schedule.

    And plan everything together.

M: Thanks for the advice.

Critical★Thinking Answers p. 5

W: My father _____ _____ _____

    I don't have many friends. He says he

    learns many things from having different

    friends. And when he has a problem,

    he can ask them all _____ _____

    _____ . But I think a few close friends

    are enough for me. When I have a

    problem, I _____ _____ _____

    _____ about it and they help me. I

    don't think I need more friends.

UNIT 07 Music

Listening ★ **Practice** Answers p. 5

1

M: You're _____ _____ _____ so

    hard.

W: The test in our music class is only a few

    days away.

M: _____ _____ _____ yet, so I'm

    very nervous.

W: Why are you worried? Don't you

    _____ _____ _____ well?

M: That was a long time ago. I won't play

    the piano this time.

W: Then _____ _____ will you play?

M: I'll play the violin instead.

2

W: My _____ _____ is Yuhki Kuramoto.

    He's from Japan. He studied science in

    college and was in the school orchestra.

    He recorded _____ _____

    _____ in 1986. The song *Lake Louise*

    was a big hit from this album. Among

    his songs, I like *Romance* _____

    _____ .

3

M: Last night, I was watching a _____

    _____ on TV. A fat, ugly woman

    came on the stage. _____ _____

    _____ _____ , I thought, 'She will

    not sing well.' But I was very surprised

    when she started to _____ _____

    _____ . Her voice was beautiful and

    her song was great.

4

W: Wow, I really _____ _____

    _____ . How about you?

M: Well, it was so-so.

W: Really? The singer _____ _____

    _____ , didn't she?

M: Yes, she did. I liked her sweet voice and

    she _____ _____ _____ to

    please us.

W: Yes, her dancing was great as well. Why

    didn't you enjoy it?

M: The concert hall was _____ _____

    and very hot.

5

M: My family is _____ _____ _____

_____. We're going to play popular jazz music. It'll be held in Denver High School hall on Friday, _____ _____ at 7 p.m. You can wear casual clothes. I hope you can come and enjoy

_____ _____ _____ _____.

6

M: Now, let's meet the next student. Could you introduce yourself?

W: My name is Michelle Williams, and I'm

_____ _____ _____.

M: How do you feel now?

W: Actually, I'm very nervous.

M: _____ _____ you'll do fine. What song are you going to sing?

W: Mariah Carey's *Hero*.

M: Okay. _____ _____ _____.

7

W: Good afternoon, everyone. This is Sarah Jones of *Music Time*. It's _____ _____. I guess many listeners are feeling low. So our first song is a lively pop song to _____ _____ _____. This is Beyonce singing, *Crazy in Love*.

8

M: ① Pop music is _____ _____ _____ among the music genres.

② The same number of teens like rock and R&B.

③ _____ _____ of teens enjoy listening to rap music.

④ Only four percent of teens _____ _____ _____.

Listening ★ Challenge Answers p. 5

A [1-2]

W: Your piano playing has improved a lot. _____ _____, David.

M: Thank you, Ms. Clinton.

W: How about _____ _____ _____ at university? You're the best player in my class.

M: I'd like to. How should I prepare?

W: You'd better attend a music academy first. Chicago Academy has famous teachers.

M: But _____ _____ _____ _____?

W: If so, Grand Academy is near here.

M: Then that academy is better for me.

W: Good. You'll do well.

M: Thank you. In the future, I want to teach students _____ _____ _____.

B [1-2]

W: Do you have a lot of stress? If so, _____ _____ _____ can help. Here's how. The most important thing is to choose the right music. Slow music can _____ _____ _____. But when you want to cheer up, listen to faster music. And get into a _____ _____. You can lie down on the floor. It's also good to take a walk while listening to your favorite music.

Critical ★ Thinking Answers p. 6

M: I'm Steve. I always listen to music when I study. It helps me _____ _____ _____ because I don't hear the noise

around me. But my mom tells me that
_____ _____. She read scientists'
research about it in the newspaper.
According to the research, our brain
can't do two things at once. So _____
_____ _____ to focus on studying
while listening to music. But I don't
really believe it.

UNIT 08 Holidays

Answers p. 6

Listening * **Practice**

1

M: Do you know about Songkran? It's a
_____ _____ _____ in Thailand.
It is from April 13th to 15th. During
Songkran, people _____ _____
onto strangers on the street to bring
good luck. They even throw water onto
people _____ _____ and buses.
But everyone smiles and enjoys the fun.

2

W: I'm going camping near Stanley Park
_____ _____ _____. Do you
want to go with me?

M: Yes, I do. When are you going?

W: How about next Thursday, _____
_____?

M: How about next Friday instead? Thursday
is my mom's birthday.

W: Okay. Sam is going too. Is that okay?

M: Of course. _____ _____ _____.

3

M: I heard you're planning to _____
_____ for a vacation. Have a great

time there!

W: Well... I'm not going. I'm _____
_____.

M: Why? Is it because of work?

W: No. Mark was going to travel with me.
But he's _____ _____ _____
now.

M: You really wanted to go, didn't you? I'm
sorry to hear that.

4

W: The day before New Year's Day, Chinese
people _____ _____ _____.
On New Year's Day, people visit their
relatives. In the evening, they _____
_____. They don't cook on this day.
They think using knives on New Year's
Day _____ _____ _____. So,
they make food the day before
New Year's Day.

5

W: _____ _____ _____ _____?

M: I'm going to the bookstore.

W: Are you going to buy comic books
again?

M: No. I'm going to buy a travel guidebook.
I'm _____ _____ _____
_____ during summer vacation.

W: Sounds great!

M: So, what are you doing during the
vacation?

W: I'm _____ _____ _____.

6

M: What are you doing _____ _____
_____, Kate?

W: I'm going to Vancouver.

M: How nice. It'll be fun _____ _____

_____ _____.

W: You don't look happy, Joe. What's up?

M: I was going to travel with friends, but
   now I can't.

W: Why not?

M: I have to _____ _____ _____.
   I got a D in math.

W: Oh, I'm sorry.

7

M: Mary, Mom is going to _____

   _____ _____ _____.

W: Great! You want a cellphone, don't you?

M: No, they're too expensive.

W: What do you want then, Tom?

M: A cheap MP3 player. How about you?

W: I _____ _____ _____.

M: You already have many sweaters. What
   about a coat?

W: No, I want a sweater. I saw a really
   pretty one _____ _____ _____.

8

W: _____ _____ _____ _____

   during the vacation.

M: Why Scotland?

W: I want to go to the Edinburgh Festival
   Fringe.

M: _____ _____?

W: It's the largest international arts festival
   in the world.

M: When is it?

W: It starts on _____ _____. It's
   usually held for three weeks.

M: Do famous people attend the festival?

W: Sure! Hugh Grant and Jude Law are
   going _____ _____.

M: Great!

Listening ⋆ Challenge Answers p. 6

A [1-2]

M: Boxing Day _____ _____

   _____. It is on the first weekday
   after Christmas. In the past, servants
   _____ _____ from their masters
   the day after Christmas. Masters put the
   presents in boxes. That's how Boxing
   Day got its name. Today, people still

   _____ _____ _____ _____

   on that day. It's also a popular shopping
   day because most stores have _____

   _____.

B [1-2]

M: When is Mother's Day in America?

W: Mother's Day is on the _____

   _____ _____ _____.

M: What do people do on that day?

W: They give carnations to their moms as
   a thank-you gift.

M: Do people celebrate Father's Day, too?

W: Yes. Father's Day is on the _____

   _____ _____ _____.

M: Do people give carnations to their
   fathers, too?

W: No. Traditionally, people gave roses
   to their fathers, but these days people
   usually give _____ _____ instead.

Critical⋆Thinking Answers p. 6

M: How was your Christmas, Linda?

W: Great. I watched TV and ate holiday
   food at home.

M: What? You just _____ _____?

W: I'm usually busy studying, so I just relax

during the holidays.

M: I'm also busy with my part-time job. But

I _____ _____ _____ .

W: What did you do, Tim?

M: I made food for poor people.

W: How nice.

M: I do it _____ _____ . I like helping

others.

W: Helping others is good. But I think the

holidays are for _____ _____

_____ .

UNIT 09 Shopping

Listening * **Practice**   Answers p. 6

1

W: Chris, is there anything you want?

M: This yogurt _____ _____ .

W: It's a little expensive, but let's get it.

Anything else?

M: We need milk for tomorrow morning.

W: And _____ _____ _____

_____ some orange juice, too.

M: We have orange juice at home. How

about _____ _____ _____

instead?

W: Okay.

2

M: Kate, _____ _____ _____

_____ about that blue jacket? It's nice.

W: I don't like the color.

M: _____ _____ _____ for three

hours already. Why don't you buy a

jacket later?

W: I must buy one today to wear for the

wedding.

M: I'm so tired. Let's _____ _____

_____ and eat some ice cream first.

W: Okay.

3

W: That cap looks good. Is it new?

M: Yes. I went to the J Mall yesterday. It

was _____ _____ .

W: How much was it?

M: It was $5.

W: Wow. That's _____ _____ . Did you

buy just one?

M: No. I bought _____ _____

_____ , too. It was $6.

4

M: When you shop, it's good to take a

friend with a good _____ _____

_____ . And think about which items

to buy before you _____ _____ .

Or, you might buy too many things.

Don't just look at clothes, but _____

_____ _____ . You might not like

them after putting them on.

5

(Telephone rings.)

M: This is CX Home Shopping.

W: Hello. I _____ _____ _____

three days ago. But I got the wrong color.

M: Okay. _____ _____ _____ ?

W: It's Kelly Louise.

M: Let's see. You ordered a black miniskirt

on Monday.

W: Yes. But I got a yellow one.

M: I'm sorry. We'll _____ _____

_____ _____ .

W: Okay.

6

W: Attention, shoppers! Right now,

_____ _____ _____ _____,

there's a brand-name sunglasses event.
You can buy one pair for $60. All the
ladies fashion shops on the fifth floor
are having _____ _____ _____.
Men's shoes are 40% off on the ninth
floor. We hope you _____ _____
with us.

7

M: Are you _____ _____ _____?

W: I'm looking for something to wear to a
party.

M: How about this yellow dress?

W: It's pretty, but too simple.

M: How about this one with the _____
_____ on it?

W: I don't like pink.

M: Then I'd like to _____ _____
_____ _____ to you.

W: Great! I'll take it.

8

M: Are you looking for the best _____
_____ _____ for teenage boys?
Visit *Mark's*. We have jackets, pants,
T-shirts, and shoes. Our products
_____ _____ _____ their
quality. We have an offline store in New
York, too. We're _____ _____
_____ _____ until this Sunday.
Visit us anytime!

Listening ★ Challenge   Answers p. 7

A [1-2]

(*Telephone rings.*)

W: _____ _____ Happy Home
Shopping.

M: Hello. I want to buy an S laptop.

W: _____ _____ do you want, silver
or black?

M: I want black.

W: Do you also need speakers or a mouse?

M: No, I don't.

W: Okay, _____ _____. How would
you like to pay?

M: I'll pay _____ _____ _____. Oh,
I'm sorry, but can I add the speakers?

W: Sure. They will be $100 more.

M: Okay. When will I get them?

W: You'll get them _____ _____
_____.

M: Thanks.

B [1-2]

W: I'm going to Hong Kong _____
_____. Where should I go shopping?

M: Visit Harbor City.

W: Ah, I heard about that place. Is it really
that big?

M: Yes. There are over 700 stores.

W: It _____ _____ _____. Any
place else?

M: Pacific Place is smaller than Harbor City.
There are _____ _____ _____
in it.

W: How about Times Square?

M: Many young people go there. There's a
large movie theater.

105

W: Pacific Place _____ _____. I want
    to shop and eat a nice meal.
M: Nice!

Critical★Thinking Answers p. 7

W: _____ _____ _____?
M: It says you're a shopaholic.
W: I thought so. I get nervous if I don't shop.
M: You need to control yourself, Lisa.
W: _____ _____ _____ _____?
M: First, you should stop using all your
    credit cards. And make some new
    hobbies.
W: Why?
M: That way, you'll have _____ _____
    _____ _____.
W: Anything else?
M: Before buying anything, ask yourself
    three times if you really need it.
W: Okay. I'll try.
M: Visit me again in a week. I want to see if
    you're _____ _____ _____.
W: Thank you.

UNIT 10 Advice

Listening ★ Practice   Answers p. 7

1

W1: My name is Jane. Every day I _____
    _____ after school. But my school
    grades are still low.
M: I'm Tom. I'm _____ _____ most
    other students. How can I become taller?
W2: I'm Susan. I want to buy some new

clothes. But my mom thinks I already
have too many clothes, so she told me
_____ _____ _____ _____.

2

W: What's wrong?
M: I heard that Jack _____ _____
    about me to some other friends.
W: Really? But Jack is your best friend, isn't
    he?
M: Yes. I'm so angry at him.
W: _____ _____. Why don't you talk
    with Jack about it?
M: Do you think I should?
W: Yes. Maybe he just _____ _____
    _____.
M: Okay. I'll do that.

3

M: I want to go to a Hilary Duff concert. All
    of my best friends will go there. But I
    _____ _____ _____ _____
    for a ticket. My parents will not buy one
    for me. They don't like me _____
    _____ _____. I'm so sad.

4

M: _____ _____ _____ _____
    the trip?
W: Almost. But I'm worried about my
    puppy. I can't find anyone to _____
    _____ him.
M: Why don't you ask your brother?
W: I already did. But he said no.
M: Well, I heard that there are _____
    _____ _____.
W: Really?
M: Yeah, people keep their dogs there
    during vacations.

W: In that case, I should _____ _____ puppy hotels on the Internet.

5

W: I _____ _____. I always fight with my brother about using the computer.

M: I understand. My family had a similar problem before.

W: Really? How did your family solve it?

M: We _____ _____ _____ for using the computer.

W: What do you mean?

M: For example, on Monday, I use the computer _____ _____ _____ _____. Then my sister uses it.

W: Wow, my family should try that, too.

6

W: During the _____ _____ _____, I saw Sally looking at Mary's paper. Cheating is wrong, so I told my teacher about it. Because of that, Sally is _____ _____ _____ and doesn't want to talk to me. I don't want to _____ _____ _____. What should I do?

7

W: What's wrong? You look so sad.

M: I want to _____ _____ _____ _____, but my mom won't allow it.

W: Why not?

M: She thinks I'll lose interest after a short time.

W: Well, maybe she's right. You stopped going to _____ _____ after two weeks.

M: That's true, but I really love dancing. I won't _____ _____.

W: Then, how about joining a free dance club and learning there instead?

M: That sounds great!

8

M: ① 20 percent of teenagers _____

_____ _____ _____.

② 10 percent of teenagers tell their father about their problems.

③ _____ _____ of teenagers talk to their friends.

④ 15 percent of teenagers don't _____ _____ _____ about their problems.

Listening ∗ Challenge   Answers p. 7

A [1-2]

W: _____ _____, I visited the Vatican Museums in Rome. There were many _____ _____. But I liked the paintings by Michelangelo the most. They were amazing. Now I've decided to _____ _____ _____ just like him. So, I want to enter a good art university. But I'm very worried because I'm _____ _____. I have only a year to prepare for the entrance exam. Can I do it?

B [1-2]

W: Mark, I have a big problem.

M: _____ _____ _____?

W: I promised Amy I would go shopping with her this Saturday. But then I _____ _____ _____.

M: Today is only Wednesday. What's the problem?

W: I also promised my boyfriend I would

_____ _____ _____ _____

with him on the same day.

M: Oh, so what are you going to do?

W: I don't know.

M: _____ _____ _____ that you

forgot about your plan with Amy. He'll

understand.

W: Okay. I'll ask him to see a movie

_____ _____ instead.

Critical ★ Thinking   Answers p. 7

M1: My girlfriend wants me to _____

_____. She thinks I'm too fat, but

I don't think I am. Anne, what do you

think?

W: Chris, she's your girlfriend. If you really

love her, you should _____ _____

_____. Also, it is healthy to lose

weight. How about you, Alex?

M2: I _____ _____ _____, Anne.

Chris, you don't need to lose weight. If

she loves you, she should accept you

_____ _____ _____ _____.

If she can't, then she doesn't really love

you.

UNIT 11 Boys & Girls

Listening ★ Practice   Answers p. 8

1

M: Hi, I'm looking for some _____

_____.

W: Is the baby a boy or a girl?

M: It's a girl.

W: How about _____ _____ _____?

M: It's cute, but I don't like pink. I don't

know why a girl should wear pink clothes.

W: I see. Then what about the blue or

yellow one?

M: I'll _____ _____ _____

_____.

2

M: Why _____ _____ _____?

W: Don't you know why?

M: I have no idea. Is it because I don't

_____ _____ _____?

W: No, it isn't. I know you're busy these

days.

M: Then what's the reason?

W: What date is it today?

M: Today is the _____ _____

_____. Why are you asking?

W: Teddy! How can you forget my birthday?

M: Oh, no! _____ _____ _____.

3

M1: I'm Sam. Every morning, my sister

takes two hours to _____ _____.

But it takes me only twenty minutes. I'm

glad I'm a boy!

M2: I'm Bill. _____ _____ _____

fashion. But there isn't a big enough

variety of clothes for boys. I really envy

girls.

M3: I'm Jack. I think my parents _____

_____ _____ my sister because

she's a girl. I wish I were a girl.

4

W: I'm 165 cm tall and my weight is _____

_____. I don't think I'm fat. But when

my friend Rio heard my weight, he said I was fat. I guess boys don't know about girls' _____ _____. They only know the weight of thin actresses.

5

W: Is it true that boys don't _____
_____ _____ _____?

M: I think it is. I still miss my first girlfriend.

W: Really? I didn't know that.

M: Don't you miss your first love?

W: No, I don't. He is just _____ _____
_____ my past.

M: Wow, that's quite surprising.

W: I only care about my _____ _____.

6

M: Today I went shopping with my girlfriend. She _____ _____ almost every blouse in the department store. But she _____ _____ _____ because she couldn't find a good one. Can you believe it? It _____ _____
_____ to buy nothing! I won't go shopping with her again.

7

M: I like Donna, but she doesn't know.

W: _____ _____ _____ tell her your feelings?

M: You know I'm shy.

W: Then just start by _____ _____
_____ by text message.

M: Small talk?

W: Yes, like asking about homework.

M: That's a good idea. I'll send her a text message _____ _____.

8

W: Finally, Johnny Gray's third book has

_____ _____! The title is
Understanding. It's about the differences between men and women. It _____ _____ _____ for those differences. This book will help couples _____ _____ _____. You can buy it from October 12th.

Listening ★ Challenge   Answers p. 8

A [1-2]

M: Valentine's Day is only _____ _____
_____ _____ away. So, today's *Challenge Show* will have lots of questions about Valentine's Day. Here's the first question. If you _____
_____ _____ _____, you'll get 10 points. Listen carefully. This is one of the most popular gifts for Valentine's Day. It is usually in a glass bottle. It smells like flowers or fruit. You can buy this in a _____ _____. What is this?

B [1-2]

W: Danny, I had a fight with my boyfriend.

M: Why?

W: He was _____ _____ _____ to other girls. I didn't like that.

M: But he's just a kind person, isn't he? Everybody knows that he only loves you.

W: _____ _____. Maybe I made a mistake.

M: Why don't you say sorry to him with a little present?

W: _____ _____ _____ present?

M: How about a comic book? He really likes those.

109

W: Well, _____ _____ _____

enough.

M: Then... how about a photo album with

pictures of you both?

W: Good idea!

Critical★Thinking   Answers p. 8

W: Jeff, I'm going to have dinner with

Jason tomorrow.

M: Again? Why do you _____ _____

_____ _____ ?

W: Last Saturday was his birthday. And I

haven't given him a present yet.

M: Amy, I _____ _____ _____

_____ . I don't like you seeing him.

W: What? He's my best friend.

M: In my opinion, boys and girls can't be

just friends.

W: We've been friends for ten years. He's

just like _____ _____ _____ .

M: But nobody knows what will happen

between you and him.

W: I _____ _____ _____ ! Don't

you trust me?

UNIT 12 Jobs

Listening ★ Practice   Answers p. 8

1

W1: I'm Nancy. I help couples _____

_____ _____ _____ . I give

them information about wedding halls,

dress shops, and photographers.

W2: I'm Rebecca. I _____ _____

_____ on a plane. I serve them food

and drinks.

W3: I'm Maria. I _____ _____ . I feel

happy when people love my songs.

2

M: What would you like to do in the future?

W: I'd like to _____ _____ _____

_____ .

M: Your own restaurant? Why? Are you

interested in cooking?

W: Yes, but that's not the _____ _____ .

M: Then, what is it?

W: I think that most restaurant owners

have a lot of _____ _____ .

3

M: What do you want to be in the future?

W: I want to _____ _____ _____ .

But I don't think I can.

M: Why not? _____ _____ _____

_____ .

W: I'm very shy. I can't sing in front of lots

of people.

M: Practice singing in front of people

_____ _____ _____ . Then you

won't feel shy anymore.

W: Okay, I'll try it.

4

(Telephone rings.)

W: Hello, this is the Beijing Garden

Restaurant.

M: Hello. I heard you're _____ _____

_____ _____ .

W: Oh, yes. Do you have any experience?

M: Well, I _____ _____ a Chinese

restaurant for six months.

W: Is that all?

M: Well, I took Chinese cooking classes for a year.

W: Um, I'm sorry. I'm afraid we want a cook _____ _____ _____ than that.

M: Okay, I understand.

5

M: I'm a barista. I _____ _____ at a coffeehouse. It's a very cool job because I can taste _____ _____ _____ coffee. Also, it's fun and interesting to meet new people. But it's a hard job because I have to stand up _____ _____ _____.

6

W: Joe, why did you become an animal doctor?

M: I _____ _____ _____ _____. I wanted to do something to help them.

W: Wow. You found the perfect job, then.

M: You're right. But I'm not always happy with my job.

W: Really? When are you _____ _____ _____?

M: Sometimes, when animals are too old or sick, I cannot help them. That _____ _____ _____ _____.

7

W: To become a bungee jumpmaster, you should have _____ _____. Bungee jumping is a dangerous sport. To help people do it safely, you must get enough training. Also, you _____ _____ _____, because you will work in very high places. And you should be _____ _____ to the bungee jumpers.

8

M: I _____ _____ _____ a basketball player. But I got hurt, so I stopped _____ _____. I started selling shoes at a store instead. One day, I met a movie director in the store. We became friends, and, with his help, I _____ _____ _____ and became an actor.

Listening * Challenge Answers p. 8

A [1-2]

W: Hello, Mr. Wilson. I'm Anna from *No.1 Magazine*.

M: _____ _____ _____ _____, Anna.

W: Let's talk about this fashion show. Where did you _____ _____ _____ for your new designs?

M: I got my ideas from the letters of Asian languages.

W: Letters?

M: Yes, I used Chinese, Korean, and Japanese letters.

W: Wow, you _____ _____ _____. I'm sure that wasn't easy.

M: No, it wasn't. It was difficult for me to learn Asian letters.

W: I guess so. They _____ _____ _____ _____ English.

B [1-2]

W: Do you want to become _____ _____ _____ _____? Our new project, "Dream with Us" will be a good chance. In this project, we'll ask you to

do various tasks for one month. The
winner will _____ _____ _____
to work at Victory Home Shopping. Any
woman under 40 can apply. Please send
us an email before _____ _____.

Critical★Thinking Answers p. 8

M: I want to be a famous singer. I _____
_____ and dancing every day with my
friends. If I'm lucky, I'll become a star like
my favorite singer, Justin Timberlake.
The _____ _____ _____ are
really nice. They earn a lot of money
easily. So, they have amazing houses,
cars and clothes. Also, they meet many
other stars and _____ _____
_____ _____. How wonderful!

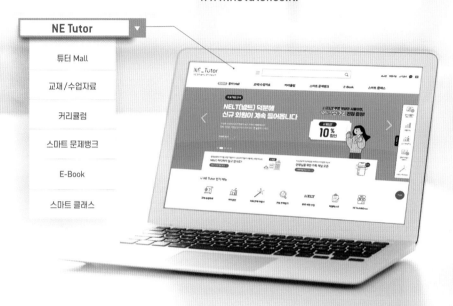

JUNIOR
LISTENING EXPERT

A Theme-Based Listening Course for Young EFL Learners

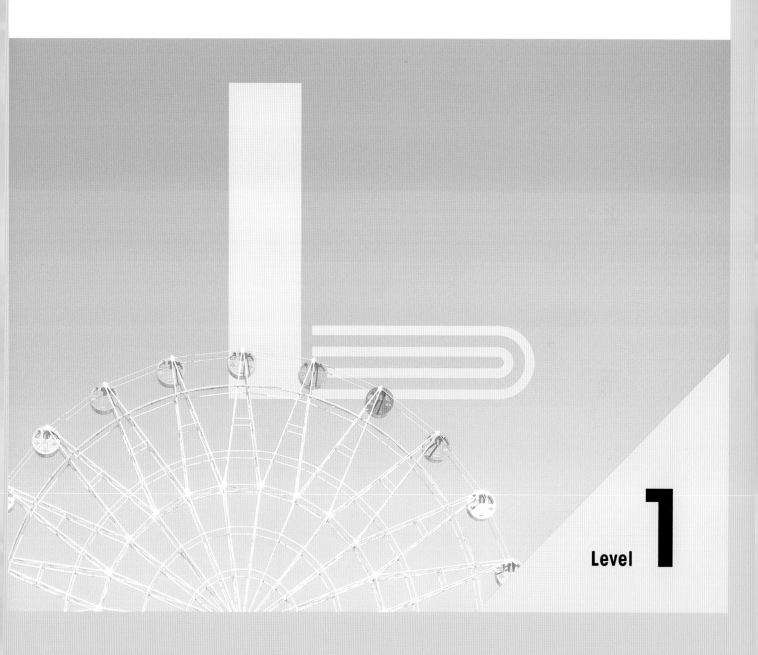

Level **1**

Answer Key

JUNIOR
LISTENING EXPERT

A Theme-Based Listening Course for Young EFL Learners

Answer Key

Level **1**

UNIT 01 Appearance

Getting ★ Ready p. 8
A 1 straight 2 sunglasses 3 necklace
  4 cap 5 curly 6 scarf
B 1 ⓓ 2 ⓔ 3 ⓐ

Listening ★ Start p. 9
1 ① / look at, wearing jeans, so cute
2 ① / my favorite actress, like, most, quite thick

Listening ★ Practice p. 10
1 ③ 2 ③ 3 (A) Changed (B) Changed
(C) Didn't change 4 ① 5 (1) ⓒ (2) ⓑ
(3) ⓐ 6 ① 7 ② 8 ③

Listening ★ Challenge p. 12
A 1 ④ 2 ② B 1 ② 2 ①

Critical ★ Thinking p. 13
1 (1) Against (2) For (3) For
2 (1) ⓑ (2) ⓒ (3) ⓐ

Dictation
Listening ★ Practice p. 88
1 long hair, wearing a tie
2 looking for, five years old, a white blouse
3 Long time no see, a little fat, like short hair
4 Why don't you, change my T-shirt
5 have straight hair, because of stress, grows
  very slowly
6 a famous rock group, wearing sunglasses,
  plays the guitar
7 looking at, How about, a bit short, shorter
  than
8 What's up, What's she like, a little short

Listening ★ Challenge p. 89
A police station, took my bag, look like,
  wearing a blue cap, in five minutes
B fashion model, have brown eyes, really
  exciting

Critical ★ Thinking p. 89
wear makeup, take care of, Is there a rule,
live freely

UNIT 02 School Life

Getting ★ Ready p. 14
A 1 ⓑ 2 ⓒ 3 ⓔ 4 ⓐ 5 ⓓ
B 1 ⓒ 2 ⓓ 3 ⓔ

Listening ★ Start p. 15
1 (1) ① (2) ③ / favorite subject, like her,
  which subject
2 ④ / this morning, wake up, missed the
  school bus

Listening ★ Practice p. 16
1 (1) Unhappy (2) Happy (3) Happy 2 ②
3 ③ 4 (1) ③ (2) ② 5 ② 6 ① 7 ③ 8 ④

Listening ★ Challenge p. 18
A 1 ④ 2 (1) Good (2) Good (3) Bad
B 1 (1) ④ (2) ① 2 ②

Critical ★ Thinking p. 19
1 (1) For (2) For (3) Against
2 (1) ⓒ (2) ⓑ (3) ⓐ

Dictation
Listening ★ Practice p. 90
1 get up early, a lot of fun, learn new things
2 Is everything okay, Don't worry, bring your
  textbooks
3 What's wrong, I'm very tired, learn so
  many subjects
4 scored a goal, How about you, saw
  wonderful paintings
5 You look tired, the first class, today was
  Wednesday
6 absent from, any homework, bring your
  dictionary

7 feeling sick, taking online classes, Get ready for school

8 group project, human body, hand it in

Listening ★ Challenge p. 91

A missed the school bus, wake you up, looked strict, many pretty girls, was disappointed with

B What happened, took it away, next week, dropped a bottle

Critical ★ Thinking p. 92

at home, what to teach, start smoking, get along with

ᴜɴɪᴛ**03** Transportation & Location

Getting ★ Ready p. 20

A 1 straight **2** across **3** next to **4** along

B 1 ⓒ **2** ⓐ **3** ⓑ   **C 1** ⓓ **2** ⓑ **3** ⓔ

Listening ★ Start p. 21

1 ② / Excuse me, turn right, on your left

2 ① / I'm going to, quicker than, Take the bus

Listening ★ Practice p. 22

1 ① **2** ① **3** ② **4** (1) ⓒ (2) ⓐ **5** ③ **6** ①

7 ③ **8** ④

Listening ★ Challenge p. 24

A 1 ③ **2** ④ **B 1** ④ **2** ①

Critical ★ Thinking p. 25

1 ② **2** ①, ③

Dictation

Listening ★ Practice p. 92

1 took off, four hours, enjoy your flight

2 Is there a bus, it's the number thirteen

3 I'm lost, turn left, next to

4 took a taxi, took the subway, by bus

5 because of, arrive thirty minutes late

6 I'm late, In about twenty minutes, too far to walk

7 how to get to, bus stop, How long does it take

8 change subway lines, take line number 7, three stops

Listening ★ Challenge p. 93

A Where to, Where are you from, good places to visit, along the street

B take the subway, get carsick, go out of, on your right

Critical ★ Thinking p. 94

on the subway, turn down the volume, has bad manners, smelled bad, act like that

ᴜɴɪᴛ**04** Seasons & Weather

Getting ★ Ready p. 26

A 1 ⓑ **2** ⓕ **3** ⓔ **4** ⓐ

B 1 ⓕ **2** ⓐ **3** ⓑ

Listening ★ Start p. 27

1 ③ / Let's go, clear up, on the weekend, shall we

2 (1) ⓒ (2) ⓐ (3) ⓑ / enjoy swimming, favorite sports, go on picnics

Listening ★ Practice p. 28

1 (1) ① (2) ④ **2** ④ **3** (1) ⓐ (2) ⓑ **4** ③

5 (1) ⓒ (2) ⓑ (3) ⓔ **6** ③ **7** ①, ② **8** ②

Listening ★ Challenge p. 30

A 1 ④ **2** ① **B 1** ③ **2** ④

Critical ★ Thinking p. 31

1 (1) Likes (2) Doesn't like (3) Likes

2 (1) ⓒ (2) ⓓ (3) ⓑ

Listening ★ Practice p. 94

1 was waiting for, how's the weather, cleared up, enjoying myself

2 an outdoor concert, it's going to rain, listen to a concert

3 favorite places, too hot to travel, In the winter

4 it's raining, changes a lot, take a walk

5 around the world, hot and sunny, snowing a lot

6 a ski resort, clear and sunny, in the snow

7 flying really low, rain soon, wait and see

8 You're from Indonesia, throughout the year, in April, November to March

Listening ★ Challenge p. 95

A there's lightning, go inside, get out

B What shall we do, How about, heavy wind, a little cloudy

Critical ★ Thinking p. 96

enjoy watching, have four seasons, enjoy different sports

UNIT 05 Family

Getting ★ Ready p. 32

A 1 ⓓ **2** ⓐ **3** ⓑ **4** ⓔ **5** ⓒ

B 1 ⓓ **2** ⓐ **3** ⓔ

Listening ★ Start p. 33

1 ④ / how many people, Do you have, younger brother

2 ② / get married, that's why, makes me laugh

Listening ★ Practice p. 34

1 ① **2** ③ **3** ①, ④ **4** ④ **5** (1) ⓕ (2) ⓓ
(3) ⓑ (4) ⓐ **6** (1) T (2) T (3) F **7** (1) ⓑ
(2) ⓒ (3) ⓐ **8** (1) ⓐ (2) ⓑ

Listening ★ Challenge p. 36

A 1 ② **2** (1) T (2) F (3) T **B 1** ② **2** ④

Critical ★ Thinking p. 37

1 ③ **2** (1) ⓑ (2) ⓒ

Listening ★ Practice p. 96

1 Let me show you, take after, I'm handsome

2 next to, introduce me to him, older brother, older than you

3 How many, younger twin sisters, When I was little, in a quiet place

4 for a present, what about sunglasses, doesn't have any

5 goes hiking, watch movies, won the first prize

6 family members, works as, in the 1960s

7 share clothes, cares about her, the only child

8 husband's family name, you got married, her husband's, don't follow it

Listening ★ Challenge p. 97

A an interesting movie, wakes up, finds out, the most important thing

B Welcome back, feel lonely, got sick, my father, having a great time

Critical ★ Thinking p. 98

Double Income No Kids, want to have children, spend their money on, choose the difficult way

UNIT 06 Friends

Getting ★ Ready p. 38

A 1 ⓖ **2** ⓐ **3** ⓔ **4** ⓕ **5** ⓒ

B 1 ⓒ **2** ⓐ **3** ⓔ

Listening ★ Start p. 39

1 ④ / best friend, What, like, free time, watch his movies

2 (1) ⓐ (2) ⓒ (3) ⓑ / near my house, be good at, would be fun

Listening ★ Practice p. 40

1 ② **2** (1) Jack, Steve (2) Jack, Steve (3) Steve **3** ③ **4** ③ **5** ① **6** (1) ③ (2) ② (3) ① **7** ④ **8** ②

Listening ★ Challenge p. 42

A 1 ① **2** ③ **B 1** (1) ⓒ (2) ⓐ **2** ③

Critical ★ Thinking p. 43

1 (1) T (2) F (3) F **2** ①, ③

Dictation

Listening ★ Practice p. 98

1 What's the matter, forget her birthday, her a good present

2 best friend, basketball players, very popular

3 look so excited, What is it, planned to meet

4 do not wait, join school clubs

5 go to a movie, had a big fight, 30 minutes late

6 three good friends, wears boy's clothes, went bungee-jumping

7 He was shopping, for a long time, moved to, why don't you

8 have some problems, wearing the same shirt, as well

Listening ★ Challenge p. 99

A make friends, the best place, over age 7, by country

B planning to travel, be very careful, On the first day, what should I do

Critical ★ Thinking p. 100

is worried that, for their help, tell my close friends

UNIT 07 Music

Getting ★ Ready p. 44

A 1 ⓐ **2** ⓓ **B 1** ⓐ **2** ⓒ **3** ⓑ **C 1** ⓕ **2** ⓑ **3** ⓔ

Listening ★ Start p. 45

1 ③ / a big fan of, be able to

2 ② / join the orchestra, play the cello, learn a lot, Sounds good

Listening ★ Practice p. 46

1 ② **2** (1) F (2) T (3) F **3** ④ **4** (1) Good (2) Good (3) Bad **5** ④ **6** ① **7** ③ **8** ④

Listening ★ Challenge p. 48

A 1 ② **2** ③ **B 1** ④ **2** ⓐ, ⓓ, ⓔ

Critical ★ Thinking p. 49

1 ① **2** (1) ⓑ (2) ⓐ

Dictation

Listening ★ Practice p. 100

1 practicing the guitar, I'm not ready, play the piano, which instrument

2 favorite pianist, his first album, the most

3 music contest, Because of her appearance, sing a song

4 enjoyed the concert, sang very well, did her best, too small

5 having a small concert, May 20th, listening to our music

6 sixteen years old, I'm sure, Let's hear it

7 raining heavily, cheer you up

8 the most popular, Twelve percent, enjoy country music

Listening ★ Challenge p. 101

A Well done, majoring in music, isn't it too far, like you do

B listening to music, help you relax, comfortable position

5

Critical ★ Thinking p. 101
focus on studying, I'm wrong, it's not possible

UNIT **08** Holidays

Getting ★ Ready p. 50
A 1 ⓔ **2** ⓓ **3** ⓕ **4** ⓒ **5** ⓐ
B 1 ⓕ **2** ⓒ **3** ⓔ

Listening ★ Start p. 51
1 (1) ② (2) ③ / making something, a kind of,
   What about, baking a pumpkin pie
2 ③ / special holiday, doing anything,
   beautiful fireworks, sounds fun

Listening ★ Practice p. 52
1 ② **2** 12 **3** ③ **4** (1) ⓒ, ⓔ (2) ⓐ, ⓓ **5** ④
6 ③ **7** (1) ⓑ (2) ⓒ **8** (1) F (2) T (3) F

Listening ★ Challenge p. 54
A 1 ④ **2** ①, ② **B 1** May 10, June 21 **2** ④

Critical ★ Thinking p. 55
1 ④ **2** ⓔ

Dictation
Listening ★ Practice p. 102
1 New Year festival, throw water, on bicycles
2 during summer vacation, June 11th, That's
   no problem
3 visit France, staying home, in the hospital
4 clean their houses, watch fireworks, brings
   bad luck
5 Where are you going, going on a trip,
   taking cooking classes
6 during the vacation, going to the beach,
   attend summer school
7 buy us Christmas presents, want a sweater,
   at the mall
8 Let's go to Scotland, What's that, August
   5th, this year

Listening ★ Challenge p. 103
A started in England, got presents, give gifts
   to workers, big sales
B second Sunday of May, third Sunday of
   June, small gifts

Critical ★ Thinking p. 103
stayed home, did something meaningful,
every Christmas, taking a rest

UNIT **09** Shopping

Getting ★ Ready p. 56
A 1 ⓔ **2** ⓐ **3** ⓑ **4** ⓒ **5** ⓓ
B 1 ⓒ **2** ⓐ **3** ⓓ

Listening ★ Start p. 57
1 ② / May I help you, kinds of, too big, I'll
   take it
2 ① / looking for, How about, How much,
   50% off

Listening ★ Practice p. 58
1 ⓐ, ⓑ, ⓓ **2** ② **3** ③ **4** ② **5** ④ **6** (1) 9th
(2) 2nd (3) 5th **7** ④ **8** (1) T (2) T (3) F

Listening ★ Challenge p. 60
A 1 ①, ④ **2** ③ **B 1** ③ **2** ②

Critical ★ Thinking p. 61
1 ② **2** ⓐ, ⓒ, ⓔ

Dictation
Listening ★ Practice p. 104
1 looks good, I'd like to get, buying tomato
   juice
2 what do you think, We've been shopping,
   take a break
3 on sale, really cheap, a white hat
4 sense of style, go out, try them on
5 ordered a miniskirt, What's your name,

exchange it for you

6 on the second floor, summer sales events, enjoy shopping

7 looking for something, big ribbon, recommend this blue dress

8 online shopping mall, are famous for, having a spring sale

Listening ★ Challenge p. 105
A This is, Which color, that's $1,400, by credit card, by this Friday
B next week, must be tiring, many good restaurants, sounds good

Critical ★ Thinking p. 106
What's the result, What should I do, less time to shop, following my advice

UNIT 10 Advice

Getting ★ Ready p. 62
A 1 ⓒ 2 ⓑ 3 ⓐ   B 1 ⓑ 2 ⓐ
C 1 ⓐ 2 ⓔ 3 ⓒ

Listening ★ Start p. 63
1 ④ / How do you feel, don't worry
2 ③ / This Saturday, I think, why don't you

Listening ★ Practice p. 64
1 (1) ⓒ (2) ⓐ (3) ⓑ 2 ③ 3 ② 4 ②
5 ④ 6 ④ 7 (1) T (2) F (3) T 8 ②

Listening ★ Challenge p. 66
A 1 ① 2 ①   B 1 ④ 2 ③

Critical ★ Thinking p. 67
1 (1) T (2) F (3) F   2 (1) ⓒ (2) ⓐ

Dictation
Listening ★ Practice p. 106
1 study hard, shorter than, not to buy any

2 told lies, Calm down, made a mistake

3 don't have enough money, going to concerts

4 Are you ready for, look after, hotels for dogs, search for

5 feel terrible, set a schedule, from six to eight

6 last English test, angry at me, lose my friend

7 attend a dance academy, swimming classes, give up

8 talk to their mother, 60 percent, talk to anybody

Listening ★ Challenge p. 107
A Last summer, famous paintings, become an artist, somewhat late
B What's the matter, forgot about it, go to a movie, Tell your boyfriend, on Sunday

Critical ★ Thinking p. 108
lose weight, follow her advice, disagree with you, just as you are

UNIT 11 Boys & Girls

Getting ★ Ready p. 68
A 1 ⓕ 2 ⓒ 3 ⓐ 4 ⓔ 5 ⓖ
B 1 ⓔ 2 ⓐ 3 ⓓ

Listening ★ Start p. 69
1 (1) Good (2) Bad / my type, see a movie, pay for
2 ④ / grow up, change your mind, like cooking

Listening ★ Practice p. 70
1 ④ 2 ④ 3 (1) Likes (2) Doesn't like
(3) Doesn't like 4 ④ 5 ② 6 ① 7 ②
8 (1) F (2) T (3) F

Listening ★ Challenge p. 72
A 1 ② 2 ③   B 1 ④ 2 ③

7

★ ★

Critical ★ Thinking p. 73
1 ③ **2** ①

Dictation
Listening ★ Practice p. 108
1 baby clothes, this pink dress, take the
yellow one
2 are you upset, call you often, 6th of
October, I'm so sorry
3 get ready, I'm interested in, care more about
4 55 kg, average weight
5 forget their first love, a part of, present
boyfriend
6 tried on, didn't buy anything, took four
hours
7 Why don't you, making small talk, right now
8 come out, explains the reasons, have
better relationships

Listening ★ Challenge p. 109
A a couple of days, get the correct answer,
cosmetics store
B acting too nice, That's true, What kind of,
that's not romantic

Critical ★ Thinking p. 110
see him so often, can't take it anymore, my
own brother, can't believe it

UNIT **12** Jobs

Getting ★ Ready p. 74
A 1 ⓓ **2** ⓐ **3** ⓔ **4** ⓑ **5** ⓒ
B 1 ⓔ **2** ⓐ **3** ⓒ

Listening ★ Start p. 75
1 ② / works at, choose the correct wine,
good wines
2 ④ / Long time no see, What do you do,
work as

Listening ★ Practice p. 76
1 (1) ⓐ (2) ⓒ (3) ⓑ **2** ③ **3** ③ **4** ②
5 (1) ⓐ, ⓓ (2) ⓒ **6** ① **7** ④ **8** ⓓ→ⓒ→ⓑ

Listening ★ Challenge p. 78
A 1 ② **2** ③   **B 1** ② **2** ①

Critical ★ Thinking p. 79
1 (1) T (2) F (3) T **2** ①, ④

Dictation
Listening ★ Practice p. 110
1 prepare their wedding day, look after
people, write songs
2 open my own restaurant, main reason, free
time
3 become a singer, You're good at singing,
whenever you can
4. looking for a cook, worked at, with more
experience
5 make drinks, many kinds of, all day long
6 love animals so much, unhappy with it,
makes me feel sad
7 certain qualities, must be brave, very
friendly
8 used to be, playing basketball, got an
audition

Listening ★ Challenge p. 111
A Nice to meet you, get the ideas, tried
something new, are very different from
B a home shopping host, get a chance,
March 12th

Critical ★ Thinking p. 112
practice singing, lives of stars, become
friends with them

8

UNIT 01 Appearance

Getting ★ Ready   p. 8

A 1 straight   2 sunglasses   3 necklace
　4 cap   5 curly   6 scarf
B 1 ⓓ   2 ⓔ   3 ⓐ

B 1 여: Michael은 말랐니?
　　남: 아니. 그는 좀 뚱뚱해.
　2 여: 그는 어떻게 생겼니?
　　남: 키가 크고 머리가 갈색이야.
　3 여: 오늘 나 어때 보여?
　　남: 멋져.

Listening ★ Start   p. 9

1 ① / look at, wearing jeans, so cute
2 ① / my favorite actress, like, most, quite thick

1

M: Mom, look at this picture of my classmates.
W: Oh, is your friend Julia in the picture?
M: Yes. She's wearing jeans.
W: You mean the girl with a hair band?
M: No, she's Nancy. Julia is wearing a
　necklace.
W: Oh, I found her. She's so cute.

남: 엄마, 우리 반 친구들 사진 좀 보세요.
여: 아, 네 친구 Julia도 사진에 있니?
남: 네. 청바지를 입고 있어요.
여: 머리띠를 한 애 말이니?
남: 아뇨. 그 애는 Nancy예요. Julia는 목걸이를 하고 있어요.
여: 아, 찾았다. 아주 귀엽게 생겼구나.

어휘
classmate[klǽsmèit] 똉 동급생   jeans[dʒiːns] 똉
청바지   mean[miːn] 똉 의미하다   hair band 머리띠
necklace[néklis] 똉 목걸이   find[faind] 똉 찾다
(find-found-found)

문제 해설
Q: 사진에서 Julia를 고르시오.
　Julia는 청바지를 입고 목걸이를 하고 있다.

2

M: Angelina is my favorite actress. She has
　beautiful big blue eyes. I like her eyes
　most. She also has very beautiful skin.
　She has a wide mouth, and her lips are
　quite thick. Some people don't like her
　lips, but I like them.

남: Angelina는 내가 제일 좋아하는 여배우예요. 그녀는 크
　고 아름다운 푸른 눈을 가지고 있지요. 나는 그녀의 눈이
　가장 좋아요. 그녀는 매우 아름다운 피부도 가지고 있어
　요. 그녀는 입이 크고, 입술은 꽤 두꺼워요. 어떤 사람들
　은 그녀의 입술을 좋아하지 않지만, 나는 좋아해요.

어휘
favorite[féivərit] 똉 가장 좋아하는   actress[ǽktris]
똉 여배우 (↔ actor)   most[moust] 뫤 가장   skin[skin]
똉 피부   wide[waid] 똉 넓은; *(눈·입이) 큰   quite
[kwait] 뫤 꽤   thick[θik] 똉 두꺼운

문제 해설
Q: 소년은 Angelina의 얼굴 중 어느 부분을 가장 좋아하는가?
　소년은 Angelina의 눈을 가장 좋아한다고 했다.

Listening ★ Practice   p. 10

1 ③   2 ③   3 (A) Changed   (B) Changed
(C) Didn't change   4 ①   5 (1) ⓒ (2) ⓑ (3) ⓐ
6 ①   7 ②   8 ③

1

W: ① He has long hair.
　② He is sitting on the chair.
　③ He is wearing a tie.
　④ He is putting on glasses.

여: ① 그는 머리가 길다.
　② 그는 의자에 앉아 있다.
　③ 그는 넥타이를 매고 있다.
　④ 그는 안경을 쓰고 있다.

어휘
tie[tai] 똉 넥타이   put on (옷을) 입다; *(안경을) 끼다;
(모자를) 쓰다

문제 해설
Q: 남자를 가장 잘 묘사한 것은?
　남자는 짧은 머리에, 넥타이를 매고 있다.

2

M: Attention, please! We're looking for a child. Her name is Tiffany and she is five years old. She has short brown hair. She is wearing a blue skirt and a white blouse. If you find her, please take her to the information center. Thank you.

남: 주목해 주십시오! 한 어린이를 찾고 있습니다. 아이의 이름은 Tiffany이고 5살입니다. 머리는 짧고 갈색입니다. 파란색 치마와 흰색 블라우스를 입고 있습니다. 아이를 발견하시면 안내소로 데리고 와주십시오. 감사합니다.

어휘
attention[əténʃən] 몡 주의, 주목 look for 찾다
brown[braun] 혱 갈색의 skirt[skəːrt] 몡 치마
white[hwait] 혱 하얀색의 blouse[blaus] 몡 블라우스
take A to B A를 B로 데려가다 information center
안내소

문제 해설
Q: 남자가 찾고 있는 아이를 고르시오.
남자가 찾고 있는 아이는 짧은 갈색 머리에, 파란색 치마와 흰색 블라우스를 입고 있다.

3

W: Oh, my god! You're Tom, aren't you?
M: Vicky? Long time no see! You've changed a lot.
W: Have I? (laughs) I was very thin, but these days I am a little fat.
M: But you look great. And you're much taller than before.
W: Yes. I grew 10 centimeters.
M: But your hairstyle is the same.
W: That's right. I like short hair.

여: 어머! 너 Tom 아니니?
남: Vicky니? 오랜만이야! 너 많이 변했구나.
여: 그래? [웃으며] 내가 정말 말랐었는데 요즘 좀 살이 쪘어.
남: 그렇지만 아주 좋아 보여. 그리고 전보다 훨씬 키가 컸네.
여: 응. 10센티미터 자랐어.
남: 근데 헤어스타일은 여전하네.
여: 맞아. 내가 짧은 머리를 좋아해서.

어휘
Long time no see! 오랜만이야! change[tʃeindʒ]
동 변하다 a lot 많이 thin[θin] 혱 마른 these

days 요즘 a little 약간 fat[fæt] 혱 뚱뚱한 grow
[grou] 동 자라다 (grow-grew-grown) centimeter
[séntəmìːtər] 몡 센티미터 hairstyle[héərstàil] 몡 머리
모양

문제 해설
Q: 각 초이스가 바뀌었는지, 바뀌지 않았는지 선택하시오.
Vicky는 살이 좀 찌고 키가 10센티미터 자랐으나, 헤어스타일은 같다고 했다.

4

M: How do I look today?
W: Umm... not so good. Why don't you change your T-shirt?
M: Why?
W: I don't think a black T-shirt looks good with your brown pants.
M: Really? Then, I'll go and change my T-shirt. I'll wear a white shirt instead.
W: Okay. I'll wait here.

남: 나 오늘 어때 보여?
여: 음… 그리 좋아 보이진 않아. 티셔츠를 갈아입는 게 어때?
남: 왜?
여: 검은색 티셔츠랑 갈색 바지가 안 어울리는 것 같아.
남: 정말? 그럼 가서 티셔츠를 갈아입고 올게. 대신에 흰색 셔츠를 입을 거야.
여: 좋아. 여기서 기다릴게.

어휘
pants[pænts] 몡 바지 instead[instéd] 부 대신에
wait[weit] 동 기다리다 [문제] jacket[dʒækit] 몡 재킷,
상의 clothes[klouðz] 몡 옷

문제 해설
Q: 남자가 다음에 할 일은?
① 티셔츠를 갈아입는다.
② 갈색 재킷을 입는다.
③ 여자와 쇼핑을 하러 간다.
④ 여자가 옷을 갈아입기를 기다린다.
남자가 흰색 셔츠로 갈아입고 온다고 하였다.

5

W1: I'm Kate. I have very curly hair. But I don't like it. I want to have straight hair.
W2: I'm Rachel. These days, I'm losing too much hair. My doctor said that it is because of stress. I'm worried about it.

W3: I'm Sarah. I have short hair. I want to have long hair, but my hair grows very slowly.

여1: 난 Kate야. 내 머리는 매우 곱슬거려. 하지만 난 그것을 좋아하지 않아. 나는 생머리를 갖고 싶어.

여2: 난 Rachel이야. 요즘 머리가 너무 많이 빠져. 의사 선생님은 스트레스 때문이라고 말씀하셨어. 그것 때문에 걱정이야.

여3: 나는 Sarah야. 난 머리가 짧아. 긴 머리를 갖고 싶지만 내 머리는 너무 천천히 자라.

어휘

curly [kə́ːrli] 형 곱슬거리는 straight [streit] 형 곧은
lose [luːz] 동 잃다 (lose-lost-lost) stress [stres] 명
스트레스 worried [wə́ːrid] 형 걱정되는 slowly
[slóuli] 부 천천히

문제 해설

Q: 각 인물에 알맞은 그림을 고르시오.
  (1) Kate는 곱슬머리라고 했다.
  (2) Rachel은 머리가 너무 많이 빠져서 걱정이라고 했다.
  (3) Sarah는 머리가 짧지만, 긴 머리를 갖고 싶어 한다.

6

W: Who are the people in this picture?
M: They are members of a famous rock group.
W: Oh, are they? I didn't know that.
M: I like Tony. He is the singer. He's wearing sunglasses.
W: I see. And who is this handsome guy?
M: Who do you mean?
W: The one wearing a white shirt and a scarf.
M: He is Danny. He plays the guitar.

여: 이 사진 속의 사람들은 누구니?
남: 유명한 록 그룹의 멤버들이야.
여: 아, 그래? 몰랐어.
남: 난 Tony를 좋아해. 그는 보컬이야. 선글라스를 끼고 있어.
여: 그렇구나. 그럼 이 잘생긴 사람은 누구야?
남: 누구 말이니?
여: 흰색 셔츠에 스카프를 매고 있는 사람.
남: 그는 Danny야. 기타를 연주해.

어휘

member [mémbər] 명 일원, 회원 famous [féiməs]
형 유명한 rock group 록 그룹 singer [síŋər] 명 가수
sunglasses [sʌ́ŋglæsiz] 명 선글라스 handsome
[hǽnsəm] 형 잘생긴 guy [gai] 명 사내 scarf [skɑːrf]
명 스카프 play [plei] 동 연주하다

문제 해설

Q: 사진에서 Danny를 고르시오.
  Danny는 흰색 셔츠를 입고 스카프를 매고 있다고 했다.

7

W: What are you doing, Mr. Spielberg?
M: I'm looking at pictures of actresses for my next movie. What do you think of them?
W: How about Katherine? She is a great actress.
M: But isn't she too tall? You know, the main actor is a bit short.
W: Oh, right. Then, what about Scarlett?
M: Good idea. She's shorter than Katherine.

여: Spielberg 씨, 뭐 하고 계세요?
남: 제 다음 영화를 위해서 여배우들 사진을 보고 있는 중이에요. 이들에 대해서 어떻게 생각해요?
여: Katherine은 어때요? 훌륭한 여배우잖아요.
남: 하지만 그녀는 키가 너무 크지 않나요? 알다시피, 남자 주연 배우가 약간 작잖아요.
여: 아, 그렇군요. 그럼. Scarlett은 어때요?
남: 좋은 생각이에요. 그녀는 Katherine보다 작으니까요.

어휘

too [tuː] 부 *너무; 역시 main [mein] 형 주
된 actor [ǽktər] 명 남자 배우 a bit 약간 [문제]
act [ækt] 동 연기하다 voice [vɔis] 명 목소리

문제 해설

Q: 남자가 Scarlett을 여자 주연 배우로 선택하는 이유는?
  ① 그녀는 연기를 잘한다.
  ② 그녀는 키가 너무 크지 않다.
  ③ 그녀는 목소리가 좋다.
  ④ 그녀는 아주 아름답다.
  Scarlett은 Katherine보다 키가 작아서 좋다고 했다.

8

(Telephone rings.)
M: Hello?
W: Hi, this is Tina.
M: Hi, Tina. What's up?
W: How about a blind date this Sunday?
M: That sounds good! Who is the girl?
W: She is my cousin, Cathy.
M: What's she like?
W: She is kind and funny. She has many friends.

11

M: Great. What does she look like?

W: She's a little short, but she is very cute. She has long blond hair.

M: I think she's my type!

(전화벨이 울린다.)

남: 여보세요?

여: 안녕, 나 Tina야.

남: 안녕, Tina. 무슨 일이야?

여: 이번 주 일요일에 소개팅 어때?

남: 좋지! 여자애가 누구야?

여: 내 사촌인 Cathy야.

남: 어떤 애야?

여: 친절하고 재미있어. 친구도 많아.

남: 좋아. 어떻게 생겼어?

여: 키는 약간 작지만 아주 귀여워. 긴 금발 머리야.

남: 내 타입인 것 같아!

어휘

What's up? 무슨 일이야?　**blind date** 소개팅　**cousin**[kʌ́zən] 명 사촌　**kind**[kaind] 형 친절한 **funny**[fʌ́ni] 형 재미있는　**blond**[bland] 형 금발의 **type**[taip] 명 형, 타입

문제 해설

Q: Cathy에 관해 사실이 <u>아닌</u> 것은?

　① 그녀는 Tina의 사촌이다.

　② 그녀는 친구가 많다.

　③ 그녀는 키가 꽤 크다.

　④ 그녀는 긴 금발 머리를 가졌다.

　Cathy는 키가 약간 작다고 했다.

Listening ★ Challenge　p. 12

A 1 ④　2 ②　B 1 ②　2 ①

A [1-2]

(*Telephone rings.*)

M: Hello, this is the police station. How can I help you?

W: My name is Leanne Parker. A man just took my bag at the Boston train station!

M: Did you see him? What did he look like?

W: He was short. And... he was wearing a brown jacket.

M: Anything else?

W: Hmm... oh, he was wearing a blue cap.

M: Okay, and could you tell me about your bag?

W: It is a big white handbag.

M: All right. Please wait at the train station. We will be there in five minutes.

(전화벨이 울린다.)

남: 여보세요, 경찰서입니다. 무엇을 도와 드릴까요?

여: 저는 Leanne Parker라고 합니다. 어떤 남자가 방금 보스턴 기차역에서 제 핸드백을 가져 갔어요!

남: 그 남자를 봤습니까? 어떻게 생겼습니까?

여: 키가 작았어요. 그리고… 갈색 재킷을 입고 있었어요.

남: 다른 건 없습니까?

여: 음… 아, 파란색 모자를 쓰고 있었어요.

남: 알겠습니다. 그리고 당신의 가방에 대해서 말씀해주시겠습니까?

여: 큰 흰색 핸드백이에요.

남: 알겠습니다. 기차역에서 기다려 주십시오. 저희가 5분 내에 거기로 가겠습니다.

어휘

police station 경찰서　**train station** 기차역　**cap** [kæp] 명 (테 없는) 모자　**handbag**[hǽndbæ̀g] 명 핸드백, 손가방

문제 해설

Q1: 여자가 말하고 있는 사람을 고르시오.

　키가 작고, 갈색 재킷을 입고 있었으며, 파란색 모자를 쓰고 있었다고 했다.

Q2: 여자가 현재 있는 곳은?

　방금 보스턴 기차역에서 핸드백을 도난당했다고 했으므로 기차역에 있음을 알 수 있다.

B [1-2]

W: My name is Melisa Brown. I'm a 21-year-old fashion model. I am 177 centimeters tall, and I weigh 60 kilograms. I have brown eyes and long red hair. I became a model when I was 16 years old. I appeared in many famous fashion shows. It was really exciting. But last year I broke my leg. So I had a year off work. Now I want to work again.

여: 제 이름은 Melisa Brown입니다. 저는 21살의 패션 모델이에요. 키는 177센티미터이고, 몸무게는 60킬로그램입니다. 전 갈색 눈에 긴 빨간 머리를 가지고 있죠. 저는

16살에 모델이 되었어요. 저는 여러 유명한 패션쇼에 출연했습니다. 정말 재미있었어요. 하지만 작년에 다리가 부러져서 일 년간 일을 쉬었습니다. 지금은 다시 일을 하고 싶습니다.

어휘

fashion[fǽʃən] 명 패션   model[mádəl] 명 모델
weigh[wei] 동 무게가 ~나가다   kilogram[kíləgræm]
명 킬로그램   become[bikʌ́m] 동 ~이 되다   appear
[əpíər] 동 나타나다; *출연하다   show[ʃou] 명 쇼
exciting[iksáitiŋ] 형 재미있는   last year 작년
break[breik] 동 부러뜨리다 (break–broke–broken)
off work 일을 쉬고 있는   again[əgén] 부 다시
[문제] hurt[həːrt] 동 다치게 하다   tired[taiərd] 형
피곤한   be interested in ~ ~에 흥미를 가지다
another[ənʌ́ðər] 형 또 다른   job[dʒab] 명 일

문제 해설

Q1: Melisa Brown에 관해 사실이 아닌 것은?
몸무게가 60킬로그램이라고 했다.

Q2: Melisa Brown이 모델 일을 그만 둔 이유는?
① 다리를 다쳐서
② 피곤해서
③ 공부를 하길 원해서
④ 다른 직업에 관심이 생겨서
다리가 부러져서 일 년간 일을 쉬었다.

Critical ★ Thinking   p. 13

1 (1) Against (2) For (3) For
2 (1) ⓑ (2) ⓒ (3) ⓐ

W1: I'm May. I feel uncomfortable when I see men who wear makeup. Men and women are different. Men look nicer when they look natural.

M: I'm Chris. These days, men also want to take care of their appearance. Makeup helps men look better.

W2: I'm Kelly. Is there a rule that men cannot wear makeup? No, there isn't. I think all people should live freely.

여1: 난 May야. 나는 화장을 한 남자를 보면 마음이 불편해. 남자와 여자는 달라. 남자는 자연스러워 보일 때가 더 괜찮아 보여.

남: 난 Chris야. 요즘에는 남자들도 자신의 외모를 가꾸고 싶어 해. 화장은 남자를 더 멋있어 보이게 해주거든.

여2: 나는 Kelly야. 남자가 화장을 하면 안 된다는 법이 있나? 아니, 없어. 나는 모든 사람이 자유롭게 살아야 한다고 생각해.

어휘

uncomfortable[ʌnkʌ́mfərtəbl] 형 불편한   makeup
[méikʌp] 명 화장   different[dífərənt] 형 다른
natural[nǽtʃərəl] 형 자연스러운   take care of ~ ~을
돌보다; *~을 신경 쓰다   appearance[əpí(ː)ərəns] 명
외모   rule[ruːl] 명 법, 규칙   live[liv] 동 살다   freely
[fríːli] 부 자유롭게   [문제] put on makeup 화장을 하
다   without[wiðáut] 전 ~ 없이

문제 해설

Q1: 각 인물이 화장을 한 남자에 대해 찬성하는지 혹은 반대하는지 ✓표 하시오.
(1) May는 남자가 화장하는 것에 대해 마음이 불편하다고 했으므로 반대하는 입장이다.
(2) Chris는 남자들도 화장을 하면 더 멋있어 보일 수 있다고 했으므로 찬성하는 입장이다.
(3) Kelly는 남자가 화장을 하면 안 된다는 법은 없다고 했으므로 찬성하는 입장이다.

Q2: 각 인물과 해당 의견을 연결하시오.
ⓐ 남자도 원한다면 화장을 할 수 있다.
ⓑ 남자는 화장을 하지 않는 게 더 잘생겨 보인다.
ⓒ 남자는 화장을 하면 더 잘생겨 보인다.
(1) May는 남자들이 화장을 안 했을 때 더 괜찮아 보인다고 했다.
(2) Chris는 남자가 화장을 하면 더 멋있어 보인다고 했다.
(3) Kelly는 모든 사람이 자유롭게 살아야 한다고 했으므로 남자도 원한다면 화장을 할 수 있다고 생각할 것이다.

UNIT 02 School Life

Getting ★ Ready   p. 14

A 1 ⓑ   2 ⓒ   3 ⓔ   4 ⓐ   5 ⓓ
B 1 ⓒ   2 ⓓ   3 ⓔ

B 1 여: 넌 어떤 과목을 좋아하니?
남: 영어를 가장 좋아해.
2 여: 언제까지 내야 해요?
남: 다음 주 금요일까지 제출하렴.
3 여: 너 왜 결석했니?
남: 많이 아팠어.

Listening ★ Start   p. 15

1 (1) ① (2) ③ / favorite subject, like her, which subject
2 ④ / this morning, wake up, missed the school bus

1

W: What is your favorite subject, David? Science?

M: No, I like history. You know, my history teacher is so pretty.

W: I like her, too, but I don't like history. There is too much homework.

M: Then, which subject do you like, Nicole?

W: My favorite subject is music.

여: David, 네가 가장 좋아하는 과목이 뭐니? 과학이야?

남: 아니. 나는 역사를 좋아해. 알다시피 우리 역사 선생님이 아주 예쁘시잖아.

여: 나도 그 선생님을 좋아하지만 역사는 안 좋아해. 숙제가 너무 많아.

남: 그럼, Nicole, 넌 어떤 과목을 좋아하니?

여: 내가 가장 좋아하는 과목은 음악이야.

어휘

favorite[féivərit] 형 매우 좋아하는   subject[sʌ́bdʒikt] 명 과목   science[sáiəns] 명 과학   history[hístəri] 명 역사   homework[hóumwə̀ːrk] 명 숙제

문제 해설

Q: 각 인물이 가장 좋아하는 과목을 고르시오.
　David는 역사를, Nicole은 음악을 가장 좋아한다고 했다.

2

W: John, I didn't see you this morning.

M: Well… I arrived at around 10 o'clock, Ms. Johnson.

W: Did you wake up late?

M: No. I was late because I met my old friend at the bus stop.

W: What happened?

M: I thought we talked for just a moment. But twenty minutes passed.

W: So you missed the school bus?

M: Yes. I'm sorry.

여: John, 오늘 아침에 널 못 봤는데.

남: 저기… Johnson 선생님, 제가 10시쯤에 도착했어요.

여: 늦게 일어났니?

남: 아니요. 버스 정류장에서 옛날 친구를 만나서 지각했어요.

여: 무슨 일 있었니?

남: 저희가 아주 잠깐 동안 얘기했다고 생각했는데 20분이 지났더라고요.

여: 그래서 학교 버스를 놓쳤니?

남: 네. 죄송해요.

어휘

arrive[əráiv] 동 도착하다   around[əráund] 부 *대략; 주위에   wake up 잠이 깨다   late[leit] 형 지각한; 부 늦게   bus stop 버스 정류장   happen[hǽpən] 동 (일·사건 등이) 일어나다   for a moment 잠시 동안   pass[pæs] 동 지나다   miss[mis] 동 *놓치다; 그리워하다   [문제] sick[sik] 형 아픈   wrong[rɔ(ː)ŋ] 형 틀린, 잘못된

문제 해설

Q: 소년이 학교에 지각한 이유는?

　① 아팠다.

　② 늦게 일어났다.

　③ 버스를 잘못 탔다.

　④ 학교 버스를 놓쳤다.

　소년은 버스 정류장에서 만난 친구와 얘기하느라 학교 버스를 놓쳐서 지각했다.

Listening ★ Practice   p. 16

1 (1) Unhappy (2) Happy (3) Happy 2 ②
3 ③ 4 (1) ③ (2) ② 5 ② 6 ① 7 ③ 8 ④

1

W1: I'm Emma. To go to school, I must get up early. I must also do a lot of homework. I hate school.

M: I'm Bill. At school, I can play with my friends. I have a lot of fun there.

W2: I'm Debbie. It is very interesting to learn new things in school. And I can try many fun activities.

여1: 난 Emma야. 학교에 가기 위해서 난 일찍 일어나야 해. 난 많은 숙제도 해야 해. 학교가 싫어.

남: 난 Bill이야. 학교에서 난 친구들이랑 놀 수 있어. 거기서 아주 즐겁게 시간을 보내지.

여2: 난 Debbie야. 학교에서 새로운 것들을 배우는 건 아주 재미있어. 그리고 재미있는 활동도 많이 해 볼 수 있어.

get up 일어나다   early[ə́ːrli] 부 일찍   a lot of 많은
hate[heit] 동 싫어하다   have fun 재미있게 놀다
interesting[íntərəstiŋ] 형 흥미로운   learn[ləːrn] 동
배우다   try[trai] 동 *시도하다; 노력하다   activity
[æktívəti] 명 활동

문제 해설
Q: 각 인물이 자신의 학교 생활에 대해 어떻게 느끼는지 ✓표
하시오.
  (1) Emma는 학교를 싫어한다고 했으므로 학교 생활이
     행복하지 않을 것이다.
  (2) Bill은 학교에서 친구들과 즐거운 시간을 보낼 수 있
     어 행복할 것이다.
  (3) Debbie는 학교에서 새로운 것을 배우고 재미있는 활
     동도 해 볼 수 있어 즐거워한다.

2

M: How's your life at school? Is everything
   okay?
W: I think so, Mr. Robinson.
M: Good. You seem to study hard.
W: I'm trying to. But I feel that some
   subjects are difficult.
M: Don't worry. I checked your exam results,
   and you're doing well.
W: Thank you.
M: But sometimes you don't bring your
   textbooks. Don't forget to prepare
   everything for class.
W: Okay, sir.

남: 학교 생활 어때? 다 괜찮니?
여: 그런 것 같아요, Robinson 선생님.
남: 다행이구나. 공부를 열심히 하는 것 같더구나.
여: 그러려고 노력하고 있어요. 하지만 몇몇 과목들은 어려
   운 것 같아요.
남: 걱정하지 마. 내가 네 시험 결과를 확인했는데 잘하고 있
   던 걸.
여: 감사해요.
남: 하지만 넌 간혹 교과서를 안 가져 오던데. 잊지 말고 수업
   에 필요한 모든 걸 챙겨오렴.
여: 알겠어요, 선생님.

어휘

everything[évriθìŋ] 대 모든 것   seem[siːm] 동 ~하
게 보이다   hard[haːrd] 부 열심히   difficult[dífikʌ̀lt]
형 어려운   check[tʃek] 동 확인하다   exam[igzǽm] 명

시험   result[rizʌ́lt] 명 결과   sometimes[sʌ́mtàimz]
부 때때로   bring[briŋ] 동 가져오다 (bring-brought-
brought)   textbook[tékstbùk] 명 교과서   forget
[fərgét] 동 잊다 (forget-forgot-forgotten)   prepare
[pripέər] 동 준비하다   [문제] parent[pέ(ː)ərənt] 명 부모

문제 해설
Q: 화자 간의 관계는?
   남자가 여자의 시험 성적을 확인해봤다고 했고, 수업 시
   간에 교과서 등 모든 것을 챙겨올 것을 당부하는 것으로
   보아 남자는 선생님이고 여자는 학생임을 알 수 있다.

3

M: How's it going, Kate?
W: Not good.
M: What's wrong? Did you have a fight with
   your friend?
W: I have to study too many subjects, so I'm
   very tired.
M: Do you have a lot of homework, too?
W: Yes. I don't know why we must learn so
   many subjects.
M: Cheer up! They'll be helpful later in life.

남: Kate, 어떻게 지내니?
여: 좋진 않아요.
남: 무슨 일 있니? 친구랑 싸웠어?
여: 너무 많은 과목들을 공부해야 해서 너무 피곤해요.
남: 숙제도 많니?
여: 네. 그렇게 많은 과목을 왜 공부해야 하는지 모르겠어요.
남: 기운 내렴! 그것들이 살면서 나중에 도움이 될 거야.

어휘

How's it going? 어떻게 지내?   fight[fait] 명 싸움
know[nou] 동 알다 (know-knew-known)   Cheer
up! 기운 내!   helpful[hélpfəl] 형 도움이 되는   later
[léitər] 부 나중에   life[laif] 명 삶, 인생   [문제] far
away 멀리 떨어진 곳에   classmate[klǽsmèit]
명 반 친구   understand[ʌ̀ndərstǽnd] 동 이해하다
(understand-understood-understood)

문제 해설
Q: Kate가 기분이 안 좋은 이유는?
  ① 학교가 너무 멀다.
  ② 반 친구와 싸웠다.
  ③ 공부할 게 너무 많다.
  ④ 몇몇 과목들이 이해하기 어렵다.
  Kate는 공부해야 할 과목이 너무 많아서 피곤해하고 있다.

4

W: Michael, when was the best time in your school life?

M: Last sports day. I scored a goal for my soccer team, and we won!

W: Right! You were great.

M: Thanks. How about you, Helen?

W: I liked the field trip most.

M: Do you mean when we went to Rose Lake?

W: No. Do you remember the art gallery in Seattle? I saw wonderful paintings by Picasso there.

여: Michael, 네가 학교 생활하면서 가장 좋았던 때가 언제야?

남: 지난 운동회 때. 내가 우리 축구팀에서 한 골을 넣어서 우승했잖아!

여: 맞아! 너 대단했지.

남: 고마워. Helen, 너는?

여: 나는 현장 학습이 가장 좋았어.

남: 우리가 Rose Lake에 갔을 때 말이니?

여: 아니. 시애틀에 있는 미술관 기억나니? 거기서 피카소가 그린 훌륭한 그림들을 봤잖아.

어휘

sports day 운동회   score[skɔːr] ⑧ 득점하다   goal [goul] ⑲ 목표; *골   soccer[sákər] ⑲ 축구   win[win] ⑧ 이기다 (win—won—won)   field trip 현장 학습   remember[rimémbər] ⑧ 기억하다   art gallery 미술관   wonderful[wʌ́ndərfəl] ⑲ 훌륭한

문제 해설

Q: 각 인물이 가장 즐거워한 학교 행사를 고르시오.

(1) Michael은 운동회 때 골을 넣었던 일에 대해 얘기하고 있다.

(2) Helen은 시애틀에 있는 미술관에서 피카소 그림을 관람한 일에 대해 얘기하고 있다.

5

W: You look tired.

M: I stayed up all night doing math homework.

W: What? We have one more day to do math homework.

M: No, we don't. Math is the first class today.

W: What are you talking about? Today's first class is French.

M: Really? Oh, no. I thought today was Wednesday.

W: That's too bad. Don't forget that we have English homework today.

여: 너 피곤해 보이는구나.

남: 수학 숙제를 하느라 밤을 새웠어.

여: 뭐라고? 수학 숙제 하는 건 하루 더 남았는데.

남: 아니야. 수학은 오늘 첫 수업인걸.

여: 무슨 말을 하는 거야? 오늘 첫 수업은 프랑스어야.

남: 정말? 이런. 난 오늘이 수요일이라고 생각했어.

여: 저런. 오늘은 영어 숙제가 있단 걸 잊지 마.

어휘

stay up all night 밤을 새우다   math[mæθ] ⑲ 수학   French[frenʧ] ⑲ 프랑스어

문제 해설

Q: 오늘은 무슨 요일인가?

여자가 오늘은 첫 시간에 프랑스어 수업이 있고, 그 외에 영어 수업이 있다고 했다.

6

(*Telephone rings.*)

W: Hello.

M: Hi, Anna. This is John.

W: John! Why were you absent from school today?

M: I had a cold, but I feel better now.

W: Then, will you come to school tomorrow?

M: I will. Anyway, is there any homework for tomorrow?

W: Yes, you should research about John F. Kennedy.

M: Anything else?

W: That's all. And bring your dictionary for English class.

M: Okay. Thanks.

(전화벨이 울린다.)

여: 여보세요.

남: Anna야, 안녕. 나 John이야.

여: John! 오늘 왜 학교에 결석했어?

남: 감기에 걸렸는데, 지금은 나아졌어.

여: 그럼 내일은 학교에 올 거니?

남: 그럴 거야. 그런데, 내일 숙제 있니?

여: 응, John F. Kennedy에 대해서 조사해야 해.

남: 다른 건 없어?

여: 그게 다야. 그리고 영어 수업 시간에 사전을 가져와.

남: 알았어. 고마워.

어휘

be absent from ~ ~을 결석하다   have a cold 감기에 걸리다   anyway[éniwèi] ⑨ 어쨌든   research [risə́ːrtʃ] ⑧ 조사하다   dictionary[díkʃənèri] ⑲ 사전 [문제] borrow[bárou] ⑧ 빌리다   plan[plæn] ⑲ 계획 together[təɡéðər] ⑨ 함께

문제 해설

Q: John이 Anna에게 전화한 이유는?

① 숙제에 대해 물어보려고

② 영어 사전을 빌리려고

③ 함께 숙제할 계획을 세우려고

④ 그녀에게 학교에 결석한 이유를 말하려고

John은 Anna에서 전화해서 숙제가 있는지 물어보고 있다.

7

M: Mom, do I have to go to school today?

W: Are you feeling sick?

M: No, I just don't want to go.

W: Are you kidding?

M: I can study at home by taking online classes. Why should I study at school?

W: I understand your point. But studying isn't everything. You can learn many other things at school.

M: But Mom...

W: Get ready for school, now!

남: 엄마, 저 오늘 학교에 꼭 가야 되요?

여: 너 아프니?

남: 아니요, 그냥 가고 싶지가 않아서요.

여: 농담하는 거니?

남: 집에서 온라인 수업 들으면서 공부할 수 있다고요. 왜 학교에서 공부해야만 하는 거죠?

여: 네 말의 요점은 알겠어. 하지만 공부가 다는 아니야. 넌 학교에서 다른 것도 많이 배울 수 있어.

남: 하지만 엄마…

여: 당장 학교 갈 준비해!

어휘

Are you kidding? 농담하니?   online[ɔ́ːnláin] ⑲ 온라인 상의   point[pɔint] ⑲ 요점   get ready 준비하다 [문제] hospital[háspitəl] ⑲ 병원

문제 해설

Q: 소년이 다음에 할 일은?

① 집에서 공부한다.

② 병원에 간다.

③ 학교에 갈 준비를 한다.

④ 온라인 수업을 듣는다.

엄마가 학교에 가야 한다고 주장하며 학교 갈 준비를 하라고 했으므로, 소년은 학교 갈 준비를 할 것이다.

8

M: Attention, students! This homework is a group project. Make groups of four members and give me a list of members by tomorrow. Your project is to choose one part of the human body and research it. You should write a three-page report. Please hand it in by next Friday.

남: 여러분, 주목해 주세요! 이 숙제는 그룹 과제예요. 네 명씩 그룹을 지어서 내일까지 구성원 명단을 저한테 주세요. 여러분의 과제는 인체의 한 부분을 골라서 조사하는 거예요. 여러분은 3장 분량의 보고서를 써야 합니다. 그걸 다음 주 금요일까지 제출해 주세요.

어휘

project[prɑ́dʒekt] ⑲ 과제   list[list] ⑲ 목록   part [pɑːrt] ⑲ 부분   human[hjúːmən] ⑱ 사람의 report[ripɔ́ːrt] ⑲ 보고서   hand in ~ ~을 제출하다 [문제] product[prɑ́dəkt] ⑲ 제품; *결과물   due date 마감 예정일

문제 해설

Q: 숙제에 관해 틀린 정보를 고르시오.

네 명씩 그룹을 지어서 인체의 한 부분에 대해 3장짜리 보고서를 작성해야 하며, 다음 주 금요일까지 제출해야 한다고 했다.

Listening ★ Challenge   p. 18

A 1 ④   2 (1) Good (2) Good (3) Bad

B 1 (1) ④   (2) ①   2 ②

A [1-2]

W: How was your first day at your new school?

M: Great. But I almost missed the school bus.

W: Why? You left home on time.

17

M: But I made a mistake. It comes at 7:10, not at 7:15.

W: Really? I'll wake you up earlier, then. So, how was your school?

M: My teacher Ms. Sullivan looked strict at first, but she's actually very friendly.

W: Good. How about your classmates?

M: There are many pretty girls in my class, so I'm happy.

W: (laughing) Good for you.

M: But I was disappointed with the school gym. It's too old.

여: 새 학교에서 첫날이 어땠니?

남: 좋았어요. 근데 학교 버스를 거의 놓칠 뻔 했어요.

여: 왜? 집에서 시간에 맞춰서 나갔잖아.

남: 하지만 제가 실수했어요. 버스가 7시 15분이 아니라 7시 10분에 오거든요.

여: 정말? 그럼 너를 더 빨리 깨워야겠구나. 그래, 학교는 어땠어?

남: 저희 Sullivan 선생님은 처음엔 엄격해 보였는데, 사실은 아주 다정하시더라고요.

여: 잘됐구나. 반 친구들은 어땠니?

남: 우리 반에 예쁜 여자애들이 많아서 행복해요.

여: [웃으며] 잘됐구나.

남: 하지만 학교 체육관에 실망했어요. 너무 낡았어요.

어휘

almost[ɔ́ːlmoust] 퇸 거의　leave[liːv] 통 떠나다 (leave-left-left)　on time *시간에 맞게; 정각에　make a mistake 실수하다　strict[strikt] 혱 엄격한　at first 처음에　actually[ǽktʃuəli] 퇸 사실　friendly [fréndli] 혱 다정다감한　disappointed[dìsəpɔ́intid] 혱 실망한　gym[dʒim] 명 체육관　[문제] correct[kərékt] 혱 올바른

문제 해설

Q1: 소년이 학교 버스를 거의 놓칠 뻔한 이유는?

　① 버스 번호를 잊었다.

　② 너무 늦게 일어났다.

　③ 잘못된 버스 정류장에서 기다렸다.

　④ 정확한 버스 시간표를 몰랐다.

　소년은 버스가 7시 10분에 오는데, 7시 15분에 오는 줄 알고 있었다.

Q2: 소년이 다음의 각각에 대해 어떻게 느끼는지 √표 하시오.

　(1) 선생님이 다정하다고 했다.

　(2) 같은 반에 예쁜 여자애들이 많아서 행복해하고 있다.

　(3) 학교 체육관이 너무 낡아 실망했다.

B [1-2]

M: Emily, I'm having a bad day!

W: What happened?

M: In my English class, my teacher saw me using my cell phone. So he took it away.

W: Did you get it back after class?

M: No, I can get it back next week.

W: That's too bad.

M: Also, in science class, I dropped a bottle, and it broke.

W: How terrible!

M: That's not all. I have a history test in the afternoon, but I can't find my notebook.

W: That's too bad.

M: This is not my day.

남: Emily, 나 오늘 일진이 사나워.

여: 무슨 일이 있었는데?

남: 영어 수업 시간에, 우리 선생님이 내가 휴대 전화 사용하는 걸 보시고는 그것을 가져가 버리셨어.

여: 수업 끝나고 그걸 돌려받았어?

남: 아니, 다음 주에 되찾을 수 있어.

여: 안됐구나.

남: 그리고 과학 수업 시간에 내가 병을 떨어뜨렸는데, 그게 깨져 버렸어.

여: 저런!

남: 그게 다가 아니야. 오후에 역사 시험을 치는데, 내 공책을 찾을 수가 없어.

여: 정말 안됐네.

남: 오늘은 정말 운이 없는 날이야.

어휘

cell phone 휴대 전화　take away ~을 가져가다　get back ~을 되찾다　drop[drɑp] 통 떨어뜨리다　bottle[bátl] 명 병　terrible[térəbl] 혱 끔찍한　[문제] wall[wɔːl] 명 벽　pour[pɔːr] 통 퍼붓다　catch[kætʃ] 통 잡다 (catch-caught-caught)　worm[wəːrm] 명 벌레

문제 해설

Q1: 각 수업 시간에 소년에게 무슨 일이 있었는지 고르시오.

　(1) 영어 수업 시간에 휴대 전화를 사용하다가 선생님에게 빼앗겼다고 했다.

　(2) 과학 시간에는 병을 떨어뜨려서 깨뜨렸다고 했다.

Q2: 소년의 상황을 가장 잘 묘사하는 것은?

　① 벽에도 귀가 있다.

　② 비가 오기만 하면 억수로 쏟아진다.

　③ 일찍 일어나는 새가 벌레를 잡는다.

④ 인생에 모든 것에는 때가 있다.

하루 동안 나쁜 일이 여러 개 겹쳐서 일어났으므로, '비가 오기만 하면 억수로 쏟아진다(=설상가상)'라는 의미의 속담이 알맞다.

Critical ★ Thinking   p. 19

1 (1) For (2) For (3) Against
2 (1) ⓒ (2) ⓑ (3) ⓐ

M1: I'm Tony. Some people teach their children at home. So, their children don't go to school. I think this homeschooling is a good idea. Parents can choose what to teach according to each child's talent.

W: I'm Julia. Many schools have poor learning environments. Also, children can start smoking or drinking alcohol because of friends. Therefore, I think homeschooling is better for children.

M2: I'm Darren. In school, children can learn how to get along with other people. Homeschooling can't teach this important thing.

남1: 난 Tony야. 어떤 사람들은 집에서 자신의 아이들을 가르쳐. 그래서 그 아이들은 학교에 가지 않지. 내 생각에 홈스쿨링은 좋은 생각인 것 같아. 부모가 각 아이의 재능에 따라 무엇을 가르칠지 선택할 수 있으니까.

여: 난 Julia야. 많은 학교들이 열악한 학습 환경을 가지고 있어. 그리고 아이들이 친구들 때문에 담배를 피우거나 술을 마시기 시작하기도 해. 그래서 내 생각에 홈스쿨링이 아이들을 위해서 더 좋은 것 같아.

남2: 난 Darren이야. 학교에서 아이들은 다른 사람들이랑 잘 지내는 방법을 배울 수 있어. 홈스쿨링은 이 중요한 걸 가르쳐줄 수가 없어.

어휘
teach[tiːtʃ] 동 가르치다 (teach-taught-taught)
homeschooling[hóumskùːliŋ] 명 홈스쿨링, 자택 학습
according to ~ ~에 따라 each[iːtʃ] 형 각각의
talent[tǽlənt] 명 재능 poor[puər] 형 나쁜, 조잡한
environment[inváiərənmənt] 명 환경 smoke
[smouk] 동 담배 피다 alcohol[ǽlkəhɔ̀(ː)l] 명 술 get
along with ~ ~와 잘 지내다 important[impɔ́ːrtənt]
형 중요한 [문제] social[sóuʃəl] 형 사회의 skill[skil]
명 기술, 능력 homeschool[hóumskùːl] 동 자택에서
교육하다

문제 해설
Q1: 각 인물이 홈스쿨링에 찬성하는지 혹은 반대하는지 √표 하시오.
 (1) Tony는 홈스쿨링이 각 학생에 맞는 수업을 제공한다고 말했다.
 (2) Julia는 학교 환경이 열악한 경우가 많으므로 홈스쿨링이 더 좋다고 생각한다.
 (3) Darren은 학교에서만 배울 수 있는 것이 있다고 했다.

Q2: 각 인물과 해당 의견을 연결하시오.
 ⓐ 학생들은 학교에서 사교 기술을 배운다.
 ⓑ 가정이 더 좋은 학습 환경이다.
 ⓒ 각 학생은 홈스쿨링을 받음으로써 자신이 배울 필요가 있는 것을 배울 수 있다.
 (1) Tony는 홈스쿨링을 통해 아이들이 자신의 재능에 맞게 배울 수 있다고 했다.
 (2) Julia는 학교보다 가정이 더 나은 학습 환경을 제공할 것이라 생각한다.
 (3) Darren은 학교에서 다른 사람과 어울리는 방법, 즉 사회성을 키울 수 있다고 생각한다.

UNIT 03 Transportation & Location

Getting ★ Ready   p. 20

A 1 straight 2 across 3 next to 4 along
B 1 ⓒ 2 ⓐ 3 ⓑ C 1 ⓓ 2 ⓑ 3 ⓔ

C 1 여: 얼마나 걸려요?
   남: 20분 정도 걸려요.
 2 여: 시청에 어떻게 가나요?
   남: 모퉁이에서 왼쪽으로 도세요. 그러면 보일 거예요.
 3 여: 센트럴 파크에 가려면 버스를 타야 하나요, 지하철을 타야 하나요?
   남: 버스를 타야 해요. 그게 더 빨라요.

Listening ★ Start   p. 21

1 ② / Excuse me, turn right, on your left
2 ① / I'm going to, quicker than, Take the bus

1

W: Excuse me. Do you know where the Guggenheim Museum is?

M: Yes. Go straight one block and turn right at the corner.

W: Turn right at the corner?

M: That's right. Then you will see it on your left.

W: I see. Thank you.

여: 실례합니다. 구겐하임 박물관이 어디인지 아세요?

남: 네. 한 블록 직진하셔서 모퉁이에서 오른쪽으로 도세요.

여: 모퉁이에서 오른쪽으로 돌라고요?

남: 맞아요. 그러면 왼편에 보일 거예요.

여: 알겠어요. 고마워요.

어휘
Excuse me. 실례합니다.　museum[mju(ː)zí(ː)əm] 명 박물관　straight[streit] 부 똑바로, 일직선으로 block[blɑk] 명 블록　turn[təːrn] 동 돌다　corner[kɔ́ːrnər] 명 모퉁이

문제 해설
Q: 지도에서 구겐하임 박물관을 고르시오.

현재 위치에서 한 블록을 곧장 간 후, 모퉁이에서 오른쪽으로 돌면 왼편에 보인다고 했다.

2

W: Where are you going?

M: I'm going to Central Park to meet Lena. But I'm late.

W: Oh, you should hurry.

M: Do you think the subway is quicker than the bus?

W: No. You have to change subway lines. Take the bus.

M: Okay. Thank you.

여: 어디 가니?

남: Lena를 만나러 센트럴 파크에 가는 중이야. 근데 늦었어.

여: 아, 서둘러야겠구나.

남: 네 생각에 지하철이 버스보다 더 빠를 것 같니?

여: 아니. 지하철은 갈아타야 하거든. 버스를 타.

남: 알았어. 고마워.

어휘
hurry[hə́ːri] 동 서두르다　subway[sʌ́bwèi] 명 지하철 quick[kwik] 형 빠른　line[lain] 명 선; *노선

문제 해설
Q: 남자는 센트럴 파크에 어떻게 갈 것인가?

여자가 버스를 타라고 조언했으므로 버스를 탈 것이다.

Listening ★ Practice　p. 22

1 ①　2 ①　3 ②　4 (1) ⓒ (2) ⓐ
5 ③　6 ①　7 ③　8 ④

1

M: Good afternoon. I'm James Parker, the pilot of this plane. We just took off and are heading for Hong Kong International Airport. It takes about four hours. Today's weather is fine. So, please enjoy your flight with us. Thank you.

남: 안녕하세요. 저는 이 비행기의 조종사인 James Parker 입니다. 우리는 이제 막 이륙해서 홍콩 국제 공항으로 향하고 있습니다. 약 네 시간이 걸릴 겁니다. 오늘의 날씨는 화창하네요. 그럼, 저희와 함께 즐거운 비행 되세요. 감사합니다.

어휘
pilot[páilət] 명 조종사　plane[plein] 명 비행기 (= airplane)　take off 이륙하다　head[hed] 명 머리; *동 향하다　international[ìntərnǽʃənəl] 형 국제의 airport[ɛ́ərpɔ̀ːrt] 명 공항　enjoy[indʒɔ́i] 동 즐기다 flight[flait] 명 비행　[문제] announcement [ənáunsmənt] 명 공고, 발표　travel agency 여행사

문제 해설
Q: 이런 종류의 방송을 들을 수 있는 곳은?

비행기 조종사가 기내 안내 방송을 하는 상황이다.

2

M: Excuse me. Is there a bus to Jurong Bird Park here?

W: No. The bus stop is just over there, across the street.

M: Oh, I see. Do you know which bus should I take?

W: I think it's the number thirteen.

M: Number thirty?

W: No, number thirteen.

M: Okay, thanks.

남: 실례합니다. 여기서 주롱 새공원으로 가는 버스가 있나요?

여: 아니요. 버스 정류장은 바로 저기, 길 건너편에 있습니다.

남: 아, 알겠습니다. 어느 버스를 타야 하는지 아세요?

여: 13번 버스인 것 같아요.

남: 30번이요?

여: 아니요, 13번이요.

남: 알겠어요, 감사합니다.

어휘

across[əkrɔ́ːs] 전 ~ 건너서   street[striːt] 명 길

문제 해설

Q: 남자는 어느 버스를 탈 것인가?

여자가 13번 버스를 타야 할 것 같다고 말했다.

3

(*Telephone rings.*)

W: Thank you for calling Star Café.

M: Hello, I'm trying to get there now, but I'm lost.

W: What can you see around you?

M: Well, there is a post office on my left.

W: Then, go straight one block and turn left.

M: Okay.

W: Then you will see the police station. The café is next to it.

(전화벨이 울린다.)

여: Star Café에 전화 주셔서 감사드립니다.

남: 안녕하세요, 제가 지금 거기로 가려고 하는데, 길을 잃었어요.

여: 주위에 뭐가 보이나요?

남: 음, 제 왼편에 우체국이 있어요.

여: 그럼 한 블록 직진하셔서 왼쪽으로 도세요.

남: 알겠어요.

여: 그러면 경찰서가 보일 거예요. 카페는 그 옆에 있어요.

어휘

try to-v ~하려고 노력하다   lost[lɔ(ː)st] 형 길을 잃은   post office 우체국   police station 경찰서   next to ~ ~ 옆에

문제 해설

Q: 지도에서 Star Café를 고르시오.

카페는 경찰서 옆에 있다고 했다.

4

W: Today was my first day in London. In the morning, I took a taxi to Big Ben. It was very tall, and I heard the bell ring. Then I took the subway to Tower Bridge. It was beautiful. After that, I went to Piccadilly Circus by bus and saw a famous musical.

여: 오늘은 런던에서의 첫날이었다. 아침에 빅벤으로 가는 택시를 탔다. 그것은 매우 높았고, 나는 종이 울리는 걸 들었다. 그리고 나서 타워 브리지로 가는 지하철을 탔다. 그것은 아름다웠다. 그런 다음, 버스를 타고 피커딜리 광장에 가서 유명한 뮤지컬을 봤다.

어휘

hear[hiər] 동 듣다 (hear-heard-heard)   bell[bel] 명 종   ring[riŋ] 동 울리다 (ring-rang-rung)   circus [sə́ːrkəs] 명 곡예; *《영》원형 광장   musical[mjúːzikəl] 명 뮤지컬   [문제] on foot 걸어서

문제 해설

Q: 여자가 각 장소에 어떻게 갔는가?

빅벤에서 지하철을 타고 타워 브리지에 갔다가 버스를 타고 피커딜리 광장으로 이동했다.

5

M: Attention, please! The train from Boston is delayed because of heavy snow. It was going to arrive at 11:00, but it will arrive thirty minutes late. Sorry for any problems. Thank you for your understanding.

남: 안내 말씀 드리겠습니다! 보스턴에서 오는 기차가 폭설로 인해 지연되고 있습니다. 기차는 11시에 도착할 예정이었으나 30분 늦게 도착할 것입니다. 불편을 끼쳐 드려 죄송합니다. 이해해 주셔서 감사합니다.

어휘

Attention, please! 여러분께 알려드립니다!   delay [diléi] 동 지연시키다   heavy snow 폭설   any[éni] 형 어떤 ~든지, 모든   problem[prábləm] 명 문제

문제 해설

Q: 기차가 역에 도착할 시간은?

원래 11시에 도착할 예정이었으나 30분 늦어질 것이라고 했으므로 11시 30분에 도착할 것이다.

6

W: Michael! I'm sorry, I'm late.

M: Oh, Lisa! The bus just left.

W: I'm really sorry! When will the next bus come?

M: In about twenty minutes. Why were you late?

W: I went to the train station to buy tickets. It took a long time.

M: I see. Let's take a taxi. The theater is too

★　★

far to walk.

W: Okay. I will pay!

여: Michael! 늦어서 미안해.

남: 아, Lisa! 버스가 방금 떠났어.

여: 정말 미안해! 다음 버스는 언제 오지?

남: 약 20분 후에. 왜 늦었어?

여: 표를 사러 기차역에 갔거든. 시간이 오래 걸렸어.

남: 그렇구나. 택시를 타자. 극장이 너무 멀어서 걸어갈 수가 없어.

여: 알았어. 내가 낼게!

어휘

ticket[tíkit] 몡 표　theater[θí(ː)ətər] 몡 극장　too ~ to-v 너무 ~해서 …할 수 없다　far[faːr] 혱 멀리 떨어진
pay[pei] 동 지불하다 (pay-paid-paid)

문제 해설

Q: 그들이 다음에 할 일은?
　① 택시를 탄다.
　② 다음 버스를 기다린다.
　③ 기차역으로 간다.
　④ 극장에 걸어서 간다.
　극장이 너무 멀어서 택시를 타기로 했다.

7

W: Henry, do you know how to get to the Louvre Museum?

M: Yes. You can get there on the number 24 bus.

W: Where is the bus stop?

M: It's across from the library.

W: Oh, so it's quite near. How long does it take?

M: It takes about thirty minutes.

W: I see. Thanks a lot.

여: Henry, 루브르 박물관에 어떻게 가는지 아니?

남: 응. 24번 버스를 타면 거기에 도착할 수 있어.

여: 버스 정류장은 어딘데?

남: 도서관 건너편에 있어.

여: 아, 꽤 가깝구나. 얼마나 걸려?

남: 약 30분 정도 걸려.

여: 알았어. 정말 고마워.

어휘

library[láibrèri] 몡 도서관　near[niər] 혱 가까운
a lot 매우, 많이

문제 해설

Q: 틀린 정보를 고르시오.
　버스 정류장은 도서관 옆이 아니고 건너편에 있다.

8

W: Excuse me. Does this line go to Times Square?

M: No. You need to change subway lines.

W: Oh, really? Which line do I need to take?

M: Let me see. You have to take line number 7 from Union Square station.

W: Union Square station? I see.

M: Times Square is just three stops from Union Square station.

여: 실례합니다. 이 노선이 타임스퀘어로 가나요?

남: 아니요. 지하철을 갈아타야 해요.

여: 아, 정말이요? 어느 노선을 타야 하나요?

남: 음, 어디 봅시다. 유니언 스퀘어 역에서 7호선을 타야겠네요.

여: 유니언 스퀘어 역이요? 알겠습니다.

남: 타임스퀘어는 유니언 스퀘어 역에서 딱 세 정거장이에요.

어휘

need[niːd] 동 ~할 필요가 있다　change[tʃeindʒ] 동 바꾸다　Let me see. 글쎄, 어디 보자.　stop[stɑp] 몡 정거장

문제 해설

Q: 타임스퀘어 역을 지도에서 고르시오.
　7호선이며 유니언 스퀘어 역에서 세 정거장 떨어져 있다.

Listening ★ Challenge　p. 24

A 1 ③　2 ④　B 1 ④　2 ①

A [1-2]

M: Good morning. Where to, ma'am?

W: To Tokyo Hotel, please. How long will it take?

M: About 15 minutes. Where are you from?

W: I'm from Canada.

M: I see. Have you ever been here before?

W: No. Are there any good places to visit?

M: What about Tokyo Tower or Disney Land? They are popular places for tourists.

W: I see. And where can I go shopping?

M: Shibuya is a good shopping place. There are many stores along the street.

W: Thank you. I'll go shopping there tomorrow.

남: 안녕하세요. 어디로 모실까요, 손님?

여: 도쿄 호텔이요. 얼마나 걸릴까요?

남: 대략 15분 정도요. 어디서 오셨어요?

여: 캐나다에서 왔어요.

남: 그렇군요. 전에 여기 와 보신 적 있어요?

여: 아니요. 어디 방문하기 좋은 곳이 있나요?

남: 도쿄 타워나 디즈니랜드 어때요? 관광객들 사이에서 인기가 많아요.

여: 그렇군요. 그리고 쇼핑은 어디서 할 수 있나요?

남: 시부야가 쇼핑하기 좋은 곳이죠. 길을 따라서 상점들이 많아요.

여: 고마워요. 내일 거기로 쇼핑하러 가야겠네요.

어휘

before[bifɔ́ːr] 분 전에 place[pleis] 명 장소 visit [vízit] 동 방문하다 popular[pápjulər] 형 인기 있는 among[əmʌ́ŋ] 전 ~ 사이에 tourist[tú(:)ərist] 명 관광객 go shopping 쇼핑하러 가다 store[stɔːr] 명 가게 along[əlɔ́(ː)ŋ] 전 ~을 따라서 [문제] staff[stæf] 명 직원 guest[gest] 명 손님 guide[gaid] 명 안내원 driver[dráivər] 명 운전사 passenger[pǽsəndʒər] 명 승객 flight attendant 비행기 승무원

문제 해설

Q1: 화자 간의 관계는?

관광객이 택시를 타서 관광과 관련된 내용을 묻고 답하는 상황이다.

Q2: 여자가 내일 가려고 하는 곳은?

남자가 소개해 준 시부야에 쇼핑하러 가려고 한다.

B [1-2]

M: Helen, do you know how I can get to Carnegie Hall?

W: Yes. You are going to take the subway, aren't you?

M: That's right. I don't like buses because I get carsick.

W: I know. Anyway, do you know 57th Street station?

M: Yes, I do.

W: Okay. There, you should go out of exit number 1.

M: Exit number 1?

W: Yes. Then, go straight for two blocks and turn left. You will see the hall on your right. You can't miss it.

남: Helen, 카네기홀에 어떻게 가는지 아니?

여: 응. 너 지하철 탈 거지, 아니야?

남: 맞아. 난 차멀미를 해서 버스를 안 좋아해.

여: 알아. 어쨌든, 57번가 역 알아?

남: 응, 알아.

여: 좋아. 거기서 1번 출구로 나가야 해.

남: 1번 출구?

여: 응. 그러고 나서 두 블록을 직진해서 왼쪽으로 돌아. 오른편에 카네기홀이 보일 거야. 금방 찾을 수 있어.

어휘

hall[hɔːl] 명 집회장, 홀 carsick[káːrsìk] 형 차멀미하는 out of ~ ~의 밖으로 exit[égzit] 명 출구 [문제] concert[kánsə(ː)rt] 명 콘서트, 음악회 nearby [níərbài] 부 가까이 cheap[tʃiːp] 형 값이 싼

문제 해설

Q1: 남자가 지하철을 타려는 이유는?

① 콘서트에 늦어서

② 지하철역이 가까이 있어서

③ 버스를 타는 것보다 더 싸서

④ 버스를 타면 멀미를 해서

남자는 버스를 타면 차멀미를 해서 버스를 좋아하지 않는다고 했다.

Q2: 지도에서 카네기홀을 찾으시오.

1번 출구로 나와서 두 블록을 직진한 후 왼쪽으로 돌면, 오른편에 있다.

Critical ★ Thinking   p. 25

1 ② 2 ①, ③

W: Dave, is something wrong? You look upset.

M: I met some rude people on the subway.

W: What happened?

M: Well, a girl was listening to music very loudly.

W: Why didn't you ask her to turn down the volume?

M: I did, but she said no. She said that it was her choice.

W: She really has bad manners.

M: That's not all.

23

W: What else?

M: A teenage boy got on the subway and started to eat a hamburger. It smelled bad.

W: Oh, dear.

M: I can't understand why they act like that. They should learn better manners.

여: Dave, 안 좋은 일 있니? 언짢아 보이는데.

남: 지하철에서 무례한 사람들을 만났어.

여: 무슨 일인데?

남: 음. 한 여자애가 음악을 아주 크게 듣고 있었거든.

여: 그 애한테 소리 좀 줄이라고 말하지 그랬어?

남: 그렇게 했는데 그 여자애가 싫다고 했어. 자기가 선택할 문제라고 말하더라고.

여: 그 애는 정말 예의가 없구나.

남: 그게 다가 아니야.

여: 또 뭔데?

남: 한 10대 남자애가 지하철에 타서 햄버거를 먹기 시작했어. 냄새가 안 좋았어.

여: 아, 저런.

남: 그 애들이 왜 그렇게 행동하는지 이해할 수가 없어. 그 애들은 예의를 좀 더 배워야 해.

어휘

upset[ʌpsét] 형 화난 rude[ruːd] 형 무례한 loudly [láudli] 부 크게 turn down 줄이다, 낮추다 volume [váljuːm] 명 음량 choice[tʃɔis] 명 선택 manner [mǽnər] 명 ((~s)) 예절 teenage[tíːnèidʒ] 형 10대의 hamburger[hǽmbə̀ːrgər] 명 햄버거 smell[smel] 동 냄새가 나다 act[ækt] 동 행동하다 [문제] sad[sæd] 형 슬픈 angry[ǽngri] 형 화난 bored[bɔːrd] 형 지루한 worried[wə́ːrid] 형 걱정되는

문제 해설

Q1: 현재 남자의 기분은?

지하철에서 무례한 사람들을 만나 화가 난 상황이다.

Q2: 남자에게 무슨 일이 있었는지 보여주는 그림을 두 개 고르시오.

지하철에서 음악을 크게 듣고 있는 소녀와 햄버거를 먹는 10대 소년을 만났다.

UNIT 04 Seasons & Weather

Getting ★ Ready p. 26

A 1 ⓑ 2 ⓕ 3 ⓔ 4 ⓐ

B 1 ⓕ 2 ⓐ 3 ⓑ

B 1 남: 언제 날씨가 갤까?

　여: 이번 금요일까지는 안 갤 거야.

2 남: 인도네시아의 날씨는 어떠니?

　여: 일년 내내 더워.

3 남: 내일 날씨는 어떨까?

　여: 비가 올 거야.

Listening ★ Start p. 27

1 ③ / Let's go, clear up, on the weekend, shall we

2 (1) ⓒ (2) ⓐ (3) ⓑ / enjoy swimming, favorite sports, go on picnics

1

W: Let's go to an amusement park this Thursday.

M: I heard it's going to be cloudy and rainy in the afternoon.

W: When will it clear up?

M: Well, not until this Friday.

W: Is it going to be sunny on the weekend?

M: No, but it won't rain.

W: Then, shall we go this Saturday?

M: Okay.

여: 이번 목요일에 놀이공원에 가자.

남: 오후에 흐리고 비가 올 거라고 들었어.

여: 언제 날씨가 갤까?

남: 글쎄. 이번 금요일까지는 안 갤거야.

여: 주말에는 날씨가 화창할까?

남: 아니. 그래도 비는 안 올 거야.

여: 그럼 이번 토요일에 갈래?

남: 좋아.

어휘

amusement park 놀이공원 cloudy[kláudi] 형 구름 낀, 흐린 rainy[réini] 형 비가 오는 clear up 날씨

가 개다   not until ~ ~까지는 아닌   sunny[sʌ́ni] 혱
화창한   weekend[wíːkènd] 몡 주말

Q: 두 사람은 놀이공원에 언제 가려고 하는가?
  토요일에 가기로 했다.

2

W1: I'm Jacky. I love hot weather because I
    can enjoy swimming in the hot sun.
M: I'm Paul. I like snow. Skiing and
    snowboarding are my favorite sports.
W2: I'm Nora. I love warm weather. I like to
    go on picnics and see lots of beautiful
    flowers.

여1: 나는 Jacky야. 나는 뜨거운 태양 아래서 수영을 즐길
    수 있어서 더운 날씨를 좋아해.
남: 나는 Paul이야. 나는 눈을 좋아해. 스키와 스노보드는
    내가 가장 좋아하는 운동이야.
여2: 나는 Nora야. 나는 따뜻한 날씨를 좋아해. 나는 소풍을
    가서 아름다운 많은 꽃들을 보는 것을 좋아해.

어휘
hot[hɑt] 혱 뜨거운; 더운   weather[wéðər] 몡 날씨
sun[sʌn] 몡 태양   snow[snou] *몡 눈; 동 눈이 오다
ski[skiː] 동 스키를 타다   snowboard[snóubɔ̀ːrd] 동
스노보드를 타다   warm[wɔːrm] 혱 따뜻한   go on a
picnic 소풍 가다   flower[fláuər] 몡 꽃

문제 해설
Q: 각 인물이 가장 좋아하는 계절을 고르시오.
  (1) Jacky는 덥고 햇빛이 쨍쨍한 계절을 좋아한다.
  (2) Paul은 스키와 스노보드를 즐길 수 있는 계절을 좋아
    한다.
  (3) Nora는 아름다운 꽃을 볼 수 있는 계절을 좋아한다.

Listening ★ Practice   p. 28

1 (1) ① (2) ④   2 ④   3 (1) ⓐ (2) ⓑ   4 ③
5 (1) ⓒ (2) ⓑ (3) ⓔ   6 ③   7 ①, ②   8 ②

1

(*Telephone rings.*)
W: Hello.
M: Hello, Mom. It's me.
W: John! I was waiting for your call.

M: Sorry, Mom. I was busy traveling.
W: So how's the weather in New York?
M: It was cloudy yesterday, but it has
    cleared up now.
W: That's good. Are you having a good time?
M: I'm enjoying myself. So, how's Seattle?
W: It's snowing a lot.

(전화벨이 울린다.)
여: 여보세요.
남: 여보세요, 엄마. 저예요.
여: John! 네 전화 기다리고 있었어.
남: 죄송해요, 엄마. 여행하느라 바빴어요.
여: 그래, 뉴욕 날씨는 어떠니?
남: 어제는 흐렸는데 지금은 날씨가 갰어요.
여: 잘됐구나. 좋은 시간 보내고 있니?
남: 재미있게 보내고 있어요. 근데, 시애틀은 어때요?
여: 눈이 많이 와.

어휘
wait for ~을 기다리다   call[kɔːl] *몡 전화; 동 전화하다
be busy v-ing ~하느라 바쁘다   travel[trǽvəl] 몡 여
행; *동 여행하다   have a good time 좋은 시간을 보내
다   enjoy oneself 즐겁게 시간을 보내다

문제 해설
Q: 뉴욕과 시애틀의 오늘 날씨를 고르시오.
  뉴욕은 날씨가 개었고, 시애틀에는 눈이 많이 오고 있다.

2

M: What will the weather be like tomorrow,
    Sandy?
W: Why do you ask?
M: I'm going to an outdoor concert.
W: Wait. Did you say it's tomorrow?
M: Yeah, is there some problem?
W: I heard it's going to rain.
M: Oh, no! Are you sure?
W: Yes. It's going to rain all day.
M: That's bad news! I don't want to listen to
    a concert in the rain.
W: That's too bad.

남: Sandy, 내일 날씨가 어떨까?
여: 왜 물어 보는 거야?
남: 야외 콘서트에 가려고.
여: 잠깐만. 그게 내일이라고?

남: 응. 무슨 문제 있니?

여: 내일 비가 올 거라고 들었거든.

남: 아, 안돼! 정말이야?

여: 응. 하루 종일 비가 올 거야.

남: 나쁜 소식이네! 빗속에서 콘서트 음악을 듣고 싶진 않은데.

여: 안됐다.

문제 해설

Q: 현재 남자의 기분은?

내일 야외 콘서트에 가려고 했는데 비가 올 거라는 소식에 실망했을 것이다.

3

M: I've traveled to many countries. My favorite places are Greece and England. Greece is nice in the spring. In the summer, it's too hot to travel there. In England, the sun stays up till 10 o'clock in the evening during summer. So it's the perfect time to travel there. In the winter, the sun sets too early.

남: 나는 많은 나라들을 여행했어. 내가 가장 좋아하는 곳은 그리스와 영국이야. 그리스는 봄에 좋지. 여름에는 너무 더워서 그곳을 여행하기 힘들어. 영국에서는 여름에 해가 밤 10시까지 떠 있어. 그래서 그곳을 여행하기에 완벽한 시기야. 겨울에는 해가 너무 빨리 져.

문제 해설

Q: 각 나라를 여행하기에 가장 좋은 계절을 고르시오.

그리스는 봄이, 영국은 여름이 여행하기 좋은 계절이다.

4

M: Oh, it's raining. I should buy an umbrella.

W: Just wait a while. I think it's just a shower.

M: Really?

W: Believe me. The weather in London changes a lot in a day.

M: Then why don't we wait in that café over there?

W: Okay. Let's go to Hyde Park and take a walk when the rain stops.

M: Great.

남: 이런, 비가 오네. 우산을 사야겠어.

여: 잠깐만 기다려 봐. 내 생각엔 그냥 소나기인 것 같아.

남: 정말?

여: 내 말 믿어 봐. 런던 날씨는 하루에도 많이 변해.

남: 그럼, 저기 있는 저 카페에서 기다리는 게 어때?

여: 그래. 비가 그치면 하이드파크에 가서 산책하자.

남: 좋아.

문제 해설

Q: 그들이 다음에 할 일은?

두 사람은 비가 그칠 때까지 카페에서 기다리기로 했다.

5

M: Let's look at the weather around the world for tomorrow. There'll be strong storms in London. Singapore will be very hot and sunny. In Seoul, it'll be gray and a little cold. And it will be snowing a lot in Vancouver.

남: 내일의 세계 날씨를 보시겠습니다. 런던에는 강한 폭풍우가 있겠고, 싱가포르는 매우 덥고 햇빛이 쨍쨍하겠습니다. 서울은 흐리고 약간 춥겠습니다. 그리고 밴쿠버에는 눈이 많이 오겠습니다.

문제 해설

Q: 각 도시의 내일 날씨를 고르시오.

런던에는 강한 폭풍우가 있을 것이고, 서울은 흐릴 것이라고 했다. 또한, 밴쿠버에는 눈이 많이 올 것이라고 했다.

6

W: I went to a ski resort yesterday. On the way to the resort, the weather was clear and sunny. But when we arrived, it started to rain. I thought I wouldn't be able to ski. But soon, the rain changed to snow. Skiing in the snow was cold, but also very nice.

여: 나는 어제 스키 리조트에 갔어. 리조트에 갈 때는 날씨가 맑고 햇빛이 쨍쨍했어. 하지만 우리가 도착하자 비가 내리기 시작했지. 스키를 못 탈 것 같았어. 하지만 곧 비가 눈으로 바뀌었어. 눈 속에서 스키를 타는 것은 춥긴 했지만 너무 좋았어.

어휘
resort[rizɔ́ːrt] 명 휴양지, 리조트   on the way to ~ ~로 가는 길에   clear[kliər] 형 맑은   soon[suːn] 부 곧   also[ɔ́ːlsou] 부 또한

문제 해설
Q: 날씨의 변화 순서가 올바른 것을 고르시오.
리조트에 가는 중에는 날씨가 맑았지만 도착하자 비가 내리기 시작했고 곧 비가 눈으로 바뀌었다.

7

W: Look at that bird. It's flying really low.
M: Is that surprising?
W: When a bird flies low, it's a sign that it will rain soon.
M: Really? Are there any other ways to know when it will rain?
W: Yes. Fish jump out of the water, and spiders come into houses.
M: That's funny. Still, I don't believe it.
W: Let's wait and see then.

여: 저 새 좀 봐. 아주 낮게 날고 있어.
남: 그게 놀라워?
여: 새가 낮게 나는 건 곧 비가 올 거라는 신호잖아.
남: 정말? 그 외에 비가 올 거라는 걸 아는 다른 방법도 있니?
여: 응. 물고기가 물 밖으로 뛰어오르고 거미가 집 안으로 들어와.
남: 재미있네. 그래도 믿기지는 않는데.
여: 그럼 지켜보자.

어휘
bird[bəːrd] 명 새   fly[flai] 동 날다   low[lou] 형 낮은; *부 낮게   surprising[sərpráiziŋ] 형 놀라운   sign[sain] 명 신호, 조짐   way[wei] 명 방법   fish[fiʃ] 명 물고기   jump[dʒʌmp] 동 뛰어오르다   spider[spáidər] 명 거미   funny[fʌ́ni] 형 재미있는   still[stil] 부 여전히; *그래도

문제 해설
Q: 비가 곧 올 거라는 두 가지 신호는 어느 것인가?
새가 낮게 나는 경우, 물고기가 물 밖으로 뛰어오르는 경우, 거미가 집 안으로 들어오는 경우이다.

8

M: You're from Indonesia, right?
W: Yes, I am.
M: How's the weather there?
W: It's hot throughout the year.
M: So is there only one season?
W: Well, we have a dry season and a rainy season.
M: When are they?
W: Dry season starts in April and ends around October, and rainy season is from November to March.
M: I see.

남: 너 인도네시아 출신이지?
여: 응, 맞아.
남: 거기 날씨는 어때?
여: 일년 내내 더워.
남: 그럼 계절이 하나뿐이야?
여: 음, 건기와 우기가 있어.
남: 그게 언제인데?
여: 건기는 4월에 시작해서 10월쯤 끝나고 우기는 11월에서 3월까지야.
남: 그렇구나.

어휘
throughout[θru(ː)áut] 전 ~ 내내   dry[drai] 형 건조한   April[éiprəl] 명 4월   end[end] 동 끝나다   October[ɑktóubər] 명 10월   November[nouvémbər] 명 11월   March[mɑːrtʃ] 명 3월

문제 해설
Q: 인도네시아의 12월 날씨는 어떠한가?
인도네시아는 일년 내내 덥고, 11월부터 3월까지가 우기라고 했으므로 12월 날씨는 덥고 비 오는 날씨일 것이다.

Listening ★ Challenge   p. 30

A 1 ④ 2 ①   B 1 ③ 2 ④

A [1-2]

M: Let's learn what we should do when there's lightning. First, it's dangerous to hold an umbrella or stand under a tree. It's safe to be in a low place. If there's a tall building, go inside. If you are in a car, stay in it to be safe. But if you are in the water, you should get out.

남: 번개가 칠 때 어떻게 해야 하는지 배워봅시다. 먼저, 우산을 들고 있거나 나무 아래에 서 있는 것은 위험합니다. 낮은 장소에 있는 것이 안전합니다. 만약 높은 건물이 있다면 안으로 들어가세요. 차 안에 있다면, 그 안에 안전하게 머무르세요. 하지만 물 속에 있다면 밖으로 나와야 합니다.

어휘
lightning[láitniŋ] 명 번개 first[fəːrst] 형 처음의; *부 먼저 dangerous[déinʤərəs] 형 위험한 hold[hould] 동 들다, 쥐다 (hold-held-held) stand[stænd] 동 서 있다 under[ʌ́ndər] 전 ~아래에 safe[seif] 형 안전한 inside[insáid] 부 내부에, 안으로 get out 밖으로 나오다 [문제] cause[kɔːz] 동 야기하다 happen[hǽpən] 동 (일·사건 등이) 일어나다, 생기다 act[ækt] 동 행동하다

문제 해설
Q1: 남자는 주로 무엇에 대해 이야기하고 있는가?
① 무엇이 번개를 일으키는가
② 언제 번개가 치는가
③ 번개가 왜 위험한가
④ 번개가 칠 때 어떻게 행동해야 하는가
남자는 번개가 칠 때 피해야 할 행동과 취해야 할 행동에 대해 이야기하고 있다.

Q2: 잘못된 행동을 하고 있는 사람은?
번개가 칠 때 나무 아래에 서 있는 것은 위험하다고 했다.

B [1-2]

W: Next Wednesday is Dad's birthday. What shall we do?
M: How about going to a nice restaurant together?
W: Well… I don't think he'd like that. How about throwing a garden party?
M: That's a good idea. But we should check the weather on the Internet first.
W: Let's see. It's going to rain with heavy wind next Wednesday.
M: That's not good. What will the weather be like this weekend?

W: It'll be a little cloudy.
M: Okay. If it doesn't rain, let's do it this Saturday.
W: Great!

여: 다음 주 수요일이 아빠 생신이야. 우리 뭘 할까?
남: 근사한 식당에 같이 가는 게 어때?
여: 글쎄… 아빠가 좋아하실 것 같지 않은데. 가든파티를 여는 게 어때?
남: 좋은 생각이야. 근데 먼저 인터넷으로 날씨를 확인해야겠어.
여: 어디 보자. 다음 주 수요일에 강한 바람을 동반한 비가 올 거라는데.
남: 좋지 않네. 이번 주말 날씨는 어떨까?
여: 약간 흐릴 거야.
남: 좋아. 비가 안 오면 이번 주 토요일에 하자.
여: 좋아!

어휘
birthday[bə́ːrθdèi] 명 생일 How about ~? ~하는 게 어때? restaurant[réstərənt] 명 음식점 throw a garden party 가든파티를 열다 heavy[hévi] 형 무거운; *심한

문제 해설
Q1: 그들은 아버지의 생신을 위해 무엇을 할 계획인가?
이번 주말에 가든파티를 열기로 했다.

Q2: 토요일의 날씨는 어떨까?
약간 흐릴 거라고 했다.

Critical ★ Thinking p. 31

1 (1) Likes (2) Doesn't like (3) Likes
2 (1) ⓒ (2) ⓓ (3) ⓑ

W1: I'm Marina. I think it's good to have four seasons. I enjoy watching the changes in each of the seasons.
M: I'm Seyoon. Because we have four seasons, we have to buy many clothes. It costs a lot of money to buy them.
W2: I'm Yuki. I like sports a lot. I like having four seasons because I can enjoy different sports during each season.

여1: 난 Marina야. 내 생각에 사계절이 있는 건 좋은 것 같아. 각 계절에 일어나는 변화를 보는 게 즐거워.

28

남: 난 세윤이야. 우리는 사계절이 있기 때문에 옷을 많이 사
　　야 해. 그것들을 사려면 돈이 많이 들어.

여2: 난 Yuki야. 나는 운동을 아주 좋아해. 난 사계절이 있는
　　게 좋아. 매 계절마다 다른 운동을 즐길 수 있으니까.

어휘

watch[wɑtʃ] 통 보다　clothes[klouðz] 명 옷
cost[kɔ(ː)st] 통 (비용 등이) 들다 (cost-cost-cost)
[문제] spend[spend] 통 쓰다, 사용하다 (spend-spent-
spent)

문제 해설

Q1: 각 인물이 사계절을 좋아하는지 좋아하지 않는지 ✓표
　　하시오.
　　Marina와 Yuki는 사계절의 좋은 점에 대해서 얘기하고
　　있고, 세윤이는 사계절의 안 좋은 점에 대해 얘기하고 있다.

Q2: 각 인물의 의견을 고르시오.
　　ⓐ 매 계절마다 멋진 옷을 사는 걸 좋아한다.
　　ⓑ 각 계절마다 다른 운동들을 즐길 수 있다.
　　ⓒ 각 계절의 변화를 즐길 수 있어 좋다.
　　ⓓ 각 계절마다 옷을 사는 데 돈을 써야 한다.

UNIT 05 Family

Getting ★ Ready　p. 32

A 1 ⓓ　2 ⓐ　3 ⓑ　4 ⓔ　5 ⓒ
B 1 ⓓ　2 ⓐ　3 ⓔ

B 1 남: 프랑스에서 외로웠니?
　　여: 응, 가족이 많이 그리웠어.
　 2 남: 형제 자매가 몇 명 있니?
　　여: 한 명도 없어. 난 외동아이야.
　 3 남: 넌 아빠랑 엄마 중에 누구를 닮았니?
　　여: 두 분 다 닮았어.

Listening ★ Start　p. 33

1 ④ / how many people, Do you have,
　younger brother
2 ② / get married, that's why, makes me
　laugh

1

W: Ted, how many people are in your family?
M: I have a big family. I'm living with my
　grandparents and my parents.
W: Do you have brothers or sisters?
M: Yes. I have one older sister and one
　younger brother.

여: Ted, 가족이 몇 명이니?
남: 우린 대가족이야. 조부모님들이랑 부모님과 함께 살고
　　있어.
여: 형제 자매도 있니?
남: 응. 누나 한 명이랑 남동생 한 명이 있어.

어휘

grandparent[grǽndpɛ̀ərənt] 명 조부모　[문제]
grandfather[grǽndfɑ̀ːðər] 명 할아버지
grandmother[grǽndmʌ̀ðər] 명 할머니

문제 해설

Q: 올바른 가계도를 고르시오.
　　Ted는 할머니, 할아버지, 어머니, 아버지와 함께 살고 있
　　으며 누나 한 명과 남동생 한 명이 있다고 했다.

2

M: Did your big sister get married?
W: Yes. She got married last year.
M: Do you like your brother-in-law?
W: Yes, I do. He often gives me pocket money.
M: (laughing) So that's why you like him!
W: The main reason is that he's so funny. He
　always makes me laugh.

남: 너희 큰 언니는 결혼했니?
여: 응. 작년에 결혼했어.
남: 넌 너희 형부를 좋아하니?
여: 응, 좋아해. 나한테 용돈을 자주 주셔.
남: [웃으며] 그래서 네가 그를 좋아하는 거구나!
여: 주된 이유는 그가 너무 재미있어서야. 항상 나를 웃게 해
　　주거든.

어휘

get married 결혼하다　brother-in-law[brʌ́ðərinlɔ̀ː]
명 형부　often[ɔ́(ː)fən] 부 자주, 종종　pocket money
용돈　main[mein] 형 주요한　reason[ríːzən] 명 이유
always[ɔ́ːlweiz] 부 항상　laugh[læf] 통 웃다　[문제]
good-looking[gúdlúkiŋ] 형 잘생긴　humorous
[hjúːmərəs] 형 유머 감각이 있는

29

문제 해설

Q: 여자가 형부를 좋아하는 주된 이유는?

① 그는 잘생겼다.

② 그는 유머 감각이 있다.

③ 그는 그녀에게 용돈을 준다.

④ 그는 그녀의 언니에게 잘해준다.

여자는 무엇보다 형부가 유머 감각이 있어 좋아한다.

Listening ★ Practice   p. 34

1 ① 2 ③ 3 ①, ④ 4 ④ 5 (1) ① (2) ⓓ
(3) ⓑ (4) ⓐ 6 (1) T (2) T (3) F 7 (1) ⓑ
(2) ⓒ (3) ⓐ 8 (1) ⓐ (2) ⓑ

1

M: My name is John. Let me show you a picture of my family. You can see my father, my mother and me. I take after both of my parents. I have my father's nose and mouth. And I have my mother's eyes. People tell me I'm handsome.

남: 내 이름은 John이야. 우리 가족 사진을 보여줄게. 우리 아버지, 어머니, 그리고 나를 볼 수 있을 거야. 나는 부모님 두 분을 다 닮았어. 나는 아버지의 코와 입을 가졌고, 어머니의 눈을 가졌어. 사람들은 나보고 잘생겼다고 얘기해.

어휘

show[ʃou] ⑧ 보여주다 picture[píktʃər] ⑲ 사진
take after ~을 닮다 both[bouθ] ⑭ 둘 다 tell[tel]
⑧ 말하다 (tell-told-told) handsome[hǽnsəm] ⑲ 잘생긴 [문제] face[feis] ⑲ 얼굴

문제 해설

Q: John의 얼굴을 고르시오.

코와 입은 아버지를 닮았고, 눈은 어머니를 닮았다고 했으므로, John은 높은 코에 큰 입, 큰 눈을 가졌을 것이다.

2

W: Tony. Do you know the boy next to Jack?

M: Oh, he's my brother, Chuck.

W: He's very handsome. Can you introduce me to him?

M: (laughing) He's much younger than you. Plus he has a girlfriend.

W: Oh, boy.

M: I have an older brother, too.

W: Really? How old is he?

M: He's nineteen. He's one year older than you.

W: Perfect!

여: Tony야. 너 Jack 옆에 있는 남자애 아니?

남: 아. 내 남동생인 Chuck이야.

여: 아주 잘생겼네. 나 좀 쟤한테 소개시켜 줄래?

남: [웃으며] 쟤는 너보다 훨씬 어려. 게다가 여자 친구도 있어.

여: 아, 이런.

남: 나 형도 있는데.

여: 정말? 몇 살인데?

남: 19살이야. 너보다 한 살 더 많지.

여: 완벽하네!

어휘

introduce[intrədjúːs] ⑧ 소개해 주다 plus[plʌs] ⑳ 게다가 perfect[pə́ːrfikt] ⑲ 완벽한

문제 해설

Q: 여자는 몇 살인가?

19살인 남자의 형보다 한 살 어리므로 18살이다.

3

W: How many brothers and sisters do you have, Dan?

M: I have two older brothers and younger twin sisters.

W: Wow. You have a large family. Do you like having many brothers and sisters?

M: Well, not always. When I was little, I had to wear old clothes from my brothers.

W: That's too bad.

M: And the house is noisy. Sometimes I want to be in a quiet place.

여: Dan, 넌 형제 자매가 몇 명 있니?

남: 형이 두 명 있고. 쌍둥이 여동생들이 있어.

여: 우와. 가족이 많구나. 형제 자매가 많아서 좋아?

남: 글쎄. 항상 그런 건 아니야. 내가 어렸을 땐 형들한테 물려 받은 낡은 옷을 입어야 했거든.

여: 안됐네.

남: 그리고 집이 시끄러워. 때로는 조용한 곳에 있고 싶어.

어휘

twin[twin] ⑲ 쌍둥이의 wear[wɛər] ⑧ 입다 (wear-wore-worn) noisy[nɔ́izi] ⑲ 시끄러운 sometimes

[sʌ́mtàimz] 🄫 때때로   quiet[kwáiət] 🄗 조용한   [문제]
care about~ ~에 대해 신경 쓰다   never[névər] 🄫
결코 ~않다   alone[əlóun] 🄫 혼자서

문제 해설

Q: Dan에 따르면 대가족이 좋지 않은 점 두 가지는 무엇인가?

　① 그의 집은 시끄럽다.

　② 그의 부모님은 여동생들만 신경 쓴다.

　③ 그는 컴퓨터를 결코 혼자서 사용할 수 없다.

　④ 그는 자신의 형들이 입던 낡은 옷을 입어야 했다.

Dan은 형들에게 낡은 옷을 물려받아 입어야 했고, 집이
시끄럽다고 했다.

4

W: Jack, Mom's birthday is tomorrow. What
　should we buy her for a present?

M: Why don't we buy her a scarf?

W: She already has so many.

M: Then, what about sunglasses? Summer
　is almost here.

W: That's a good idea. She doesn't have any.

M: Let's go to the shopping mall now to buy
　them.

W: Okay.

여: Jack, 엄마 생신이 내일이야. 선물로 뭘 사드려야 할까?

남: 스카프를 사드리는 게 어때?

여: 이미 너무 많이 가지고 계셔.

남: 그러면, 선글라스는 어때? 거의 여름이 다 됐잖아.

여: 좋은 생각이야. 엄마가 하나도 안 가지고 계시니까.

남: 지금 그걸 사러 쇼핑몰에 가자.

여: 그래.

어휘

present[prézənt] 🄗 선물   already[ɔːlrédi] 🄫 이미
shopping mall 쇼핑몰

문제 해설

Q: 그들이 사려고 하는 선물은?

　그들은 선글라스를 사기로 했다.

5

W: My family members have various hobbies.
　My father goes hiking in the mountains
　every weekend. My mother likes to watch
　movies. She loves action movies. My
　brother loves rollerblading. He won the
　first prize in a rollerblading contest. I enjoy

cooking. I like to make delicious food for
my family.

여: 우리 가족들은 다양한 취미를 가지고 있어. 아버지는 주
말마다 산으로 하이킹을 가셔. 어머니는 영화 보는 것을
좋아하시는데, 액션 영화를 좋아하셔. 우리 오빠는 롤러
블레이드 타는 걸 좋아해. 롤러블레이드 시합에서 1등 상
을 탔어. 나는 요리하는 걸 좋아해. 가족을 위해 맛있는
음식을 만드는 걸 좋아하지.

어휘

various[vɛ́(ː)əriəs] 🄗 다양한   hobby[hábi] 🄗 취미
hike[haik] 🄫 하이킹하다, 도보 여행하다   mountain
[máuntən] 🄗 산   movie[múːvi] 🄗 영화   action
movie 액션 영화   rollerblade[róulərblèid] 🄫 롤러블
레이드를 타다   prize[praiz] 🄗 상   contest[kántest]
🄗 경연 대회   cook[kuk] 🄫 요리하다   delicious
[dilíʃəs] 🄗 맛있는   food[fuːd] 🄗 음식

문제 해설

Q: 각 인물에 알맞은 취미를 고르시오.

　아버지는 하이킹을, 어머니는 영화 보기를, 오빠는 롤러
블레이드 타기를, 나는 요리하는 것을 좋아한다.

6

M: Do you know that Angelina Jolie's family
members are famous like her? Her father,
Jon Voight, won an Academy Award for
Best Actor. Her older brother, James Haven,
works as an actor and producer. Her uncle,
Chip Taylor, was a famous singer in the
1960s.

남: Angelina Jolie의 가족들이 그녀처럼 유명하다는 거 아
세요? 그녀의 아버지인 Jon Voight는 아카데미 남우주
연상을 수상했습니다. 그녀의 오빠인 James Haven은
영화배우이자 프로듀서로 활동합니다. 그녀의 삼촌인
Chip Taylor는 1960년대에 유명한 가수였습니다.

어휘

Academy Award 아카데미상   actor[ǽktər] 🄗 남
자 배우   producer[prədjúːsər] 🄗 프로듀서, 제작자
uncle[ʌ́ŋkl] 🄗 삼촌

문제 해설

Q: 사실이면 T, 사실이 아니면 F에 ✓표 하시오.

　(1) Angelina Jolie의 아버지는 배우이다.

　(2) Angelina Jolie는 오빠가 있다.

　(3) Angelina Jolie의 삼촌은 1970년대에 유명했다.

31

7

W1: I'm Linda. I only have brothers. I want to share clothes with an older sister.

W2: I'm Jenny. My friend Lily has an older brother. He cares about her so much. I'd like to have a brother like him.

M: I'm Tom. I'm the only child. I want to have a cute younger sister.

여1: 난 Linda야. 난 남자 형제들만 있어. 난 언니와 옷을 함께 입고 싶어.

여2: 난 Jenny야. 내 친구인 Lily는 오빠가 있어. 그는 그녀를 정말 많이 신경 써 줘. 나도 그와 같은 오빠가 있으면 좋겠어.

남: 난 Tom이야. 난 외아들이야. 귀여운 여동생이 있으면 좋겠어.

어휘
share[ʃɛər] 동 나누다, 같이 쓰다　only child 외아들, 외동딸　cute[kju:t] 형 귀여운

문제 해설
Q: 각 인물과 그들의 바람을 연결하시오.
　ⓐ 나는 여동생이 있으면 좋겠어.
　ⓑ 나는 언니가 있으면 좋겠어.
　ⓒ 나는 오빠가 있으면 좋겠어.
　(1) Linda는 언니와 함께 옷을 입고 싶다고 했다.
　(2) Jenny는 자신을 신경 써 줄 오빠가 있기를 바란다.
　(3) Tom은 귀여운 여동생이 있기를 바란다.

8

M: May, is your husband's family name Pitt?

W: Yes.

M: That's the same family name as yours.

W: In America, each woman usually uses her husband's family name.

M: What was your family name before you got married?

W: It was Smith.

M: How about Cathy? Cathy's family name is Stevens, but her husband's is Jones.

W: Using the husband's family name is a tradition. But some women don't follow it.

남: May, 너의 남편 성이 Pitt니?

여: 응.

남: 너랑 성이 같구나.

여: 미국에서는 각각의 결혼한 여성은 대개 남편의 성을 사용해.

남: 결혼하기 전에는 네 성이 뭐였니?

여: Smith였어.

남: Cathy는? Cathy의 성은 Stevens지만 그녀의 남편의 성은 Jones잖아.

여: 남편 성을 사용하는 게 전통이긴 하지만 어떤 여성들은 그걸 안 따르기도 해.

어휘
husband[hʌ́zbənd] 명 남편　family name 성　same[seim] 형 같은, 동일한　usually[júːʒuəli] 부 보통, 대개　tradition[trədíʃən] 명 전통　follow[fálou] 동 따르다

문제 해설
Q: May와 Cathy의 현재 성명은?
　May는 남편의 성인 Pitt를 사용한다고 했으므로 'May Pitt', Cathy는 원래 자신의 성인 Stevens를 사용한다고 했으므로 'Cathy Stevens'일 것이다.

Listening ★ Challenge　p. 36

A 1 ② 　2 (1) T 　(2) F 　(3) T 　B 1 ② 　2 ④

A [1-2]

W: Yesterday, I saw an interesting movie. In the movie, a man lives a successful single life. One day, everything changes. He wakes up and has a wife and children. He's not a successful careerman anymore. But he enjoys his new life. In the end, he finds out that his family life was just his dream. He finally realizes that family is the most important thing in life.

여: 어제 재미있는 영화를 보았어. 그 영화에서 한 남자가 성공한 독신 생활을 하지. 어느 날 모든 것이 변해. 그가 깨어 보니 아내와 아이들이 있는 거야. 그는 더 이상 성공한 직장인이 아닌 거야. 하지만 그는 자신의 새로운 삶을 즐겨. 결국 그는 자신의 가정 생활이 꿈이었을 뿐이라는 것을 알게 되지. 그는 마침내 가족이 인생에서 가장 중요한 것이라는 점을 깨닫게 돼.

어휘
successful[səksésfəl] 형 성공적인　single[síŋgl] 형 단 하나의; *독신의　one day 어느 날　wake up 잠에

★ ★

서 깨다 **wife**[waif] 명 아내 **careerman**[kəríərmən] 명 직업인 **anymore**[ènimɔ́ːr] 부 더 이상 **in the end** 결국 **find out** 알아내다 **finally**[fáinəli] 부 마침내 **realize**[rí(ː)əlàiz] 동 깨닫다 [문제] **power**[páuər] 명 힘 **importance**[impɔ́ːrtəns] 명 중요성 **role**[roul] 명 역할 **real**[ríːəl] 형 실제의

문제 해설
Q1: 이 영화의 주제는?
① 사랑의 힘
② 가족의 중요성
③ 한 가정에서의 아버지의 역할
④ 자녀들에게 있어 행복한 가정의 중요성
한 남자가 꿈에서 겪은 일을 통해 가족의 소중함에 대해 깨닫게 되었다는 내용의 영화이다.

Q2: 사실이면 T, 사실이 아니면 F에 ✓표 하시오.
(1) 이 영화는 성공한 직장인의 꿈에 관한 것이다.
(2) 남자는 현실에서 결혼을 했다.
(3) 남자는 꿈에서 자신의 삶을 즐겼다.
이 영화는 성공한 직장인의 꿈에 관한 영화라고 했다. 남자는 실제로 결혼한 것이 아니라 꿈 속에서 결혼을 한 것이며, 꿈 속에서 새로운 삶을 즐겼다.

B [1-2]

W: Welcome back! How was your life in France?
M: Well, I lived alone in a small apartment.
W: So, did you feel lonely?
M: Yes. I missed talking with my family. I also missed my mom's food.
W: I heard you got sick there, too.
M: Yes. I had a bad cold.
W: That's too bad!
M: At that time, I really missed being taken care of by my father.
W: So, are you having fun with your family now?
M: Of course! I'm having a great time at home. I love my family!

여: 돌아온 걸 환영해! 프랑스에서의 생활은 어땠어?
남: 음, 작은 아파트에 혼자 살았어.
여: 그럼, 외로웠겠구나?
남: 응, 우리 가족이랑 대화를 나누었던 게 그리웠어. 엄마의 요리도 그리웠고.
여: 네가 거기서 아팠다는 말도 들었어.

남: 응. 독감에 걸렸어.
여: 저런!
남: 그때 아버지의 보살핌을 받는 게 정말 그리웠어.
여: 그래서 지금은 가족이랑 즐겁게 지내고 있니?
남: 물론이지! 집에서 좋은 시간 보내고 있어. 가족이 너무 좋아!

어휘
apartment[əpáːrtmənt] 명 아파트 **lonely**[lóunli] 형 외로운 **miss**[mis] 동 그리워하다 **have a cold** 감기에 걸리다 **at that time** 그 당시에 **take care of** ~을 돌보다 [문제] **attention**[əténʃən] 명 주의; *배려, 돌봄 **describe**[diskráib] 동 묘사하다 **situation**[sìtʃuéiʃən] 명 상황 **build**[bild] 동 짓다 (build-built-built)

문제 해설
Q1: 남자가 그리워했다고 말하지 않은 것을 고르시오.
가족의 넓은 아파트에 대해서는 언급하지 않았다.

Q2: 상황을 가장 잘 묘사한 것은?
① 로마는 하루 아침에 지어지지 않았다.
② 늦더라도 안 하느니보다는 낫다.
③ 무소식이 희소식이다.
④ 집보다 좋은 곳은 없다.
남자가 집을 떠나 있으면서 집이 얼마나 그리웠는지에 대해 얘기하고 있으므로, '집보다 좋은 곳은 없다.'라는 뜻의 속담이 알맞다.

Critical ★ Thinking p. 37

1 ③ 2 (1) ⓑ (2) ⓒ

M: Jill, what does "DINK" mean?
W: It means "Double Income No Kids." In other words, it's a working couple without kids.
M: So, they both work but don't want to have children?
W: Yes. Think about the money people spend on their kids. Without kids, couples can spend their money on their hobbies.
M: Even so, I think they'll feel lonely without children.
W: I don't think so, Paul. DINK couples can have fun with all their friends. Why should they choose the difficult way?

남: Jill, 'DINK'가 무슨 의미야?

여: '아이 없는 맞벌이 부부'라는 뜻이지. 다른 말로 하자면, 아이 없이 일하는 부부야.

남: 그러니까, 둘 다 일하지만 아이는 원하지 않는다는 거지?

여: 응. 사람들이 그들의 아이들에게 쓰는 돈을 생각해 봐. 아이들이 없으면 부부는 자기들의 취미에 돈을 쓸 수 있잖아.

남: 그렇다고 해도 아이가 없으면 외로울 것 같아.

여: Paul, 난 그렇게 생각하지 않아. DINK 부부는 자기들의 친구들과 즐겁게 지낼 수 있어. 그들이 왜 어려운 길을 선택해야 하겠니?

어휘

double[dʌ́bl] 형 2중의　income[ínkʌm] 명 수입　kid[kid] 명 아이　in other words 다른 말로 하자면　couple[kʌ́pl] 명 한 쌍; *부부　choose[tʃuːz] 동 선택하다 (choose-chose-chosen)　[문제] grow up 자라다

문제 해설

Q1: DINK 부부는 어느 부부인가?

① 우리는 둘 다 직업을 가지고 있고 아들이 한 명 있어요.

② 내 남편만 직업이 있어요. 우리는 아이를 가질 계획이 없어요.

③ 우리는 둘 다 직업이 있어요. 우리는 아이를 갖길 원하지 않아요.

DINK는 부부가 둘 다 직업을 가지고 있지만 아이는 원하지 않는 부부를 가리킨다고 했다.

Q2: 각 인물의 의견을 고르시오.

ⓐ 자식이 자라는 걸 보면 행복할 것이다.

ⓑ 자식이 있으면 외롭지 않을 것이다.

ⓒ 자식이 없어도 인생을 즐겁게 보낼 수 있다.

(1) Paul은 아이가 없으면 외로울 거라고 생각한다.

(2) Jill은 아이가 없어도 즐겁게 지낼 수 있다고 생각한다.

UNIT 06 Friends

Getting ★ Ready p. 38

A 1 ⓖ　2 ⓐ　3 ⓔ　4 ⓕ　5 ⓒ

B 1 ⓒ　2 ⓐ　3 ⓔ

B 1 여: 너랑 가장 친한 친구는 어떤 애니?

　　남: 상냥하고 재미있어.

2 여: 요즘에 Angela 자주 보니?

　　남: 아니. 우린 크게 싸웠어.

3 여: Bill이 너의 가장 친한 친구니?

　　남: 응. 우리는 많은 공통점이 있어.

1 ④ / best friend, What, like, free time, watch his movies

2 (1) ⓐ　(2) ⓒ　(3) ⓑ / near my house, be good at, would be fun

1

M: Who is your best friend?

W: My best friend is Jenny. She comes from Korea.

M: What is she like?

W: She is shy but humorous. She likes to travel to new places in her free time.

M: I see. What do you do when you see her?

W: We're big fans of Johnny Depp. So we usually watch his movies.

남: 너의 가장 친한 친구는 누구니?

여: 내 가장 친한 친구는 Jenny야. 그 애는 한국에서 왔어.

남: 그 애는 어떠니?

여: 그 애는 수줍음이 많지만 재미있어. 여가 시간에는 새로운 곳으로 여행가는 걸 좋아해.

남: 그렇구나. 넌 그 애를 만나면 뭘 하니?

여: 우린 Johnny Depp의 열렬한 팬이야. 그래서 우리는 주로 그의 영화를 봐.

어휘

shy[ʃai] 형 수줍은　humorous[hjúːmərəs] 형 유머러스한　fan[fæn] 명 팬　[문제] take a trip 여행을 하다

문제 해설

Q: Jenny에 관해 사실이 아닌 것은?

① 그녀는 한국 출신이다.

② 그녀는 여행하는 걸 좋아한다.

③ 그녀는 Johnny Depp을 좋아한다.

④ 그녀는 새로운 사람과 얘기하는 걸 좋아한다.

Jenny가 새로운 사람과 대화하는 것을 좋아한다는 말은 하지 않았다.

2

M1: I'm Roy. I want my friend to live near my house. Then, we could easily spend time together.

W: I'm Sue. I want my friend to be good at science. Then, he or she could help me study.

M2: I'm Tim. I want my friend to like sports. It would be fun to go to the gym together.

남1: 나는 Roy야. 나는 내 친구가 우리 집 근처에 살았으면 좋겠어. 그러면, 우리는 쉽게 함께 시간을 보낼 수 있을 거야.

여: 나는 Sue야. 나는 내 친구가 과학을 잘했으면 좋겠어. 그러면, 그 애는 내가 공부하는 걸 도와줄 수 있을 거야.

남2: 나는 Tim이야. 나는 내 친구가 운동을 좋아했으면 좋겠어. 함께 체육관에 가면 재미있을 거야.

어휘
easily[í:zəli] 부 쉽게 spend[spend] 동 (시간·돈 등을) 쓰다 (spend-spent-spent) be good at ~ ~에 능숙하다 gym[dʒim] 명 체육관

문제 해설
Q: 각 인물이 원하는 친구의 유형을 고르시오.
  (1) Roy는 친구가 자신의 집 근처에 살기를 바란다.
  (2) Sue는 과학을 잘하는 친구가 있기를 바란다.
  (3) Tim은 운동을 좋아하는 친구가 있기를 바란다.

Listening ★ Practice   p. 40

1 ②   2 (1) Jack, Steve (2) Jack, Steve
(3) Steve 3 ③   4 ③   5 ①   6 (1) ③ (2) ②
(3) ① 7 ④   8 ②

1

M: Mom, what's the date today?
W: It's May 11th.
M: Oh, my god!
W: What's the matter?
M: Yesterday was Helen's birthday.
W: She is one of your best friends. How could you forget her birthday?
M: I thought today was May 10th. What should I do?
W: Give her a good present. And explain why you missed her birthday.
M: Okay.

남: 엄마, 오늘 날짜가 어떻게 되죠?
여: 5월 11일이야.
남: 아, 이런!

여: 무슨 일인데?
남: 어제가 Helen의 생일이었어요.
여: 그 애는 너랑 가장 친한 친구 중 한 명이잖아. 어떻게 그 애 생일을 잊을 수 있니?
남: 전 오늘이 5월 10일이라고 생각했어요. 어떻게 해야 하죠?
여: 그 애한테 좋은 선물을 주렴. 그리고 네가 그 애 생일을 지나친 이유를 설명하고.
남: 알았어요.

어휘
date[deit] 명 날짜 matter[mǽtər] 명 문제 forget [fərgét] 동 잊다 (forget-forgot-forgotten) explain [ikspléin] 동 설명하다 miss[mis] 동 그리워하다; *놓치다 [문제] tired[taiərd] 형 피곤한

문제 해설
Q: 현재 남자의 기분은?
  친한 친구의 생일을 지나쳐서 미안한 심정일 것이다.

2

M: My name is Jack. My best friend is Steve. We have many things in common. We both like comic books and computer games. Also, we are basketball players at our school. He is handsome and kind, so he is very popular with girls. But I'm not.

남: 내 이름은 Jack이야. 나의 가장 친한 친구는 Steve야. 우리는 공통점이 많아. 우린 둘 다 만화책과 컴퓨터 게임을 좋아하지. 또한, 우리는 우리 학교 농구 선수야. 그는 잘생겼고 친절해서 여자애들에게 인기가 많아. 하지만 난 그렇지 않아.

어휘
have ~ in common ~을 공통으로 가지고 있다
comic book 만화책 basketball[bǽskitbɔ̀:l] 명 농구
popular[pápjulər] 형 인기 있는

문제 해설
Q: 각 인물에 관한 정보로 옳은 것에 ✓표 하시오.
  (1) 만화책을 좋아한다
  (2) 학교 농구 선수이다
  (3) 여자애들 사이에서 인기가 있다
  Jack과 Steve가 만화책을 좋아하고 학교 농구 선수라는 점은 같다고 했다. 그러나 Steve는 여자애들 사이에서 인기가 있지만 Jack은 그렇지 않다고 했다.

3

M: You look so excited. What's up?

W: I have a great plan for today.

M: What is it?

W: I'm going to meet Julie. She is my friend on the Internet.

M: Oh, is this your first time to meet her?

W: Yes. We planned to meet last month, but she was sick then.

M: I see. Have a good time!

남: 너 아주 신나 보이는구나. 무슨 일이야?

여: 오늘 멋진 계획이 있거든.

남: 그게 뭔데?

여: Julie를 만날 거야. 그 애는 인터넷으로 만난 친구야.

남: 아, 이번이 그 앨 처음 만나는 거니?

여: 응. 우린 지난 달에 만나기로 했었는데 그 애가 그때 아팠어.

남: 그렇구나. 좋은 시간 보내!

어휘

What's up? 무슨 일이야?   plan[plæn] 명 계획; 동 계획하다   [문제] online[ɔ́nlàin] 형 온라인 상의; 부 온라인으로

문제 해설

Q: 여자가 오늘 할 일은?

인터넷을 통해 알게 된 Julie를 만나기로 했다.

4

M: Do you want to make many new friends at your new school? Then, do not wait until other people talk to you. You should make the first move. And smile! It makes you look friendly. It's also helpful to join school clubs. You can meet people with the same interests.

남: 여러분은 새 학교에서 새로운 친구를 많이 사귀고 싶나요? 그러면 다른 사람이 여러분에게 말을 걸 때까지 기다리지 마세요. 여러분이 먼저 다가가야 해요. 그리고 미소를 지으세요! 그렇게 하면 다정다감해 보입니다. 학교 동아리에 가입하는 것도 도움이 됩니다. 같은 관심사를 가진 사람들을 만날 수 있으니까요.

어휘

until[əntíl] 접 ~할 때까지   make the first move 발단을 만들다, 개시하다   friendly[fréndli] 형 다정다감한

helpful[hélpfəl] 형 도움이 되는   join[dʒɔin] 동 참가하다, 가입하다   club[klʌb] 명 클럽, 동아리   interest [íntərəst] 명 관심사   [문제] tip[tip] 명 사례금; *조언

문제 해설

Q: 남자는 주로 무엇에 대해 이야기하고 있는가?

① 좋은 친구가 되는 방법

② 친구의 중요성

③ 새로운 친구를 만드는 방법

④ 동아리에 가입하는 것의 중요성

남자는 새로운 친구를 사귀는 여러 가지 방법에 대해 이야기하고 있다.

5

M: Mom, I'm home.

W: You came home too early. Didn't you go to a movie with Catherine?

M: Yeah, I planned to. But we had a big fight.

W: What happened?

M: We were going to meet at 3, but she was 30 minutes late.

W: Oh, no! I understand why you are angry with her.

남: 엄마, 저 집에 왔어요.

여: 너 집에 너무 일찍 왔네. Catherine이랑 영화 보러 안 갔니?

남: 네, 그러려고 했는데 크게 싸웠거든요.

여: 무슨 일이 있었니?

남: 3시에 만나기로 했는데, 그 애가 30분 늦었어요.

여: 아, 저런! 그 애한테 왜 화가 났는지 이해가 되는구나.

어휘

fight[fait] 명 싸움   understand[ʌ̀ndərstǽnd] 동 이해하다 (understand-understood-understood)   [문제] on time 시간에 맞게

문제 해설

Q: 남자가 Catherine에게 화가 난 이유는?

① 그녀가 제시간에 오지 않았다.

② 그녀가 그를 기다리지 않았다.

③ 그녀가 다른 친구와 그 영화를 봤다.

④ 그녀가 다른 영화를 보고 싶어 했다.

남자는 Catherine이 30분이나 늦어서 화가 났다.

6

W: When I went to France, I made three good friends. Gina is good at making funny faces. She made me laugh a lot. Kelly is very pretty, but she has short hair and wears boy's clothes. Rachel is very short and thin, but she is brave. She even went bungee-jumping!

여: 내가 프랑스에 갔을 때, 나는 좋은 친구를 세 명 사귀었어. Gina는 우스꽝스러운 표정을 잘 지어. 그 애가 날 많이 웃게 했어. Kelly는 아주 예쁘지만 짧은 머리를 하고 남자애 옷을 입고 다녀. Rachel은 아주 작고 말랐지만 용감해. 그 애는 심지어 번지 점프를 하러 갔어!

어휘
thin[θin] 휑 마른 brave[breiv] 휑 용감한 even [íːvən] 휜 심지어 bungee-jump[bʌ́ndʒiːdʒʌ̀mp] 동 번지 점프를 하다

문제 해설
Q: 사진에서 각 인물을 고르시오.
(1) Gina는 재미있는 표정을 잘 짓는 친구라고 했다.
(2) Kelly는 짧은 머리에 남자애처럼 옷을 입는다고 했다.
(3) Rachel은 키가 작고 말랐다고 했다.

7

W: Nick, I saw Billy last Saturday.
M: Billy? Where?
W: He was shopping at the department store.
M: Oh, I really miss him. I haven't seen him for a long time.
W: Really? I thought you and Billy were close friends.
M: We were. But he moved to North Carolina last year. He got into a college there.
W: Then, why don't you call him?
M: I will.

여: Nick, 나 지난 토요일에 Billy를 봤어.
남: Billy? 어디서?
여: 그 애가 백화점에서 쇼핑을 하고 있더라고.
남: 아, 그 애가 정말 그리워. 오랫동안 그 애를 못 봤거든.
여: 정말? 난 너랑 Billy가 친한 친구인 줄 알았는데.
남: 그랬었지. 근데 그 애가 지난 해에 노스캐롤라이나로 이사를 갔어. 그 애가 그곳에 있는 대학에 갔거든.
여: 그럼, 그 애한테 전화해보지 그래?
남: 그렇게 할 거야.

어휘
department store 백화점 close[klous] 휑 가까운;

*친한 move[muːv] 동 이사하다 college[kálidʒ] 명 대학 call[kɔːl] 동 *전화하다; 부르다 [문제] reason [ríːzən] 명 이유 city[síti] 명 도시

문제 해설
Q: Nick이 Billy를 만나지 못한 이유는?
① Nick은 아주 바빴다.
② Nick은 Billy와 싸웠다.
③ Nick은 노스캐롤라이나로 이사 갔다.
④ Billy는 다른 도시에서 학교를 다닌다.
Billy가 노스캐롤라이나에 있는 대학에 진학하기 위해 이사를 갔다고 했다.

8

M: I like my friend Matt, but we have some problems. When I do something, he does the same thing. The other day, I bought a shirt. The next day, he was wearing the same shirt. When I started swimming lessons, he joined the swimming class as well.

남: 나는 내 친구 Matt을 좋아하지만 우리는 문제가 좀 있어. 내가 뭔가를 하면 그 애도 똑같이 하는 거지. 일전에, 내가 셔츠를 샀어. 그 다음 날에 그 애가 똑같은 셔츠를 입고 있었어. 내가 수영 강습을 시작하니까, 그 애도 수영 수업에 참가했어.

어휘
the other day 일전에 lesson[lésən] 명 수업 as well ~도, 또한 [문제] lie[lai] *명 거짓말; 동 거짓말하다 copy[kápi] 동 복사하다; *모방하다 choice[tʃɔis] 명 선택

문제 해설
Q: 남자의 문제는 무엇인가?
① 그의 친구가 거짓말을 한다.
② 그의 친구가 그를 따라 한다.
③ 그는 친구를 만날 시간이 없다.
④ 그는 친구가 선택하는 패션을 좋아하지 않는다.
남자는 자신의 친구인 Matt이 자신이 하는 것을 똑같이 따라 하는 것이 문제라고 했다.

Listening ★ Challenge p. 42

A 1 ① 2 ③   B 1 (1) ⓒ (2) ⓐ 2 ③

A [1-2]

M: Do you want to make friends from all over the world? If so, *Friends.com* is the best place on the Internet. This website opened in 2005. Now we have thousands of members from over 150 countries. Anyone over age 7 can become a member of this site. After you join us, you can find new friends easily by country, age, and interests. Join now and be our friend.

남: 전 세계의 친구들을 사귀고 싶나요? 그렇다면, 'Friends. com'이 인터넷 상에 있는 최고의 장소예요. 이 웹 사이트는 2005년에 오픈했어요. 이제 우리는 150개 이상 국가의 수천 명의 회원을 가지고 있어요. 7세 이상이면 누구나 이 사이트의 회원이 될 수 있답니다. 여러분이 우리 사이트에 가입하면, 나라별, 나이별, 흥미별로 쉽게 새로운 친구들을 찾을 수 있어요. 지금 가입하셔서 우리의 친구가 되세요.

어휘
website[wébsàit] 몡 웹 사이트(= site) age[eidʒ] 몡 나이 [문제] chat[tʃæt] 동 잡담하다; *채팅하다 childhood[tʃáildhùd] 몡 어린 시절 allow[əláu] 동 허락하다

문제 해설
Q1: 이 웹 사이트에서 할 수 있는 것은?
　① 새로운 친구를 사귄다.
　② 친구들과 동호회에 가입한다.
　③ 반 친구들과 채팅한다.
　④ 어린 시절의 옛 친구를 찾는다.
　전 세계의 친구들을 만날 수 있는 웹 사이트라고 했다.

Q2: 이 웹 사이트에 관해 사실이 아닌 것은?
　① 2005년에 시작했다.
　② 수천 명의 회원이 있다.
　③ 9세 이상의 회원들만 허용한다.
　④ 나라, 나이, 흥미별로 친구를 찾도록 도와준다.
　7세 이상이면 누구나 이 사이트의 회원이 될 수 있다고 했다.

B [1-2]

W: You look excited, Ricky.

M: I'm planning to travel with my friend. We're going to Spain!

W: Great! But you should be very careful. When I travelled with my friend, we had many problems.

M: What were the problems, Sarah?

W: On the first day, for example, I wanted to go shopping and she wanted to go skiing. So, I spent the whole day fighting with her.

M: So what should I do?

W: Before you travel, talk about the schedule. And plan everything together.

M: Thanks for the advice.

여: Ricky, 너 신나 보여.
남: 내 친구랑 여행갈 계획을 하고 있어. 우린 스페인에 갈 거야!
여: 좋겠다! 근데 너 아주 조심해야 할 거야. 내가 내 친구랑 여행했을 때 우린 문제가 많았거든.
남: Sarah, 문제가 뭐였는데?
여: 예를 들면, 첫째 날에 난 쇼핑을 하러 가고 싶었는데 그 애는 스키를 타러 가고 싶어 했어. 그래서 난 온종일 친구랑 싸우면서 보냈어.
남: 그럼 내가 어떻게 해야 하지?
여: 여행하기 전에 일정에 대해서 얘기해. 그리고 모든 계획을 함께 세워.
남: 조언해줘서 고마워.

어휘
careful[kɛ́ərfəl] 혱 주의 깊은, 조심스러운 for example 예를 들어 whole[houl] 혱 전체의 schedule[skédʒuːl] 몡 스케줄, 일정 advice[ədváis] 몡 조언 [문제] discuss[diskʌ́s] 동 토론하다, 상의하다 collect[kəlékt] 동 모으다

문제 해설
Q1: Sarah와 그녀의 친구가 여행 첫 날에 하고 싶어한 것은?
　Sarah는 쇼핑을 하고 싶어 했으나 그녀의 친구는 스키를 타러 가고 싶어 했다.

Q2: Ricky를 위한 Sarah의 조언은 무엇인가?
　① 혼자 여행해라.
　② 여행 일정을 바꿔라.
　③ 일정을 친구와 상의해라.
　④ 스페인에 대한 정보를 더 많이 모아라.
　여행하기 전에 일정에 대해서 얘기하고 모든 계획을 함께 세우라고 조언해 주었다.

Critical ★ Thinking　p. 43

1 (1) T (2) F (3) F 2 ①, ③

38

W: My father is worried that I don't have many friends. He says he learns many things from having different friends. And when he has a problem, he can ask them all for their help. But I think a few close friends are enough for me. When I have a problem, I tell my close friends about it and they help me. I don't think I need more friends.

여: 아버지는 내가 친구들이 많이 없어서 걱정하셔. 아버지는 여러 친구들로부터 많은 것을 배운다고 말씀하셔. 그리고 아버지에게 문제가 생겼을 때 아버지는 그들 모두에게 도움을 요청할 수 있으시다는 거야. 하지만 나는 몇몇의 가까운 친구만으로도 충분하다고 생각해. 내게 문제가 있을 때 가까운 친구들에게 그것에 대해서 얘기하면 그들은 나를 도와주거든. 나는 더 많은 친구가 필요하다고 생각하지 않아.

어휘
worried[wɔ́:rid] 혱 걱정하는   ask[æsk] 동 묻다; *요청하다   a few 몇몇의   enough[ináf] 혱 충분한   [문제] social skill 사회성

문제 해설
Q1: 사실이면 T, 사실이 아니면 F에 ✓표 하시오.
  (1) 그녀는 친한 친구가 몇 명 밖에 없다.
  (2) 그녀는 그녀의 문제에 대해 주로 부모님에게 얘기한다.
  (3) 그녀는 친구가 더 많이 필요하다고 생각한다.
Q2: 여자의 아버지에 따르면, 친구가 많은 것의 두 가지 좋은 점은 무엇인가?
  ① 그들로부터 많은 것을 배울 수 있다.
  ② 사회성을 더 기를 수 있다.
  ③ 그들로부터 도움을 받을 수 있다.
  ④ 그들과 더 재밌게 지낼 수 있다.
  여자의 아버지는 여러 친구들로부터 많은 것을 배울 수 있고, 그들에게 도움을 요청할 수 있다고 했다.

UNIT 07 Music

Getting ★ Ready   p. 44

A 1 ⓐ 2 ⓓ   B 1 ⓐ 2 ⓒ 3 ⓑ
C 1 ① 2 ⓑ 3 ⓔ

C 1 여: 넌 뭘 연주할 거니?
   남: 첼로를 연주할 거야.
 2 여: 넌 Usher의 콘서트에 갈 거니?
   남: 응. 난 그의 광팬이잖아.
 3 여: 넌 공부할 때 음악을 듣니?
   남: 응. 공부에 집중하는 데 도움이 되거든.

Listening ★ Start   p. 45

1 ③ / a big fan of, be able to
2 ② / join the orchestra, play the cello, learn a lot, Sounds good

1

M: I'm going to go to Usher's concert tomorrow. I'm a big fan of his. I bought all of his CDs and I can sing all of his songs. I can't believe that I'm going to see him tomorrow. I don't think I'll be able to sleep tonight!

남: 나는 내일 Usher의 콘서트에 갈 거예요. 나는 그의 광팬이거든요. 나는 그의 CD를 모두 다 샀고 그의 노래는 모두 다 부를 수 있어요. 내일 그를 보게 된다는 게 믿기지 않아요. 오늘 밤에 잠을 잘 수 있을 것 같지 않네요!

어휘
fan[fæn] 몡 (영화·스포츠 등의) 팬   believe[bilíːv] 동 믿다   sleep[sliːp] 동 자다 (sleep–slept–slept)   tonight[tənáit] 붼 오늘밤

문제 해설
Q: 현재 남자의 기분은?
  내일 자신이 좋아하는 Usher의 콘서트에 갈 수 있어서 아주 신나고 설레는 상황이다.

2

W: Daniel, look at this! The school orchestra is looking for new members.
M: Oh, I want to join the orchestra and play the flute again. Are you interested?
W: Yes. I don't play the cello very well, but I want to try.
M: That's a good idea. You can learn a lot in the orchestra.
W: The auditions are this Thursday. Let's go together.
M: Sounds good.

39

여: Daniel, 이것 좀 봐! 학교 오케스트라에서 새로운 멤버를 찾고 있어.

남: 아, 오케스트라에 들어가서 다시 플루트를 연주하고 싶어. 넌 관심 있니?

여: 응. 난 첼로 연주를 아주 잘 하는 건 아니지만 시도해 보고 싶어.

남: 좋은 생각이야. 오케스트라에서 많이 배울 수 있을 거야.

여: 오디션이 이번 목요일이네. 같이 가자.

남: 좋아.

어휘

orchestra[ɔ́ːrkəstrə] 명 오케스트라   look for 찾다
flute[fluːt] 명 플루트   interested[íntərəstid] 형 관심
있는 cello[tʃélou] 명 첼로   audition[ɔːdíʃən] 명 오디션

문제 해설

Q: 목요일에 그들이 할 일은?

두 사람은 이번 목요일에 오케스트라의 오디션에 함께 가기로 했다.

Listening ★ Practice   p. 46

1 ②   2 (1) F (2) T (3) F   3 ④   4 (1) Good
(2) Good (3) Bad   5 ④   6 ①   7 ③   8 ④

1

M: You're practicing the guitar so hard.

W: The test in our music class is only a few days away.

M: I'm not ready yet, so I'm very nervous.

W: Why are you worried? Don't you play the piano well?

M: That was a long time ago. I won't play the piano this time.

W: Then which instrument will you play?

M: I'll play the violin instead.

남: 너 기타 연습을 아주 열심히 하는구나.

여: 음악 수업 시간에 칠 시험이 며칠밖에 안 남았잖아.

남: 난 아직 준비가 안 되어 있어서 아주 긴장돼.

여: 왜 걱정하는 거야? 너 피아노 잘 치지 않니?

남: 그건 오래 전이지. 이번엔 피아노 안 칠 거야.

여: 그럼 어떤 악기를 연주할 거야?

남: 대신에 바이올린을 연주할 거야.

어휘

practice[prǽktis] 동 연습하다   test[test] 명 시험
ready[rédi] 형 준비된   yet[jet] 부 아직   nervous

[nə́ːrvəs] 형 긴장된   instrument[ínstrəmənt] 명 악기
violin[vàiəlín] 명 바이올린   instead[instéd] 부 대신에

문제 해설

Q: 남자는 어떤 악기를 연주할 것인가?

남자가 이번에는 바이올린을 연주할 거라고 했다.

2

W: My favorite pianist is Yuhki Kuramoto. He's from Japan. He studied science in college and was in the school orchestra. He recorded his first album in 1986. The song *Lake Louise* was a big hit from this album. Among his songs, I like *Romance* the most.

여: 내가 가장 좋아하는 피아니스트는 유키 구라모토예요. 그는 일본인이지요. 그는 대학에서 과학을 공부하고 학교 오케스트라에 있었어요. 1986년에 첫 번째 앨범을 녹음했지요. 이 앨범에서 'Lake Louise'라는 곡이 크게 히트했어요. 그의 곡 중에서 나는 'Romance'를 가장 좋아해요.

어휘

pianist[piǽnist] 명 피아노 연주자   science[sáiəns]
명 과학   record[rikɔ́ːrd] 동 녹음하다   album[ǽlbəm]
명 앨범   hit[hit] 동 때리다; *명 히트 작품   among
[əmʌ́ŋ] 전 ~ 중에서   [문제] major in ~을 전공하다

문제 해설

Q: 유키 구라모토에 관해 사실이면 T, 사실이 아니면 F에 ✓표 하시오.

(1) 그는 대학에서 음악을 전공했다.

(2) 그의 첫 번째 앨범은 1986년에 만들어졌다.

(3) 여자는 그의 곡 중에 'Lake Louise'를 가장 좋아한다.

3

M: Last night, I was watching a music contest on TV. A fat, ugly woman came on the stage. Because of her appearance, I thought, 'She will not sing well.' But I was very surprised when she started to sing a song. Her voice was beautiful and her song was great.

남: 어젯밤에 나는 TV에서 음악 콘테스트를 보고 있었어. 한 뚱뚱하고 못생긴 여자가 무대에 나온 거야. 그녀의 외모 때문에 나는 '저 여자는 노래를 잘 못할 거야'라고 생각했

어. 하지만 그녀가 노래를 부르기 시작했을 때 나는 정말 놀랐어. 그녀의 목소리는 아름다웠고 그녀의 노래도 훌륭했거든.

어휘

fat[fæt] 형 뚱뚱한   ugly[ʌ́gli] 형 못생긴   stage[steidʒ] 명 무대   appearance[əpí(:)ərəns] 명 외모   surprised [sərpráizd] 형 놀란   voice[vɔis] 명 목소리   [문제] easy [í:zi] 형 쉬운; *부 쉽게   judge[dʒʌdʒ] 동 판단하다 cover[kʌ́vər] 명 표지

문제 해설

Q: 상황을 가장 잘 묘사한 것은?

① 쉽게 들어온 것은 쉽게 나간다.

② 무소식이 희소식이다.

③ 로마는 하루 아침에 지어지지 않았다.

④ 겉만 보고 판단하지 마라.

한 여자의 외모만 보고 노래를 잘 못할 거라 생각했는데 알고 보니 그렇지 않았다는 내용이다. 따라서 '겉만 보고 판단하지 마라'라는 속담이 알맞다.

4

W: Wow, I really enjoyed the concert. How about you?

M: Well, it was so-so.

W: Really? The singer sang very well, didn't she?

M: Yes, she did. I liked her sweet voice and she did her best to please us.

W: Yes, her dancing was great as well. Why didn't you enjoy it?

M: The concert hall was too small and very hot.

여: 우와, 콘서트 정말 재미있었어. 넌 어땠어?

남: 글쎄, 그저 그랬어.

여: 정말? 가수가 노래를 정말 잘하던데, 안 그랬니?

남: 응, 그랬어. 그녀의 감미로운 목소리가 좋았어. 그리고 그녀가 우리를 즐겁게 해주려고 최선을 다했지.

여: 응, 춤도 멋졌잖아. 넌 왜 즐겁지 않았던 거야?

남: 콘서트 홀이 너무 작고 아주 더웠거든.

어휘

so-so[sóusòu] 형 좋지도 나쁘지도 않은   sweet[swi:t] 형 달콤한, 감미로운   do one's best 최선을 다하다 please[pli:z] 동 기쁘게 하다

문제 해설

Q: 남자가 콘서트에 대해 어떻게 느꼈는지 ✓표 하시오.

남자는 가수의 감미로운 목소리와 무대 매너는 마음에 들었으나 콘서트 홀이 너무 작고 더워서 마음에 들지 않았다.

5

M: My family is having a small concert. We're going to play popular jazz music. It'll be held in Denver High School hall on Friday, May 20th at 7 p.m. You can wear casual clothes. I hope you can come and enjoy listening to our music.

남: 저희 가족이 작은 콘서트를 열려고 합니다. 저희는 대중적인 재즈 음악을 연주할 거예요. 콘서트는 5월 20일 금요일 저녁 7시에 Denver 고등학교 강당에서 열릴 예정이에요. 평상복을 입고 오셔도 됩니다. 오셔서 저희의 음악을 즐겨주셨으면 해요.

어휘

jazz[dʒæz] 명 재즈   hold[hould] 동 열다, 개최하다 (hold-held-held)   casual[kǽʒuəl] 형 평상복의 [문제] location[loukéiʃən] 명 위치, 장소   dress code 복장 규정   formal[fɔ́:rməl] 형 격식을 차린

문제 해설

Q: 콘서트에 관해 틀린 정보를 고르시오.

복장은 평상복을 입고 와도 된다고 하였다.

6

M: Now, let's meet the next student. Could you introduce yourself?

W: My name is Michelle Williams, and I'm sixteen years old.

M: How do you feel now?

W: Actually, I'm very nervous.

M: I'm sure you'll do fine. What song are you going to sing?

W: Mariah Carey's *Hero*.

M: Okay. Let's hear it.

남: 이제 다음 학생을 만나봅시다. 본인 소개를 해주시겠습니까?

여: 제 이름은 Michelle Williams이고, 16살입니다.

남: 지금 기분이 어떤가요?

여: 사실, 아주 긴장됩니다.

남: 분명히 잘하실 거예요. 어떤 노래를 부르실 거예요?

여: 머라이어 캐리의 'Hero'요.

남: 알겠습니다. 들어봅시다.

어휘

introduce[ìntrədjúːs] 통 소개하다   actually[ǽktʃuəli]
부 사실   [문제] conversation[kànvərséiʃən] 명 대화
take place (사건 등이) 일어나다   classical[klǽsikəl]
형 클래식의

문제 해설

Q: 대화가 일어나고 있는 곳은?

여자가 노래 대회에 참가해 본인 소개를 하고, 노래를 부르려고 하는 상황이다.

7

W: Good afternoon, everyone. This is Sarah Jones of *Music Time*. It's raining heavily. I guess many listeners are feeling low. So our first song is a lively pop song to cheer you up. This is Beyonce singing, *Crazy in Love*.

여: 안녕하세요, 여러분. 'Music Time'의 Sarah Jones입니다. 비가 매우 많이 내리고 있네요. 많은 청취자분들이 우울해하실 것 같은데요. 그래서 첫 번째 곡은 여러분의 기운을 북돋아 줄 경쾌한 팝송입니다. 비욘세가 부르는 'Crazy in Love'입니다.

어휘

heavily[hévili] 부 심하게   guess[ges] 통 추측하다
listener[lísnər] 명 청취자   low[lou] 형 낮은; *기운 없는, 침울한   lively[láivli] 형 생기에 넘친; *경쾌한
cheer up 기운을 북돋우다

문제 해설

Q: 여자의 직업은?

라디오 DJ가 라디오 방송에서 음악을 틀어주는 상황이다.

8

M: ① Pop music is the most popular among the music genres.
  ② The same number of teens like rock and R&B.
  ③ Twelve percent of teens enjoy listening to rap music.
  ④ Only four percent of teens enjoy country music.

〈십대들이 가장 즐기는 음악 종류〉

남: ① 팝 음악은 음악 장르 중에서 가장 인기 있다.
  ② 록과 R&B를 좋아하는 십대의 수는 같다.
  ③ 십대 중 12퍼센트가 랩 음악 듣기를 즐긴다.
  ④ 4퍼센트의 십대만 컨트리 음악을 즐긴다.

어휘

pop music 팝 음악   genre[ʒɑ́ːŋrə] 명 장르
percent[pərsént] 명 퍼센트   rap music 랩 음악
country music 컨트리 음악

문제 해설

Q: 아래 그래프에 관해 사실이 아닌 것은?

컨트리 음악을 즐기는 십대는 6퍼센트이다.

Listening ★ Challenge   p. 48

A 1 ② 2 ③   B 1 ④ 2 ⓐ, ⓓ, ⓔ

A [1-2]

W: Your piano playing has improved a lot. Well done, David.

M: Thank you, Ms. Clinton.

W: How about majoring in music at university? You're the best player in my class.

M: I'd like to. How should I prepare?

W: You'd better attend a music academy first. Chicago Academy has famous teachers.

M: But isn't it too far?

W: If so, Grand Academy is near here.

M: Then that academy is better for me.

W: Good. You'll do well.

M: Thank you. In the future, I want to teach students like you do.

여: 피아노 연주가 많이 좋아졌구나. 잘했다, David.

남: 감사합니다, Clinton 선생님.

여: 대학에서 음악을 전공하는 게 어떻겠니? 넌 우리 반에서 피아노 실력이 제일 좋은데.

남: 그러고 싶어요. 어떻게 준비해야 될까요?

여: 먼저 음악 학원에 다녀보는 게 좋을 것 같구나. Chicago Academy에 유명한 선생님들이 계셔.

남: 하지만 너무 멀지 않나요?

여: 그렇다면, Grand Academy가 여기 근처에 있는데.

남: 그럼 그 학원이 저한테 더 낫겠네요.

여: 좋아. 넌 잘할 거야.

남: 감사합니다. 앞으로 선생님처럼 학생들을 가르치고 싶어요.

어휘

improve[imprúːv] 통 나아지다   university

[jùːnəvə́ːrsəti] 몡 대학　prepare[pripέər] 됭 준비하다
had better ~하는 편이 낫다　attend[əténd] 됭 참석하
다, 출석하다; *(학교 등에) 다니다　academy[əkǽdəmi]
몡 학원　far[fɑːr] 혱 멀리 떨어진　future[fjúːtʃər] 몡
미래　[문제] relationship[riléiʃənʃip] 몡 관계

문제 해설
Q1: 화자 간의 관계는?
　남자가 마지막에 "I want to teach students like you
　do."라고 했으므로 남자는 학생이고 여자는 선생님임을
　짐작할 수 있다.
Q2: 남자가 Grand Academy를 선택하는 이유는?
　남자는 Grand Academy가 근처에 있어서 Chicago
　Academy보다 더 나을 것 같다고 했다.

B [1-2]

W: Do you have a lot of stress? If so, listening to music can help. Here's how. The most important thing is to choose the right music. Slow music can help you relax. But when you want to cheer up, listen to faster music. And get into a comfortable position. You can lie down on the floor. It's also good to take a walk while listening to your favorite music.

여: 여러분은 스트레스를 많이 받나요? 그렇다면 음악을 듣는 게 도움이 됩니다. 여기에 방법이 있습니다. 가장 중요한 것은 올바른 음악을 선택하는 겁니다. 느린 음악은 긴장을 푸는 데 도움이 됩니다. 하지만 기운을 북돋우고 싶을 때는 더 빠른 음악을 들으세요. 그리고 편안한 자세를 취하세요. 바닥에 누워도 됩니다. 여러분이 좋아하는 음악을 들으며 산책하는 것도 좋습니다.

어휘
stress[stres] 몡 스트레스　relax[rilǽks] 됭 긴장을 풀다
comfortable[kʌ́mfərtəbl] 혱 편안한　position[pəzíʃən]
몡 위치; *자세　lie down 눕다　floor[flɔːr] 몡 바닥
take a walk 산책하다　[문제] reduce[ridjúːs] 됭 감소
시키다　headphone[hédfòun] 몡 헤드폰　earphone
[íərfòun] 몡 이어폰　more than ~ 이상으로　based
on ~에 근거하여　mood[muːd] 몡 기분, 감정

문제 해설
Q1: 여자는 주로 무엇에 대해 이야기하고 있는가?
　① 숙면을 위한 음악
　② 음악을 들어야 하는 이유
　③ 좋은 음악을 고르는 방법

④ 음악으로 스트레스를 줄이는 방법
　스트레스를 풀기 위해 음악을 듣는 게 좋다고 얘기하면서 이와 관련된 구체적인 방법들을 제시하고 있다.
Q2: 여자의 조언을 모두 고르시오.
　ⓐ 음악을 들으며 산책을 해라.
　ⓑ 헤드폰이나 이어폰을 사용해라.
　ⓒ 30분 이상 음악을 들어라.
　ⓓ 기분에 따라 다른 음악을 선택해라.
　ⓔ 음악을 들으면서 편안한 자세를 취해라.
　여자는 좋아하는 음악을 들으며 산책을 해도 좋다고 했다. 또한, 긴장을 풀려면 느린 음악을, 기운을 북돋우고 싶을 때는 빠른 음악을 듣고, 음악을 들을 때는 편안한 자세를 취하라고 했다.

Critical ★ Thinking　p. 49

1 ①　2 (1) ⓑ　(2) ⓐ

M: I'm Steve. I always listen to music when I study. It helps me focus on studying because I don't hear the noise around me. But my mom tells me that I'm wrong. She read scientists' research about it in the newspaper. According to the research, our brain can't do two things at once. So it's not possible to focus on studying while listening to music. But I don't really believe it.

남: 전 스티브예요. 저는 공부할 때에는 항상 음악을 들어요. 내 주위의 소음이 들리지 않기 때문에 공부에 집중하는 데 도움이 되거든요. 하지만 우리 엄마는 내가 잘못 생각한다고 말씀하시죠. 엄마는 신문에서 그것에 대한 과학자들의 연구를 읽으셨대요. 그 연구에 따르면 우리의 뇌는 두 가지 일을 동시에 할 수 없다는 거예요. 그래서 음악을 들으면서 공부에 집중하는 것은 가능하지 않대요. 하지만 나는 그 말을 정말 믿을 수 없어요.

어휘
focus on ~에 집중하다　noise[nɔiz] 몡 소음
research[risə́ːrtʃ] 몡 연구　newspaper[njúːzpèipər]
몡 신문　according to ~에 따르면　brain[brein] 몡
두뇌　at once 동시에　possible[pásəbl] 혱 가능한
[문제] bother[báðər] 됭 괴롭히다, 성가시게 하다
outside[àutsáid] 혱 외부의　pay attention to ~에
주의를 기울이다

43

문제 해설

Q1: Steve는 주로 무엇에 대해 이야기하고 있는가?

    ① 음악이 공부에 도움이 되는가?

    ② 어떻게 공부에 집중할 수 있는가?

    ③ 음악을 듣는 것이 왜 좋은가?

    ④ 음악을 들을 때 뇌는 어떻게 작용하는가?

    음악을 들으면서 공부하는 것이 집중하는 데 도움이 되는가에 관해 얘기하고 있다.

Q2: 각 인물의 의견을 고르시오.

    ⓐ 우리의 뇌는 한 번에 한 가지 일에만 집중할 수 있다.

    ⓑ 우리는 음악을 들을 때 외부 소음에 방해받지 않는다.

    ⓒ 음악을 들으며 공부를 하면 주로 음악에 더 주의를 기울이게 된다.

    (1) Steve는 공부하면서 음악을 들으면 주위의 소음이 들리지 않아서 집중하는 데 도움이 된다고 생각한다.

    (2) Steve의 어머니는 우리의 뇌가 두 가지 일을 동시에 할 수 없다고 생각한다.

UNIT 08 Holidays

Getting ★ Ready p. 50

A 1 ⓔ 2 ⓓ 3 ⓕ 4 ⓒ 5 ⓐ
B 1 ⓕ 2 ⓒ 3 ⓔ

B 1 남: 오늘이 특별한 공휴일이니?

    여: 응. 독립기념일이야.

  2 남: 넌 방학 중에 뭘 할 거니?

    여: Stanley Park 근처에 야영갈 거야.

  3 남: 네가 방학 때 프랑스에 방문할 계획이라고 들었어.

    여: 아니, 그렇지 않아. 집에 있을 거야.

Listening ★ Start p. 51

1 (1) ② (2) ③ / making something, a kind of, What about, baking a pumpkin pie
2 ③ / special holiday, doing anything, beautiful fireworks, sounds fun

1

M: Cindy, are you making something for Thanksgiving?

W: Yes. I'm going to cook yams.

M: What are they?

W: They're a kind of sweet potato. They are really yummy.

M: I see. What about the turkey?

W: My parents will cook it. How about you, Jake?

M: I'm going to try baking a pumpkin pie.

W: Wow! Good luck.

남: Cindy, 추수감사절 때 뭔가 만들 거니?

여: 응. 참마 요리를 할 거야.

남: 그게 뭔데?

여: 일종의 고구마야. 정말 맛있어.

남: 그렇구나. 칠면조는 어떻게 할 거야?

여: 우리 부모님이 요리하실 거야. Jake 너는?

남: 난 호박 파이를 구워보려고.

여: 우와! 행운을 빌어.

어휘

Thanksgiving[θæ̀ŋksgívìŋ] 몡 추수감사절 yam[jæm]
몡 참마 sweet potato 고구마 yummy[jʌ́mi] 혱
맛있는 turkey[tə́ːrki] 몡 칠면조 bake[beik] 동 굽다
pumpkin[pʌ́mpkin] 몡 호박 pie[pai] 몡 파이

문제 해설

Q: 그들은 추수감사절에 어떤 음식을 만들 것인가?

    Cindy는 참마 요리를 하고, Jake는 호박 파이를 구울 거라고 했다.

2

W: Look, there's a parade. Is today a special holiday in America?

M: Yes. Today is American Independence Day.

W: Oh, I see.

M: Are you doing anything this evening?

W: Not really. I was going to stay home and watch TV.

M: There'll be beautiful fireworks downtown tonight. Let's go and watch them together.

W: Sure. That sounds fun!

여: 봐, 퍼레이드를 하네. 오늘이 미국에서 특별한 공휴일이니?

남: 응. 오늘은 미국 독립기념일이야.

여: 아, 그렇구나.

남: 오늘 저녁에 무슨 할 일 있니?

여: 아니. 집에서 TV 보려고 했어.

남: 오늘 밤에 시내에서 아름다운 불꽃놀이를 할 거야. 같이
　　가서 보자.

여: 좋아. 재미있겠다!

어휘
parade[pəréid] 명 행렬, 퍼레이드　holiday[hálədèi]
명 공휴일　Independence Day 독립기념일　stay
[stei] 통 머무르다　firework[fáiərwə̀ːrk] 명 불꽃놀이
downtown[dáuntáun] 부 도심지에서

문제 해설
Q: 그들이 저녁에 할 일은?
　　두 사람은 함께 불꽃놀이를 보러 가기로 했다.

Listening ★ Practice　p. 52

1 ② 　2 12 　3 ③ 　4 (1) ⓒ, ⓔ (2) ⓐ, ⓓ 　5 ④
6 ③ 　7 (1) ⓑ (2) ⓒ 　8 (1) F (2) T (3) F

1

M: Do you know about Songkran? It's a New
　　Year festival in Thailand. It is from April
　　13th to 15th. During Songkran, people
　　throw water onto strangers on the street
　　to bring good luck. They even throw water
　　onto people on bicycles and buses. But
　　everyone smiles and enjoys the fun.

남: Songkran에 대해서 아시나요? 그것은 태국의 새해 축제
　　랍니다. 4월 13일부터 15일까지예요. Songkran 중에는
　　행운을 가져오기 위해 사람들이 길에서 낯선 사람들에게
　　물을 끼얹었습니다. 그들은 심지어 자전거와 버스를 탄 사
　　람들에게도 물을 끼얹었습니다. 하지만 모든 사람들이 웃으
　　며 즐긴답니다.

어휘
festival[féstəvəl] 명 축제　throw[θrou] 통 던지다;
*(물을) 뿌리다 (throw-threw-thrown)　stranger
[stréindʒər] 명 낯선 사람　bring[briŋ] 통 가지고 오다
bicycle[báisikl] 명 자전거

문제 해설
Q: Songkran을 나타내는 사진을 고르시오.
　　Songkran 중에는 사람들이 거리에서 모르는 사람들에게
　　물을 끼얹었다고 했다.

2

W: I'm going camping near Stanley Park
　　during summer vacation. Do you want to
　　go with me?

M: Yes, I do. When are you going?

W: How about next Thursday, June 11th?

M: How about next Friday instead? Thursday
　　is my mom's birthday.

W: Okay. Sam is going too. Is that okay?

M: Of course. That's no problem.

여: 난 여름 방학 동안 Stanley Park 근처에 야영갈 거야.
　　너도 나랑 같이 갈래?

남: 응. 그래. 언제 갈 거야?

여: 다음 목요일. 6월 11일 어때?

남: 그 대신 다음 금요일이 어때? 목요일은 엄마 생신이거든.

여: 알았어. Sam도 갈 거야. 괜찮아?

남: 물론이지. 전혀 문제 없어.

어휘
camp[kæmp] 통 야영하다　vacation[veikéiʃən] 명 방학

문제 해설
Q: 두 사람이 야영을 가기로 한 날에 동그라미 하시오.
　　다음 금요일인 6월 12일에 야영을 갈 것이다.

3

M: I heard you're planning to visit France for
　　a vacation. Have a great time there!

W: Well... I'm not going. I'm staying home.

M: Why? Is it because of work?

W: No. Mark was going to travel with me.
　　But he's in the hospital now.

M: You really wanted to go, didn't you? I'm
　　sorry to hear that.

남: 네가 방학 때 프랑스에 방문할 계획이라고 들었어. 거기
　　서 좋은 시간 보내!

여: 음… 나 안 가. 집에 있을 거야.

남: 왜? 일 때문에?

여: 아니. Mark가 나랑 여행 가기로 했는데 지금 입원해 있
　　잖아.

남: 너 정말 가고 싶어 했잖아, 그렇지 않니? 그 말 들으니
　　안됐네.

어휘
hospital[háspitəl] 명 병원

문제 해설
Q: 여자가 여행을 가지 않기로 한 이유는?
　　① 그녀는 입원해 있다.
　　② 그녀는 할 일이 많다.

45

③ 그녀의 친구가 아프다.

④ 그녀는 돈이 충분히 없다.

여자는 함께 여행 가기로 한 친구가 지금 입원해 있다고 했다.

4

W: The day before New Year's Day, Chinese people clean their houses. On New Year's Day, people visit their relatives. In the evening, they watch fireworks. They don't cook on this day. They think using knives on New Year's Day brings bad luck. So, they make food the day before New Year's Day.

여: 한 해의 마지막 날, 중국 사람들은 집을 청소해요. 새해 첫날에는 친척을 방문하죠. 저녁에는 불꽃놀이를 구경해요. 그들은 이 날에는 요리를 하지 않는답니다. 새해 첫날에 칼을 사용하면 불행을 가져올 거라고 생각하거든요. 그래서 그들은 그 전날 음식을 만들어요.

어휘

New Year's Day 새해 첫날   clean[kliːn] 동 청소하다   relative[rélətiv] 명 친척   knife[naif] 명 칼

문제 해설

Q: 각각의 날에 중국 사람들이 하는 일을 고르시오.

(1) 한 해의 마지막 날에는 집 청소와 요리를 한다고 했다.

(2) 새해 첫날에는 친척을 방문하고, 불꽃놀이를 구경한다고 했다.

5

W: Where are you going?

M: I'm going to the bookstore.

W: Are you going to buy comic books again?

M: No. I'm going to buy a travel guidebook. I'm going on a trip during summer vacation.

W: Sounds great!

M: So, what are you doing during the vacation?

W: I'm taking cooking classes.

여: 너 어디 가니?

남: 서점에 가는 길이야.

여: 또 만화책 사려고?

남: 아니. 여행 안내서를 살 거야. 여름 방학 동안 여행을 갈

거거든.

여: 좋겠다!

남: 근데. 넌 방학 때 뭐 할 거야?

여: 요리 수업을 들을 거야.

어휘

bookstore[búkstɔːr] 명 서점   guidebook[gáidbùk] 명 안내서

문제 해설

Q: 남자는 무슨 책을 사려고 하는가?

남자는 여행 안내서를 살 거라고 했다.

6

M: What are you doing during the vacation, Kate?

W: I'm going to Vancouver.

M: How nice. It'll be fun going to the beach.

W: You don't look happy, Joe. What's up?

M: I was going to travel with friends, but now I can't.

W: Why not?

M: I have to attend summer school. I got a D in math.

W: Oh, I'm sorry.

남: Kate, 너 방학 때 뭐 할 거야?

여: 밴쿠버에 갈 거야.

남: 정말 좋겠다. 바닷가에 가면 재미있겠다.

여: Joe, 넌 행복해 보이지 않는데. 무슨 일 있어?

남: 친구들이랑 여행을 가기로 했는데 이제 못 가게 됐어.

여: 왜 못 가?

남: 여름 학교에 다녀야 하거든. 수학에서 D를 받았어.

여: 아, 안됐구나.

어휘

beach[biːtʃ] 명 해변, 바닷가   attend[əténd] 동 출석하다; *(학교 등에) 다니다

문제 해설

Q: Joe가 방학 중에 할 일은?

Joe는 여름 학교에 다녀야 한다고 했다.

7

M: Mary, Mom is going to buy us Christmas presents.

W: Great! You want a cellphone, don't you?

M: No, they're too expensive.

W: What do you want then, Tom?

M: A cheap MP3 player. How about you?

W: I want a sweater.

M: You already have many sweaters. What about a coat?

W: No, I want a sweater. I saw a really pretty one at the mall.

남: Mary, 엄마가 우리에게 크리스마스 선물을 사주실 거야.

여: 잘됐다! 너 휴대전화 갖고 싶어 했잖아?

남: 아니야, 그건 너무 비싸.

여: 그럼 Tom, 넌 뭘 원하는데?

남: 저렴한 MP3 플레이어. 넌?

여: 난 스웨터가 갖고 싶어.

남: 너 스웨터는 이미 많이 가지고 있잖아. 코트는 어때?

여: 아니, 난 스웨터가 갖고 싶어. 쇼핑몰에서 정말 예쁜 걸 봤거든.

어휘

present[prézant] 명 선물 cellphone[sélfòun] 명 휴대전화 expensive[ikspénsiv] 형 비싼 sweater[swétər] 명 스웨터 coat[kout] 명 코트

문제 해설

Q: Tom과 Mary가 원하는 선물을 고르시오.

　　Tom은 MP3 플레이어를, Mary는 스웨터를 받고 싶어 한다.

8

W: Let's go to Scotland during the vacation.

M: Why Scotland?

W: I want to go to the Edinburgh Festival Fringe.

M: What's that?

W: It's the largest international arts festival in the world.

M: When is it?

W: It starts on August 5th. It's usually held for three weeks.

M: Do famous people attend the festival?

W: Sure! Hugh Grant and Jude Law are going this year.

M: Great!

여: 방학 때 스코틀랜드에 가자.

남: 스코틀랜드에 왜?

여: Edinburgh Festival Fringe에 가고 싶어.

남: 그게 뭔데?

여: 세계에서 가장 큰 국제적인 예술 축제야.

남: 언제 해?

여: 8월 5일에 시작해. 보통 3주 동안 열려.

남: 유명한 사람들도 축제에 오니?

여: 물론이지! 올해는 Hugh Grant랑 Jude Law가 갈 거야.

남: 멋진 걸!

어휘

international[ìntərnǽʃənəl] 형 국제적인 art[ɑːrt] 명 예술 hold[hould] 동 잡다; 지속하다; *(회의 등을) 개최하다 [문제] star[stɑːr] 명 별; *인기 스타

문제 해설

Q: Edinburgh Festival Fringe에 관해 사실이면 T, 사실이 아니면 F를 쓰시오.

　(1) 세계에서 가장 오래된 예술 축제이다.

　(2) 유명한 스타들이 참석할 것이다.

　(3) 7월에 3주 동안 열린다.

　Edinburgh Festival Fringe는 세계에서 가장 오래된 예술 축제가 아니라 규모가 가장 큰 축제라고 했다. 이 축제는 8월에 3주 동안 열리고, 유명한 스타들도 참여한다.

Listening ★ Challenge　p. 54

A 1 ④　2 ①, ②　B 1 May 10, June 21　2 ④

A [1-2]

M: Boxing Day started in England. It is on the first weekday after Christmas. In the past, servants got presents from their masters the day after Christmas. Masters put the presents in boxes. That's how Boxing Day got its name. Today, people still give gifts to workers on that day. It's also a popular shopping day because most stores have big sales.

남: Boxing Day는 영국에서 시작되었어요. 그것은 크리스마스가 지난 후 첫 번째 평일이지요. 옛날에 하인들은 크리스마스 다음 날 자신의 주인에게서 선물을 받았어요. 주인이 상자에 선물을 넣어두었지요. 그렇게 해서 Boxing Day라는 이름이 붙은 거예요. 오늘날에도 여전히 그날이 되면 사람들은 노동자들에게 선물을 준답니다. 그날은 대부분의 가게들이 대규모 할인을 하기 때문에 대중적으로 쇼핑하는 날이기도 해요.

어휘

weekday[wíːkdèi] 명 평일 past[pæst] 명 과거

47

servant[sə́ːrvənt] 명 하인 master[mǽstər] 명 주인
put[put] 동 놓다, 두다 (put-put-put) box[baks] 명
상자 gift[gift] 명 선물 worker[wə́ːrkər] 명 노동자
popular[pápjulər] 형 인기있는, 대중적인 sale[seil] 명
세일, 할인 [문제] neighbor[néibər] 명 이웃

문제 해설
Q1: Boxing Day에 대해 언급되지 <u>않은</u> 것은?
　　사람들이 그날 무엇을 사는지에 대해서는 언급되지 않았다.
Q2: 사람들이 Boxing Day에 하는 일을 모두 고르시오.
　　요즘에는 Boxing Day에 노동자에게 선물을 주기도 하고,
　　쇼핑을 하기도 한다고 했다.

B [1-2]

M: When is Mother's Day in America?
W: Mother's Day is on the second Sunday of May.
M: What do people do on that day?
W: They give carnations to their moms as a thank-you gift.
M: Do people celebrate Father's Day, too?
W: Yes. Father's Day is on the third Sunday of June.
M: Do people give carnations to their fathers, too?
W: No. Traditionally, people gave roses to their fathers, but these days people usually give small gifts instead.

남: 미국에서는 어머니날이 언제야?
여: 어머니날은 5월의 두 번째 일요일이야.
남: 사람들이 그날에 뭘 하니?
여: 자신의 엄마에게 감사의 선물로 카네이션을 드려.
남: 아버지날도 기념하니?
여: 응. 아버지날은 6월의 세 번째 일요일이야.
남: 아버지에게도 카네이션을 드리니?
여: 아니. 전통적으로 아버지께 장미를 드렸었는데, 요즘에는
　　대신 작은 선물을 드려.

어휘
carnation[kɑːrnéiʃən] 명 카네이션 celebrate
[séləbrèit] 동 기념하다 traditionally[trədíʃənəli] 부
전통적으로 rose[rouz] 명 장미 these days 요즘
instead[instéd] 부 대신에 [문제] calendar[kǽləndər]
명 달력

문제 해설
Q1: 어머니날과 아버지날을 달력에서 동그라미 하시오.

어머니날은 5월의 두 번째 일요일이므로 5월 10일이고,
아버지날은 6월의 세 번째 일요일이라고 했으므로 6월
21일이다.
Q2: 어머니날에는 어머니에게 어떤 꽃을 주는가?
　　어머니날에는 카네이션을 준다고 했다.

Critical ★ Thinking p. 55

1 ④　2 ⓔ

M: How was your Christmas, Linda?
W: Great. I watched TV and ate holiday food at home.
M: What? You just stayed home?
W: I'm usually busy studying, so I just relax during the holidays.
M: I'm also busy with my part-time job. But I did something meaningful.
W: What did you do, Tim?
M: I made food for poor people.
W: How nice.
M: I do it every Christmas. I like helping others.
W: Helping others is good. But I think the holidays are for taking a rest.

남: Linda, 크리스마스 어땠니?
여: 좋았어. 집에서 TV 보고, 명절 음식을 먹었어.
남: 뭐라고? 그냥 집에 있었다고?
여: 보통 공부하느라 바빠서 휴일에는 그냥 쉬어.
남: 나도 파트타임 일로 바쁘지만 뭔가 의미 있는 걸 했다고.
여: Tim, 넌 뭘 했는데?
남: 불쌍한 사람들을 위해서 음식을 만들었어.
여: 정말 멋지다.
남: 난 크리스마스 때마다 그렇게 해. 다른 사람들을 돕는 걸
　　좋아하거든.
여: 다른 사람들을 돕는 건 좋지. 하지만 난 휴일은 휴식을
　　위한 거라고 생각해.

어휘
relax[rilǽks] 동 긴장을 풀다, 쉬다 part-
time[páːrttàim] 형 파트타임의; 부 파트타임으로
meaningful[míːniŋfəl] 형 의미 있는 take a rest 휴
식을 취하다

문제 해설
Q1: 그들은 주로 무엇에 대해 이야기하고 있는가?
　　① 크리스마스 휴일이 어떻게 시작되었는지

② 다음 크리스마스 휴일에 무엇을 할지

③ 크리스마스 휴일의 진정한 의미가 무엇인지

④ 크리스마스 휴일을 어떻게 보내야 하는지

두 사람은 크리스마스 휴일을 어떻게 보내야 하는지, 그리고 각자 어떻게 보냈는지 서로 이야기하고 있다.

Q2: Tim이 크리스마스 휴일에 한 일을 고르시오.

　　Tim은 불쌍한 사람들을 위해 음식을 만들었다고 했다.

UNIT 09 Shopping

Getting ★ Ready　p. 56

A 1 ⓔ　2 ⓐ　3 ⓑ　4 ⓒ　5 ⓓ

B 1 ⓒ　2 ⓐ　3 ⓓ

B 1 남: 어느 게 가장 인기 있나요?

　　여: 이 분홍색 것이 가장 잘 팔려요.

　2 남: 찾으시는 게 있나요?

　　여: 남동생이 신을 신발을 사고 싶은데요.

　3 남: 지불은 어떻게 하시겠어요?

　　여: 신용카드로요.

Listening ★ Start　p. 57

1 ② / May I help you, kinds of, too big, I'll take it

2 ① / looking for, How about, How much, 50% off

1

M: Hello. May I help you?

W: Yes. I'm looking for a digital camera.

M: Here are some different kinds of digital cameras.

W: Which ones are popular?

M: This pink one and that silver one sell best.

W: I like the silver color, but it's too big.

M: The pink camera is easier to carry around.

W: Okay. I'll take it.

남: 어서 오세요. 뭘 도와드릴까요?

여: 네. 디지털 카메라를 찾고 있어요.

남: 여기 여러 종류의 디지털 카메라가 있어요.

여: 어느 게 인기가 있어요?

남: 여기 분홍색이랑 저기 은색이 가장 잘 팔려요.

여: 은색이 마음에 드는데. 너무 크네요.

남: 분홍색 카메라가 가지고 다니기에는 더 편해요.

여: 그래요. 그걸로 할게요.

어휘

digital camera 디지털 카메라　silver[sílvər] 형 은색의　sell[sel] 통 팔다; *팔리다 (sell-sold-sold)

carry[kǽri] 통 나르다; *지니고 다니다

문제 해설

Q: 여자는 어떤 카메라를 살 것인가?

　가지고 다니기 편한 분홍색 카메라를 산다고 했다.

2

W: Are you looking for something?

M: Yes. I want to buy some shoes for my girlfriend.

W: How about these?

M: I think my girlfriend will like them. How much are they?

W: They're $40.

M: Wow. That's expensive.

W: They were $80, but they're 50% off now.

M: Really? Then I'll take them.

여: 찾으시는 게 있나요?

남: 네. 여자 친구가 신을 신발을 사고 싶어요.

여: 이건 어때요?

남: 제 여자 친구가 좋아할 것 같네요. 얼마예요?

여: 40달러예요.

남: 우와. 비싸네요.

여: 그건 80달러였는데 지금은 50퍼센트 할인된 거예요.

남: 정말이요? 그럼 그걸로 할게요.

어휘

off[ɔːf] 부 (얼마를) 할인하여

문제 해설

Q: 남자는 얼마를 지불할 것인가?

　남자가 사려고 하는 신발의 원래 가격은 80달러지만, 현재 50퍼센트 할인하고 있으므로 40달러를 지불하면 된다.

Listening ★ Practice　p. 58

1 ⓐ, ⓑ, ⓓ　2 ②　3 ③　4 ②　5 ④　6 (1) 9th (2) 2nd　(3) 5th　7 ④　8 (1) T　(2) T　(3) F

1

W: Chris, is there anything you want?

M: This yogurt looks good.

W: It's a little expensive, but let's get it. Anything else?

M: We need milk for tomorrow morning.

W: And I'd like to get some orange juice, too.

M: We have orange juice at home. How about buying tomato juice instead?

W: Okay.

여: Chris, 뭐 사고 싶은 거 있니?

남: 이 요구르트가 괜찮아 보여.

여: 조금 비싸긴 하지만 사자. 다른 건 없어?

남: 내일 아침에 마실 우유도 필요해.

여: 그리고 난 오렌지 주스도 사고 싶은데.

남: 오렌지 주스는 집에 있어. 대신에 토마토 주스를 사는 게 어때?

여: 좋아.

어휘

yogurt [jóuɡərt] 명 요구르트   instead [instéd] 부 대신에

문제 해설

Q: 그들이 살 것을 모두 쇼핑카트에 넣으시오.

　　두 사람은 요구르트와 우유, 토마토 주스를 사기로 했다.

2

M: Kate, what do you think about that blue jacket? It's nice.

W: I don't like the color.

M: We've been shopping for three hours already. Why don't you buy a jacket later?

W: I must buy one today to wear for the wedding.

M: I'm so tired. Let's take a break and eat some ice cream first.

W: Okay.

남: Kate, 저 파란 재킷 어떻게 생각해? 괜찮은데.

여: 색깔이 마음에 안 들어.

남: 우린 이미 세 시간 동안 쇼핑했어. 재킷은 나중에 사는 게 어때?

여: 결혼식에 입을 걸 오늘 꼭 사야 해.

남: 난 너무 피곤해. 좀 쉬면서 아이스크림부터 먹자.

여: 알았어.

어휘

later [léitər] 부 나중에   wedding [wédiŋ] 명 결혼식
take a break 잠깐 쉬다

문제 해설

Q: 두 사람이 다음에 할 일은?

　　두 사람은 좀 쉬면서 아이스크림을 먹을 것이다.

3

W: That cap looks good. Is it new?

M: Yes. I went to the J Mall yesterday. It was on sale.

W: How much was it?

M: It was $5.

W: Wow. That's really cheap. Did you buy just one?

M: No. I bought a white hat, too. It was $6.

여: 그 모자 괜찮네. 새 거야?

남: 응. 어제 J Mall에 갔거든. 이게 할인 중이더라고.

여: 그게 얼마였는데?

남: 5달러였어.

여: 우와. 정말 싸네. 하나만 샀어?

남: 아니. 하얀색 모자도 샀어. 그건 6달러였어.

어휘

cap [kæp] 명 (테가 없는) 모자   on sale 할인 중인
cheap [tʃiːp] 형 값이 싼   hat [hæt] 명 (테가 있는) 모자
[문제] in total 전체로, 총

문제 해설

Q: 남자가 총 지불한 금액은?

　　5달러짜리 모자와 6달러짜리 모자를 샀으므로 총 11달러를 지불했을 것이다.

4

M: When you shop, it's good to take a friend with a good sense of style. And think about which items to buy before you go out. Or, you might buy too many things. Don't just look at clothes, but try them on. You might not like them after putting them on.

남: 쇼핑을 할 때는 스타일 감각이 좋은 친구를 데려가는 게 좋아요. 그리고 나가기 전에 어떤 물건을 살지 생각해봐야 해요. 그렇지 않으면 너무 많은 것을 살지도 몰라요. 옷을 보기만 하지 말고 입어 보세요. 입어보고 나면 마음에 들지 않을 수도 있어요.

어휘

sense[sens] 몡 감각   style[stail] 몡 스타일, 유행
item[áitem] 몡 물건   look at ~을 보다   try on 입
어 보다   put on 입다   [문제] place[pleis] 몡 장소
point[pɔint] 몡 점, 요점

문제 해설

Q: 남자는 주로 무엇에 대해 이야기하고 있는가?

　① 쇼핑하기 가장 좋은 장소

　② 옷을 쇼핑하는 방법

　③ 저렴한 옷을 살 수 있는 곳

　④ 친구와 쇼핑을 하는 것의 좋은 점

남자는 옷을 살 때 알아두어야 할 점들에 대해 이야기하고 있다.

5

(*Telephone rings.*)

M: This is CX Home Shopping.

W: Hello. I ordered a miniskirt three days ago. But I got the wrong color.

M: Okay. What's your name?

W: It's Kelly Louise.

M: Let's see. You ordered a black miniskirt on Monday.

W: Yes. But I got a yellow one.

M: I'm sorry. We'll exchange it for you.

W: Okay.

(전화벨이 울린다.)

남: CX 홈쇼핑입니다.

여: 여보세요. 제가 3일 전에 미니스커트를 주문했는데요. 색상이 잘못된 걸 받았어요.

남: 알겠습니다. 성함이 어떻게 되시나요?

여: Kelly Louise입니다.

남: 확인해 보겠습니다. 월요일에 검은색 미니스커트를 주문하셨네요.

여: 네. 그런데 노란색이 왔어요.

남: 죄송합니다. 교환해 드리겠습니다.

여: 알겠습니다.

어휘

order[ɔ́ːrdər] 동 주문하다   miniskirt[míniskə̀ːrt] 몡 미니스커트   exchange[ikstʃéindʒ] 동 교환하다
[문제] get money back 환불받다   size[saiz] 몡 사이즈   complain[kəmpléin] 동 불평하다

문제 해설

Q: 여자가 전화를 건 이유는?

　① 돈을 환불받으려고

　② 치마를 주문하려고

　③ 안 좋은 서비스에 대해 불평하려고

　④ 구입한 치마를 교환하려고

여자는 검은색 미니스커트를 주문했는데 노란색이 와서 교환하려고 하고 있다.

6

W: Attention, shoppers! Right now, on the second floor, there's a brand-name sunglasses event. You can buy one pair for $60. All the ladies fashion shops on the fifth floor are having summer sales events. Men's shoes are 40% off on the ninth floor. We hope you enjoy shopping with us.

여: 손님 여러분께 안내 말씀 드리겠습니다! 바로 지금, 2층에서 유명 브랜드 선글라스 행사가 있습니다. 한 개당 60달러에 사실 수 있습니다. 5층에 있는 모든 여성복 매장에서는 여름 할인 행사를 하고 있습니다. 남성 신발은 9층에서 40퍼센트 할인을 하고 있습니다. 저희와 함께 즐거운 쇼핑 되시기를 바랍니다.

어휘

floor[flɔːr] 몡 방바닥; *(건물의) 층   brand-name[bréndnèim] 형 유명 상표의   event[ivént] 몡 행사
pair[pɛər] 몡 한 쌍

문제 해설

Q: 각 인물이 갈 층을 쓰시오.

　(1) Tom: 난 아버지께 드릴 신발을 사고 싶어.

　(2) Harry: 난 여름에 쓸 선글라스가 필요해.

　(3) Sally: 난 예쁜 치마를 입어보고 싶어.

　(1) Tom은 아버지의 신발을 구매하기 위해 남성 신발 할인 행사를 하는 9층으로 갈 것이다.

　(2) Harry는 선글라스를 구매하기 위해 선글라스 행사를 하는 2층으로 갈 것이다.

　(3) Sally는 스커트를 입어 보기 위해 여성 의류 할인 행사가 있는 5층으로 갈 것이다.

7

M: Are you looking for something?

W: I'm looking for something to wear to a party.

M: How about this yellow dress?

W: It's pretty, but too simple.

M: How about this one with the big ribbon on it?

W: I don't like pink.

M: Then I'd like to recommend this blue dress to you.

W: Great! I'll take it.

남: 찾으시는 게 있나요?

여: 파티에 입고 갈 걸 찾고 있어요.

남: 이 노란색 드레스는 어때요?

여: 예쁘긴 한데 너무 단순해요.

남: 여기 큰 리본이 달려 있는 건 어때요?

여: 전 분홍색을 안 좋아해요.

남: 그러면, 이 파란색 드레스를 추천해 드릴게요.

여: 좋아요! 그걸로 할게요.

어휘

dress[dres] 명 옷; *드레스 simple[símpl] 형 단순한
ribbon[ríbən] 명 리본 recommend[rèkəménd] 동
추천하다

문제 해설

Q: 여자가 살 드레스는?

여자는 파란색 드레스를 사기로 했다.

8

M: Are you looking for the best online shopping mall for teenage boys? Visit *Mark's*. We have jackets, pants, T-shirts, and shoes. Our products are famous for their quality. We have an offline store in New York, too. We're having a spring sale until this Sunday. Visit us anytime!

남: 십대 소년들을 위한 최고의 온라인 쇼핑몰을 찾고 있나요? 'Mark's'를 방문해 보세요. 재킷, 바지, 티셔츠와 신발 등이 있습니다. 저희 상품은 좋은 품질로 유명합니다. 뉴욕에 오프라인 매장도 있습니다. 이번 일요일까지 봄 세일을 하고 있습니다. 언제든지 들러주세요!

어휘

teenage[tí:nèidʒ] 형 10대의 pants[pænts] 명 바지
product[prádəkt] 명 상품 be famous for ~로 유명
하다 quality[kwáləti] 명 품질; *양질, 우수성 offline
[ɔ́:flàin] 형 오프라인의 anytime[énitàim] 부 언제든지

문제 해설

Q: Mark's에 관해 사실이면 T, 사실이 아니면 F를 쓰시오.

(1) Mark's는 소년들을 위한 물건들을 판다.

(2) Mark's는 온라인과 오프라인 매장을 둘 다 가지고 있다.

(3) 이번 일요일부터 봄 세일을 할 것이다.

Listening ★ Challenge p. 60

A 1 ①, ④ 2 ③ B 1 ③ 2 ②

A [1-2]

(*Telephone rings.*)

W: This is Happy Home Shopping.

M: Hello. I want to buy an S laptop.

W: Which color do you want, silver or black?

M: I want black.

W: Do you also need speakers or a mouse?

M: No, I don't.

W: Okay, that's $1,400. How would you like to pay?

M: I'll pay by credit card. Oh, I'm sorry, but can I add the speakers?

W: Sure. They will be $100 more.

M: Okay. When will I get them?

W: You'll get them by this Friday.

M: Thanks.

(전화벨이 울린다.)

여: Happy 홈쇼핑입니다.

남: 여보세요. S 노트북을 사고 싶은데요.

여: 은색이랑 검은색 중에 어떤 색을 원하시나요?

남: 검은색이요.

여: 스피커나 마우스도 필요하세요?

남: 아니요, 필요 없어요.

여: 알겠습니다. 1,400달러군요. 지불은 어떻게 하시겠습니까?

남: 신용카드로 지불할게요. 아, 죄송하지만 스피커를 추가해도 될까요?

여: 물론이죠. 그럼 100달러를 더 내셔야 하겠네요.

남: 알겠습니다. 언제 받아볼 수 있을까요?

여: 이번 금요일까지는 받으실 수 있을 거예요.

남: 감사합니다.

어휘

laptop[læptàp] 명 노트북 컴퓨터 speaker[spí:kər]
명 말하는 사람; *스피커, 확성기 mouse[maus] 명 생쥐;
*마우스 credit card 신용카드 add[æd] 동 더하다,
추가하다

문제 해설

Q1: 남자가 구매하는 물건을 모두 고르시오.

　　남자는 노트북과 스피커를 사기로 했다.

Q2: 남자가 지불할 금액은?

　　노트북이 1,400달러이고 스피커가 100달러이므로 총
　　1,500달러를 지불할 것이다.

B [1-2]

W: I'm going to Hong Kong next week.
　　Where should I go shopping?

M: Visit Harbor City.

W: Ah, I heard about that place. Is it really
　　that big?

M: Yes. There are over 700 stores.

W: It must be tiring. Any place else?

M: Pacific Place is smaller than Harbor City.
　　There are many good restaurants in it.

W: How about Times Square?

M: Many young people go there. There's a
　　large movie theater.

W: Pacific Place sounds good. I want to
　　shop and eat a nice meal.

M: Nice!

여: 나 다음 주에 홍콩에 갈 거야. 어디로 쇼핑을 하러 가야
　　할까?

남: Harbor City에 가 봐.

여: 아, 그곳에 대해서 들어봤어. 정말 그렇게 커?

남: 응. 매장이 700개가 넘게 있어.

여: 분명 힘들 텐데. 다른 곳은 없어?

남: Pacific Place가 Harbor City보다 작아. 거기에 좋은 음
　　식점이 많아.

여: Times Square는 어때?

남: 거기엔 젊은 사람들이 많이 가지. 큰 영화관도 있어.

여: Pacific Place가 좋은 것 같네. 쇼핑하고 근사한 식사도
　　하고 싶거든.

남: 좋지!

어휘

tiring[táiəriŋ] 형 힘드는　restaurant[réstərənt] 명 음
식점　theater[θí(ː)ətər] 명 극장　meal[miːl] 명 식사

문제 해설

Q1: 여자가 쇼핑하러 갈 곳은?

　　여자는 Pacific Place가 좋은 것 같다고 했다.

Q2: 사실이 <u>아닌</u> 것은?

　　① Harbor City에 700개 이상의 매장이 있다.

② Pacific Place는 Harbor City보다 더 크다.

③ Pacific Place에는 먹기 좋은 장소가 많다.

④ Times Square는 젊은 사람들에게 인기 있다.

　　Pacific Place는 Harbor City보다 작다고 했다.

Critical ★ Thinking　p. 61

1 ②　2 ⓐ, ⓒ, ⓔ

W: What's the result?

M: It says you're a shopaholic.

W: I thought so. I get nervous if I don't shop.

M: You need to control yourself, Lisa.

W: What should I do?

M: First, you should stop using all your credit
　　cards. And make some new hobbies.

W: Why?

M: That way, you'll have less time to shop.

W: Anything else?

M: Before buying anything, ask yourself
　　three times if you really need it.

W: Okay. I'll try.

M: Visit me again in a week. I want to see if
　　you're following my advice.

W: Thank you.

여: 결과가 어때요?

남: 당신은 쇼핑 중독자라고 나오네요.

여: 저도 그렇게 생각했어요. 쇼핑을 안 하면 초조해지거든요.

남: Lisa, 당신은 스스로를 통제할 필요가 있어요.

여: 제가 어떻게 해야 하죠?

남: 먼저, 모든 신용카드 사용을 그만두어야 합니다. 그리고
　　새로운 취미를 만드세요.

여: 왜요?

남: 그렇게 하면 당신이 쇼핑하는 데 시간을 더 적게 쓸 테
　　니까요.

여: 다른 건요?

남: 어떤 걸 사기 전에 그게 정말 필요한지 스스로에게 세
　　번 물어보세요.

여: 알았어요. 노력해 볼게요.

남: 일주일 후에 다시 저에게 찾아오세요. 당신이 제 조언을
　　따르고 있는지 봐야 하니까요.

여: 감사합니다.

어휘

result[rizʌ́lt] 명 결과　shopaholic[ʃɑpəhɑ́lik] 명 쇼
핑 중독자　nervous[nə́ːrvəs] 형 초조한　control

[kəntróul] 통 억제하다 hobby[hábi] 명 취미
follow[fálou] 통 따르다 [문제] counselor[káunsələr]
명 상담자 owner[óunər] 명 소유주 host[houst] 명
사회자 channel[tʃǽnəl] 명 채널 carefully[kέərfəli]
부 주의 깊게

문제 해설
Q1: 남자의 직업은?
　남자는 여자의 쇼핑 중독 상태를 진단해주고, 여자에게
　조언을 해주고 있으므로 상담사임을 추측할 수 있다.

Q2: 남자의 조언을 모두 고르시오.
　ⓐ 신용카드를 사용하지 않도록 애써라.
　ⓑ 친구와 함께 쇼핑해라.
　ⓒ 새로운 취미를 찾아라.
　ⓓ 홈쇼핑 채널을 보지 마라.
　ⓔ 물건을 사기 전에 신중히 생각해라.

UNIT 10 Advice

Getting ★ Ready   p. 62

A 1 ⓒ 2 ⓑ 3 ⓐ   B 1 ⓑ 2 ⓐ
C 1 ⓐ 2 ⓔ 3 ⓒ

C 1 여: 너 컴퓨터 사용하는 일정을 세우는 게 어때?
　　　남: 알았어. 그렇게 해 봐야겠어.
　2 여: 무슨 일이야?
　　　남: 공부를 충분히 안 해서 걱정 돼.
　3 여: 왜 제가 그 학원에 다니는 걸 허락하지 않으세요?
　　　남: 네가 곧 흥미를 잃을 것 같아.

Listening ★ Start   p. 63

1 ④ / How do you feel, don't worry
2 ③ / This Saturday, I think, why don't you

1

W: Tomorrow is your first day of high school.
　How do you feel?
M: I'm nervous.
W: Why? What's the matter?
M: My friends all went to different schools. I
　won't know anyone.

W: Oh, don't worry. You'll make a lot of new
　friends soon.

여: 내일이 고등학교에서의 첫날이네. 기분 어때?
남: 긴장돼.
여: 왜? 무슨 문제 있어?
남: 내 친구들이 모두 다른 학교로 갔거든. 아는 사람이 아무
　도 없을 거야.
여: 아, 걱정 마. 곧 새 친구를 많이 사귈 거야.

어휘
nervous[nə́ːrvəs] 형 긴장 되는 anyone[éniwÀn] 대
누군가; *아무도 soon[suːn] 부 곧 [문제] fight[fait]
*명 싸움; 통 싸우다 subject[sÁbdʒikt] 명 과목

문제 해설
Q: 남자의 문제는 무엇인가?
　① 그는 친구와 싸웠다.
　② 그의 새로운 고등학교가 너무 멀리 떨어져 있다.
　③ 그는 많은 과목을 공부하는 것을 어려워한다.
　④ 그는 새로운 학교에 아는 사람이 없다.
　남자는 새 학교에 아는 사람이 아무도 없어 걱정하고 있다.

2

W: This Saturday is Valentine's Day. I need
　something for my boyfriend.
M: How about Christina Aguilera's new CD?
　He likes her songs.
W: Well, I think he already has it. And I want
　something more special.
M: Then, why don't you make him some
　cookies yourself? It's not very difficult.
W: That's a good idea.

여: 이번 토요일이 발렌타인 데이야. 남자 친구를 위해서 뭔
　가 필요한데.
남: Christina Aguilera의 새 CD는 어때? 그 애가 그 가수
　노래를 좋아하잖아.
여: 음, 그 애가 그걸 이미 가지고 있는 것 같아. 그리고 난
　뭔가 더 특별한 걸 원하는데.
남: 그럼, 네가 직접 쿠키를 좀 만들어 보는 게 어때? 그리
　어렵지 않잖아.
여: 좋은 생각이야.

어휘
Valentine's Day 발렌타인 데이 already[ɔːlrédi] 부
이미 cookie[kúki] 명 쿠키

문제 해설

Q: 여자는 남자 친구에게 어떤 선물을 주려고 하는가?

여자는 남자 친구에게 쿠키를 만들어 주기로 했다.

Listening ★ Practice   p. 64

1 (1) ⓒ (2) ⓐ (3) ⓑ   2 ③   3 ②   4 ②
5 ④   6 ④   7 (1) T (2) F (3) T   8 ②

1

W1: My name is Jane. Every day I study hard after school. But my school grades are still low.

M: I'm Tom. I'm shorter than most other students. How can I become taller?

W2: I'm Susan. I want to buy some new clothes. But my mom thinks I already have too many clothes, so she told me not to buy any.

여1: 내 이름은 Jane이야. 매일 나는 방과 후에 열심히 공부해. 하지만 학교 성적이 여전히 낮아.

남: 나는 Tom이야. 나는 대부분의 다른 학생들보다 키가 작아. 어떻게 하면 더 클 수 있을까?

여2: 나는 Susan이야. 나는 새 옷을 사고 싶어. 하지만 우리 엄마는 내가 이미 옷을 너무 많이 가지고 있다고 생각하셔서 나보고 아무것도 사지 말라고 하셨어.

어휘

grade[greid] 몡 성적   most[moust] 혱 대부분의
[문제] wish[wiʃ] *몡 바람, 소망; 똥 희망하다

문제 해설

Q: 각 인물과 그들의 소망을 연결하시오.

(1) Jane은 학교 성적이 낮아서 고민이므로 성적을 더 잘 받기를 원할 것이다.

(2) Tom은 키가 더 컸으면 한다.

(3) Susan은 새 옷을 사고 싶어 한다.

2

W: What's wrong?

M: I heard that Jack told lies about me to some other friends.

W: Really? But Jack is your best friend, isn't he?

M: Yes. I'm so angry at him.

W: Calm down. Why don't you talk with Jack about it?

M: Do you think I should?

W: Yes. Maybe he just made a mistake.

M: Okay. I'll do that.

여: 무슨 문제 있어?

남: Jack이 나에 대해서 몇몇 다른 친구들한테 거짓말했다고 들었어.

여: 정말? 하지만 Jack은 너랑 가장 친한 친구 아냐?

남: 응. 난 그 애한테 너무 화가 나.

여: 진정해. Jack이랑 그것에 대해서 얘기해 보는 게 어때?

남: 넌 내가 그렇게 해야 한다고 생각해?

여: 응. 어쩌면 그 애가 그냥 실수했을지도 모르잖아.

남: 알았어. 그렇게 할게.

어휘

tell a lie 거짓말하다   calm down 진정하다
maybe[méibi:] 뿐 아마도   make a mistake 실수하다   [문제] matter[mǽtər] 몡 문제, 일   explain
[ikspléin] 똥 설명하다

문제 해설

Q: 여자의 조언은?

① Jack에게 먼저 미안하다고 말해라.

② 새로운 친한 친구를 사귀어라.

③ Jack과 그 문제에 대해 이야기해라.

④ 다른 친구들에게 Jack이 거짓말했다고 설명해 줘라.

여자는 남자에게 Jack과 얘기해 보기를 권하고 있다.

3

M: I want to go to a Hilary Duff concert. All of my best friends will go there. But I don't have enough money for a ticket. My parents will not buy one for me. They don't like me going to concerts. I'm so sad.

남: 나는 Hilary Duff 콘서트에 가고 싶어요. 나랑 친한 친구들은 모두 거기에 갈 거예요. 하지만 나는 티켓을 살 충분한 돈이 없어요. 우리 부모님은 나에게 표를 사주지 않으실 거예요. 내가 콘서트에 가는 걸 좋아하지 않으시거든요. 난 너무 슬퍼요.

어휘

ticket[tíkit] 몡 표, 입장권   [문제] lose[lu:z] 똥 잃다
(lose-lost-lost)

문제 해설

Q: 남자의 문제는?

① 그는 콘서트 표를 잃어버렸다.

② 그에게 콘서트가 너무 비싸다.

③ 그의 부모님이 Hilary Duff를 좋아하지 않는다.

④ 그의 친구들이 그와 함께 콘서트에 가고 싶어하지 않는다.

남자는 Hilary Duff 콘서트에 가고 싶지만 표를 살 돈이 충분치 않다.

4

M: Are you ready for the trip?

W: Almost. But I'm worried about my puppy. I can't find anyone to look after him.

M: Why don't you ask your brother?

W: I already did. But he said no.

M: Well, I heard that there are hotels for dogs.

W: Really?

M: Yeah, people keep their dogs there during vacations.

W: In that case, I should search for puppy hotels on the Internet.

남: 여행 갈 준비는 됐니?

여: 거의. 근데 우리 강아지 때문에 걱정이야. 얘를 돌봐 줄 사람을 찾을 수가 없어.

남: 네 오빠에게 부탁해보는 게 어때?

여: 이미 그렇게 했지. 근데 싫대.

남: 음, 강아지들을 위한 호텔이 있다고 들었는데.

여: 정말?

남: 응. 휴가 때 사람들이 자기 개를 그곳에 맡긴대.

여: 그렇다면 인터넷에서 애견 호텔을 검색해 봐야겠어.

어휘

ready[rédi] 형 준비된 trip[trip] 명 여행 worried [wə́:rid] 형 걱정스러운 puppy[pʌ́pi] 명 강아지 look after ~을 돌보다 keep[ki:p] 동 보관하다 (keep-kept -kept) in that case 그렇다면 search for ~을 검색하다 [문제] probably[prάbəbli] 부 아마도

문제 해설

Q: 여자가 다음에 할 일은?

여자가 마지막에 인터넷에서 애견 호텔을 검색해 봐야겠다고 했다.

5

W: I feel terrible. I always fight with my brother about using the computer.

M: I understand. My family had a similar problem before.

W: Really? How did your family solve it?

M: We set a schedule for using the computer.

W: What do you mean?

M: For example, on Monday, I use the computer from six to eight. Then my sister uses it.

W: Wow, my family should try that, too.

여: 너무 기분 나빠. 우리 오빠랑 컴퓨터 사용하는 것 때문에 항상 싸워.

남: 나도 이해해. 우리 가족도 전에 비슷한 문제가 있었거든.

여: 정말? 너희 가족은 그걸 어떻게 해결했어?

남: 우린 컴퓨터 사용하는 일정을 만들었어.

여: 무슨 뜻이야?

남: 예를 들면, 월요일엔 내가 6시부터 8시까지 컴퓨터를 사용해. 그러고 나서 내 여동생이 사용하는 거지.

여: 우와, 우리 가족도 그렇게 해 봐야겠다.

어휘

terrible[térəbl] 형 끔찍한 similar[símələr] 형 비슷한 solve[salv] 동 해결하다 set a schedule 일정을 만들다 [문제] library[láibrèri] 명 도서관 weekend [wí:kènd] 명 주말

문제 해설

Q: 남자의 가족은 문제를 어떻게 해결했는가?

① 컴퓨터를 한 대 더 삼으로써

② 도서관에서 컴퓨터를 사용함으로써

③ 컴퓨터를 주말에만 이용함으로써

④ 컴퓨터를 사용하는 일정을 만듦으로써

남자의 가족은 컴퓨터를 사용하는 것에 대한 일정을 세웠다고 했다.

6

W: During the last English test, I saw Sally looking at Mary's paper. Cheating is wrong, so I told my teacher about it. Because of that, Sally is angry at me and doesn't want to talk to me. I don't want to lose my friend. What should I do?

여: 지난번 영어 시험을 칠 때 나는 Sally가 Mary의 시험지를 보는 걸 봤어. 부정 행위를 하는 건 잘못된 것이니까 나는 선생님께 그것에 대해 말씀드렸지. 그것 때문에 Sally는 나한테 화가 나서 나하고 말하고 싶어하지 않아. 나는 내 친구를 잃고 싶지 않아. 어떻게 해야 할까?

어휘
cheat[tʃiːt] 동 속이다, 부정 행위를 하다 [문제] bored
[bɔːrd] 형 지루한

문제 해설
Q: 현재 여자의 기분은?
여자는 Sally와의 관계 때문에 걱정하고 있다.

7

W: What's wrong? You look so sad.
M: I want to attend a dance academy, but my mom won't allow it.
W: Why not?
M: She thinks I'll lose interest after a short time.
W: Well, maybe she's right. You stopped going to swimming classes after two weeks.
M: That's true, but I really love dancing. I won't give up.
W: Then, how about joining a free dance club and learning there instead?
M: That sounds great!

여: 무슨 일이야? 너무 슬퍼 보여.
남: 난 댄스 학원에 다니고 싶은데 엄마가 허락하시질 않아.
여: 왜?
남: 엄마는 내가 금방 흥미를 잃을 거라고 생각하셔.
여: 음, 그분 말씀이 옳을지도 모르지. 넌 수영 강습도 2주 뒤에 그만뒀잖아.
남: 그건 사실이지만 정말 춤을 좋아한단 말이야. 포기 안 할 거야.
여: 그럼 대신에 무료 댄스 동호회에 가입해서 거기서 배워 보는 게 어때?
남: 좋아!

어휘
attend[əténd] 동 참석하다, 다니다   academy
[əkǽdəmi] 명 학원   allow[əláu] 동 허락하다
interest[íntərəst] 명 흥미   stop[stɑp] 동 멈추다
give up 포기하다   free[friː] 형 무료의

문제 해설
Q: 사실이면 T, 사실이 아니면 F에 ✓표 하시오.
 (1) 남자의 어머니는 그가 댄스 학원에 다니는 걸 원치 않는다.
 (2) 남자는 약 두 달 동안 수영 강습을 받았다.
 (3) 남자는 무료 댄스 동호회에 가입할 것이다.

8

M: ① 20 percent of teenagers talk to their mother.
 ② 10 percent of teenagers tell their father about their problems.
 ③ 60 percent of teenagers talk to their friends.
 ④ 15 percent of teenagers don't talk to anybody about their problems.

〈십대들이 그들의 문제를 이야기하는 사람〉
남: ① 십대 중 20퍼센트가 어머니에게 말을 한다.
 ② 십대 중 10퍼센트가 아버지에게 자신의 문제에 대해 이야기한다.
 ③ 십대 중 60퍼센트가 자신의 친구들에게 말을 한다.
 ④ 십대 중 15퍼센트가 자신의 문제에 대해 아무에게도 말하지 않는다.

어휘
teenager[tíːnèidʒər] 명 십대

문제 해설
Q: 아래 그래프에 관해 사실이 아닌 것은?
아버지에게 자신의 문제에 대해 이야기하는 십대는 5퍼센트이다.

Listening ★ Challenge p. 66

A 1 ① 2 ① B 1 ④ 2 ③

A [1-2]

W: Last summer, I visited the Vatican Museums in Rome. There were many famous paintings. But I liked the paintings by Michelangelo the most. They were amazing. Now I've decided to become an artist just like him. So, I want to enter a good art university. But I'm very worried because I'm somewhat late. I have only a year to prepare for the entrance exam. Can I do it?

여: 지난 여름에 나는 로마에 있는 바티칸 박물관을 방문했어요. 유명한 그림이 많이 있었지만 나는 미켈란젤로가 그린 그림이 가장 마음에 들었어요. 그것들은 정말 놀라웠거든요. 이제 나는 그와 같은 화가가 되기로 결심했어요. 그래서 나는 좋은 예술 대학교에 들어가고 싶어요.

하지만 내가 조금 늦었기 때문에 아주 걱정돼요. 입학 시험을 준비할 시간이 일 년밖에 남지 않아서요. 내가 할 수 있을까요?

어휘

museum[mju(ː)zí(ː)əm] 몡 박물관   Rome[roum] 몡 로마   painting[péintiŋ] 몡 그림   amazing[əméiziŋ] 혱 놀라운   decide[disáid] 동 결정하다, 결심하다   artist[áːrtist] 몡 예술가; *미술가   enter[éntər] 동 입학하다   somewhat[sʌ́mʰwʌ̀t] 뷔 다소, 약간   prepare [pripέər] 동 준비하다   entrance exam 입학 시험 [문제] painter[péintər] 몡 화가   musician[mju(ː)zíʃən] 몡 음악가   travel guide 여행 안내원   road[roud] 몡 길   lead[liːd] 동 지도하다; *이르게 하다   smoke [smouk] 몡 연기

문제 해설

Q1: 여자가 장래에 하고 싶어 하는 것은?

여자는 미켈란젤로와 같은 화가가 되고 싶다고 했다.

Q2: 여자에게 가장 좋은 조언을 골라라.

① 늦더라도 안 하는 것보다는 낫다.

② 모든 길은 로마로 통한다.

③ 혼자보다 여럿의 머리가 낫다.

④ 아니 땐 굴뚝에 연기날까.

여자는 대학 입학 시험을 준비할 시간이 얼마 안 남아서 걱정하고 있으므로, '늦더라도 안 하는 것보다는 낫다'라는 조언을 해주는 것이 적절할 것이다.

B [1-2]

W: Mark, I have a big problem.

M: What's the matter?

W: I promised Amy I would go shopping with her this Saturday. But then I forgot about it.

M: Today is only Wednesday. What's the problem?

W: I also promised my boyfriend I would go to a movie with him on the same day.

M: Oh, so what are you going to do?

W: I don't know.

M: Tell your boyfriend that you forgot about your plan with Amy. He'll understand.

W: Okay. I'll ask him to see a movie on Sunday instead.

여: Mark, 나 큰 문제가 생겼어.

남: 무슨 문제야?

여: 이번 토요일에 Amy랑 쇼핑하러 가기로 약속했는데, 그러고 나서 그걸 잊어버렸어.

남: 오늘은 수요일밖에 안됐잖아. 뭐가 문제야?

여: 같은 날에 남자 친구랑 영화 보러 가기로 또 약속해 버렸어.

남: 아, 그래서 넌 어떻게 할 건데?

여: 모르겠어.

남: 네 남자 친구한테 네가 Amy와 계획한 걸 잊어버렸다고 얘기해. 그 애도 이해할 거야.

여: 알았어. 대신 남자 친구한테 일요일에 영화 보러 가자고 해야겠어.

어휘

promise[prámis] 동 약속하다   forget[fərgét] 동 잊다 (forget-forgot-forgotten)   instead[instéd] 뷔 대신에

문제 해설

Q1: 여자의 문제는 무엇인가?

① 그녀는 남자 친구와 크게 싸웠다.

② 그녀는 Amy와 쇼핑을 하러 가길 원하지 않는다.

③ Amy와 그녀의 남자 친구가 서로 좋아하지 않는다.

④ 그녀는 같은 날에 두 개의 다른 계획을 잡았다.

여자는 토요일에 Amy와 약속한 것을 잊어버리고 남자 친구와도 약속을 잡아버렸다.

Q2: 토요일에 여자는 무엇을 할 것인가?

남자 친구와의 약속을 미루기로 했으므로 Amy와 약속한 대로 쇼핑하러 갈 것이다.

Critical ★ Thinking   p. 67

1 (1) T (2) F (3) F   2 (1) ⓒ (2) ⓐ

M1: My girlfriend wants me to lose weight. She thinks I'm too fat, but I don't think I am. Anne, what do you think?

W: Chris, she's your girlfriend. If you really love her, you should follow her advice. Also, it is healthy to lose weight. How about you, Alex?

M2: I disagree with you, Anne. Chris, you don't need to lose weight. If she loves you, she should accept you just as you are. If she can't, then she doesn't really love you.

남1: 내 여자 친구는 내가 몸무게를 줄이기를 원해. 그 애는 내가 너무 뚱뚱하다고 생각하지만 난 그렇다고 생각하지 않거든. Anne, 넌 어떻게 생각해?

여: Chris, 그 애는 네 여자 친구야. 네가 정말 그 애를 사랑한다면 넌 그 애의 조언을 따라야지. 또, 몸무게를 줄이는 게 건강에 좋잖아. Alex, 넌 어떻게 생각해?

남2: Anne, 난 너랑 의견이 달라. Chris, 넌 몸무게를 줄일 필요가 없어. 그 애가 너를 사랑한다면 너를 있는 그대로 받아줘야지. 그 애가 그럴 수 없다면 그 애는 너를 정말 사랑하는 게 아니야.

어휘

lose weight 몸무게를 줄이다　fat[fæt] 형 뚱뚱한
follow[fálou] 동 따르다　healthy[hélθi] 형 건강한;
*건강에 좋은　disagree[dìsəgríː] 동 의견이 다르다
accept[əksépt] 동 받아들이다　[문제] be on a diet
다이어트를 하다, 식이 요법을 하다

문제 해설

Q1: 사실이면 T, 사실이 아니면 F에 ✓표 하시오.
　(1) Chris는 그가 뚱뚱하다고 생각하지 않는다.
　(2) Chris는 다이어트 중이다.
　(3) Chris는 자신의 여자 친구가 자신을 사랑하지 않을까 봐 걱정한다.

Q2: 각 인물과 그들의 의견을 연결하시오.
　ⓐ Chris의 여자 친구는 그를 있는 그대로 사랑해야 한다.
　ⓑ Chris는 여자 친구에게 자신이 살을 빼는 걸 도와달라고 부탁해야 한다.
　ⓒ Chris가 자신의 여자 친구를 사랑한다면 살을 빼도록 노력해야 한다.
　(1) Anne은 Chris가 여자 친구를 사랑한다면 그녀의 조언을 따라야 한다고 했다.
　(2) Alex는 Chris의 여자 친구가 Chris를 사랑한다면 Chris를 있는 그대로 받아줘야 한다고 했다.

UNIT 11 Boys & Girls

Getting ★ Ready　p. 68

A 1 ⓕ　2 ⓒ　3 ⓐ　4 ⓔ　5 ⓖ
B 1 ⓔ　2 ⓐ　3 ⓓ

B 1 여: 소개팅 어땠어?
　　남: 그다지 좋진 않았어. 그 애는 내 타입같지 않아.
　2 여: 넌 남자여서 좋니?
　　남: 아니. 내가 여자이면 좋겠어.
　3 여: 넌 네 첫사랑이 그립니?
　　남: 응. 그 애를 절대 못 잊을 거야.

Listening ★ Start　p. 69

1 (1) Good　(2) Bad / my type, see a movie, pay for
2 ④ / grow up, change your mind, like cooking

1

W: I'm Alice. When I first saw him, I didn't think he was my type. But when we talked, I thought he was very kind. We're going to see a movie this Sunday.
M: I'm Jim. I saw a movie and had dinner with a pretty girl today. But she wouldn't pay for anything. I don't want to see her again.

여: 나는 Alice야. 내가 그를 처음 봤을 때 그가 내 타입이라고 생각하진 않았어. 하지만 얘기를 해보고 나는 그가 아주 친절하다고 생각했어. 이번 일요일에 우린 영화를 보러 갈 거야.
남: 나는 Jim이야. 오늘 예쁜 여자애랑 영화를 보고 저녁을 먹었어. 하지만 그 애는 어떤 것에도 돈을 내지 않았어. 나는 그 애를 다시는 만나고 싶지 않아.

어휘

type[taip] 명 유형; *~타입의 사람　pay[pei] 동 지불하다　[문제] blind date 소개팅

문제 해설

Q: 각 소개팅의 결과에 동그라미 하시오.
　(1) 소개팅한 남자에 대한 첫 인상은 좋지 않았지만 얘기하면서 호감을 가지게 되었다.
　(2) 소개팅한 여자가 돈을 전혀 내지 않아서 불쾌해 하고 있다.

2

W: What do you want to be when you grow up?
M: Well, when I was young, I wanted to be a painter.
W: Did you change your mind?
M: Yes. Now I want to be a homemaker like my mom.
W: Really? That's interesting.
M: I just like cooking and cleaning.

여: 넌 커서 뭐가 되고 싶니?

남: 음, 어렸을 땐 화가가 되고 싶었지.

여: 마음이 바뀌었어?

남: 응. 지금은 우리 엄마와 같은 주부가 되고 싶어.

여: 정말? 흥미로운 걸.

남: 난 그냥 요리하고 청소하는 게 좋아.

어휘

grow up 자라다 **painter**[péintər] 몡 화가 **mind**
[maind] 몡 마음 **homemaker**[hóummèikər] 몡 주부,
전업 남편 **cook**[kuk] *동 요리하다; 몡 요리사
clean[kli:n] 동 청소하다 [문제] **engineer**[èndʒəníər]
몡 기술자 **househusband**[háushʌ̀zbənd] 몡 전업 남편

문제 해설

Q: 남자는 장래에 무엇이 되고 싶어 하는가?

　엄마와 같은 주부가 되고 싶다고 했다.

Listening ★ Practice p. 70

1 ④　2 ④　3 (1) Likes (2) Doesn't like
(3) Doesn't like　4 ④　5 ②　6 ①　7 ②
8 (1) F (2) T (3) F

1

M: Hi, I'm looking for some baby clothes.

W: Is the baby a boy or a girl?

M: It's a girl.

W: How about this pink dress?

M: It's cute, but I don't like pink. I don't know
　why a girl should wear pink clothes.

W: I see. Then what about the blue or yellow
　one?

M: I'll take the yellow one.

남: 안녕하세요. 전 아기 옷을 찾고 있어요.

여: 남자 아기예요, 여자 아기예요?

남: 여자애예요.

여: 이 분홍색 원피스는 어때요?

남: 귀엽긴 한데 전 분홍색을 안 좋아해요. 왜 여자애는 분
　홍색을 입어야 하는지 모르겠어요.

여: 알겠어요. 그럼 파란색이나 노란색 옷은 어때요?

남: 노란색 옷으로 할게요.

어휘

clothes[klouðz] 몡 옷 **cute**[kju:t] 혱 귀여운

문제 해설

Q: 남자가 사려고 하는 것은?

　남자는 노란색 옷을 사겠다고 했다.

2

M: Why are you upset?

W: Don't you know why?

M: I have no idea. Is it because I don't call
　you often?

W: No, it isn't. I know you're busy these days.

M: Then what's the reason?

W: What date is it today?

M: Today is the 6th of October. Why are you
　asking?

W: Teddy! How can you forget my birthday?

M: Oh, no! I'm so sorry.

남: 왜 화가 난 거야?

여: 왜 그런지 모르겠어?

남: 전혀 모르겠어. 내가 전화를 자주 안 해서 그러는 거야?

여: 아니, 그런 건 아니야. 네가 요즘 바쁜 거 아니까.

남: 그럼 이유가 뭐야?

여: 오늘이 며칠이지?

남: 오늘은 10월 6일이지. 왜 물어보는데?

여: Teddy! 너 어떻게 내 생일을 잊을 수가 있니?

남: 아, 이런! 정말 미안해.

어휘

upset[ʌpsét] 혱 화가 난 **often**[ɔ́(:)fən] 뷔 자주, 종종
these days 요즘 **reason**[rí:zən] 몡 이유 **October**
[aktóubər] 몡 10월 [문제] **express**[iksprés] 동 표현하다

문제 해설

Q: 여자가 남자에게 화가 난 이유는?

　① 그는 너무 바쁘다.

　② 그는 그녀에게 자주 전화를 하지 않는다.

　③ 그는 사랑을 표현하지 않는다.

　④ 그는 그녀의 생일을 기억하지 못했다.

　오늘이 여자의 생일인데 남자가 잊어서 화가 났다.

3

M1: I'm Sam. Every morning, my sister takes
　two hours to get ready. But it takes me
　only twenty minutes. I'm glad I'm a boy!

M2: I'm Bill. I'm interested in fashion. But
　there isn't a big enough variety of clothes
　for boys. I really envy girls.

M3: I'm Jack. I think my parents care more about my sister because she's a girl. I wish I were a girl.

남1: 나는 Sam이야. 매일 아침 내 여동생은 준비하는 데 두 시간이 걸려. 하지만 나는 20분밖에 안 걸리지. 나는 내가 남자라서 좋아!

남2: 나는 Bill이야. 나는 패션에 관심이 있어. 하지만 남자애들 옷은 종류가 충분히 다양하지가 않아. 나는 여자애들이 정말 부러워.

남3: 나는 Jack이야. 내 생각에 우리 부모님께서는 내 여동생이 여자애라서 더 신경을 쓰시는 것 같아. 나는 내가 여자이면 좋겠어.

어휘

be interested in ~에 흥미가 있다   a variety of 갖가지   envy[énvi] ⑧ 질투하다, 부러워하다   care about ~에 마음쓰다, ~에 관심을 가지다

문제 해설

Q: 각 인물이 남자인 것을 좋아하는지, 싫어하는지 ✓표 하시오.

(1) Sam은 여동생보다 자신이 외출 준비를 하는 데 시간이 훨씬 적게 걸려서 남자라는 점을 좋게 생각한다.

(2) Bill은 남자 옷이 다양하지 않아서 여자를 부러워한다.

(3) Jack은 부모님이 여동생에게 더 신경 쓰시는 것 같아서 자신이 여자였으면 한다.

4

W: I'm 165 cm tall and my weight is 55 kg. I don't think I'm fat. But when my friend Rio heard my weight, he said I was fat. I guess boys don't know about girls' average weight. They only know the weight of thin actresses.

여: 내 키는 165cm이고 몸무게는 55kg이야. 나는 내가 뚱뚱하다고 생각하지 않아. 하지만 내 친구 Rio가 내 몸무게를 듣고 나보고 뚱뚱하다고 말했어. 남자애들은 여자애들의 평균 몸무게를 모르는 것 같아. 그들은 마른 여배우들의 몸무게만 알고 있어.

어휘

weight[weit] ⑲ 몸무게   average[ǽvəridʒ] ⑲ 평균의   actress[ǽktris] ⑲ 여배우   [문제] healthy[hélθi] ⑲ 건강한   diet[dáiət] ⑲ 식단   normal[nɔ́ːrməl] ⑲ 표준의; *평균의

문제 해설

Q: 이야기의 주제는?

① 건강한 식단이 중요하다.

② 대부분의 여배우들은 너무 말랐다.

③ 모든 사람은 어떤 면에서 아름답다.

④ 남자애들은 여자애들의 평균 몸무게를 모른다.

남자애들이 여자애들의 평균 몸무게를 잘 모르는 것 같다는 얘기를 하고 있다.

5

W: Is it true that boys don't forget their first love?

M: I think it is. I still miss my first girlfriend.

W: Really? I didn't know that.

M: Don't you miss your first love?

W: No, I don't. He is just a part of my past.

M: Wow, that's quite surprising.

W: I only care about my present boyfriend.

여: 남자는 첫사랑을 잊지 못한다는 게 사실이야?

남: 그런 것 같아. 난 내 첫 여자 친구가 아직도 그리워.

여: 정말? 난 몰랐는데.

남: 넌 네 첫사랑이 그립지 않니?

여: 아니, 그렇지 않아. 그는 내 과거의 일부일 뿐이야.

남: 우와, 그거 꽤 놀라운데.

여: 나는 내 현재의 남자 친구만 신경 써.

어휘

miss[mis] ⑧ 그리워하다   part[pɑːrt] ⑲ 부분   past[pæst] ⑲ 과거   quite[kwait] ⑨ 꽤   surprising[sərpráiziŋ] ⑲ 놀라운   present[prézənt] ⑲ 현재의

문제 해설

Q: 여자와 같은 의견을 가진 사람은?

① Iris: 여자애들은 첫사랑을 잊지 못해.

② Helen: 내 현재의 사랑만이 중요해.

③ Tina: 여자애들은 마지막 사랑을 잊지 못해.

여자는 현재의 사랑에 충실하므로 Helen과 의견이 같다.

6

M: Today I went shopping with my girlfriend. She tried on almost every blouse in the department store. But she didn't buy anything because she couldn't find a good one. Can you believe it? It took four hours to buy nothing! I won't go shopping with her again.

61

남: 오늘 나의 여자 친구와 쇼핑을 하러 갔어. 그 애는 백화 점에 있는 거의 모든 블라우스를 입어 봤어. 하지만 그 애 는 괜찮은 걸 찾지 못해서 아무것도 사지 않았어. 믿겨져? 아무것도 사지 않는 데 4시간이 걸린 거야! 다시는 그 애 와 쇼핑하러 가지 않을 거야.

어휘

try on 입어보다 almost[ɔ́ːlmoust] ⒝ 거의 blouse [blaus] ⒨ 블라우스 department store 백화점 believe[bilíːv] ⒟ 믿다

문제 해설

Q: 현재 남자의 심정은?
남자는 여자 친구가 네 시간 동안 쇼핑하고 아무것도 사 지 않아서 화가 났다.

7

M: I like Donna, but she doesn't know.
W: Why don't you tell her your feelings?
M: You know I'm shy.
W: Then just start by making small talk by text message.
M: Small talk?
W: Yes, like asking about homework.
M: That's a good idea. I'll send her a text message right now.

남: 나는 Donna가 좋은데 그 애는 몰라.
여: 그 애한테 네 감정을 얘기하지 그래?
남: 나 수줍음 많은 거 알잖아.
여: 그럼 문자 메시지로 가벼운 이야기를 하는 걸로 시작해 봐.
남: 가벼운 이야기?
여: 응. 숙제에 대해서 물어본다든지 말이야.
남: 좋은 생각이야. 지금 바로 그 애한테 문자 메시지를 보내 야겠어.

어휘

feeling[fíːliŋ] ⒨ 감정 small talk 가벼운 대화. 잡담 text message 문자 메시지

문제 해설

Q: 남자가 보낼 문자 메시지로 맞는 것을 고르시오.
여자가 숙제를 물어보는 것과 같은 가벼운 이야기로 시작 해 보라고 조언을 해주었다.

8

W: Finally, Johnny Gray's third book has come out! The title is *Understanding*. It's about

the differences between men and women. It explains the reasons for those differences. This book will help couples have better relationships. You can buy it from October 12th.

여: 드디어 Johnny Gray의 세 번째 책이 나왔습니다! 제목 은 〈Understanding〉입니다. 그것은 남자와 여자의 차 이점에 관한 내용입니다. 그것은 그러한 차이점이 생기 는 이유를 설명해주고 있습니다. 이 책은 연인들이 더 좋 은 관계를 가질 수 있도록 도와줄 것입니다. 10월 12일부 터 구매할 수 있습니다.

어휘

finally[fáinəli] ⒝ 드디어. 마침내 title[táitl] ⒨ 제목 difference[dífərəns] ⒨ 차이점 explain[ikspléin] ⒟ 설명하다 relationship[riléiʃənʃip] ⒨ 관계

문제 해설

Q: 〈Understanding〉이라는 책에 관해 사실이면 T, 사실이 아니면 F를 쓰시오.
(1) 그것은 Johnny Gray의 첫 번째 책이다.
(2) 그것은 남자와 여자가 다른 이유에 관한 것이다.
(3) 그것은 10월 20일부터 판매될 것이다.
〈Understanding〉은 Johnny Gray의 세 번째 책이고, 남자와 여자의 차이점이 왜 존재하는지 설명해주고 있다. 이 책은 10월 12일부터 사볼 수 있다고 했다.

Listening ★ Challenge p. 72

A 1 ② 2 ③ B 1 ④ 2 ③

A [1-2]

M: Valentine's Day is only a couple of days away. So, today's *Challenge Show* will have lots of questions about Valentine's Day. Here's the first question. If you get the correct answer, you'll get 10 points. Listen carefully. This is one of the most popular gifts for Valentine's Day. It is usually in a glass bottle. It smells like flowers or fruit. You can buy this in a cosmetics store. What is this?

남: 발렌타인 데이가 이틀밖에 남지 않았습니다. 그래서 오 늘의 'Challenge Show'에서는 발렌타인 데이에 관한 질문이 많을 것입니다. 첫 번째 질문입니다. 정답을 맞히

시면 10점을 얻게 됩니다. 주의해서 들어주시기 바랍니다. 이것은 가장 인기 있는 발렌타인 데이 선물 중 하나입니다. 그것은 보통 유리병에 들어 있습니다. 그것은 꽃이나 과일 향이 납니다. 여러분은 이것을 화장품 가게에서 사실 수 있습니다. 이것은 무엇입니까?

어휘

a couple of 둘의   **question**[kwéstʃən] 몡 질문
correct[kərékt] 혱 옳은, 정확한   **point**[pɔint] 몡 점수
glass[glæs] 혱 유리의   **bottle**[bátl] 몡 병   **fruit**[fruːt]
몡 과일   **cosmetics**[kɑzmétiks] 몡 화장품   [문제]
newscast[njúːzkæst] 몡 뉴스 방송

문제 해설

Q1: 이것은 어떤 종류의 프로그램인가?

퀴즈가 나오고, 정답을 맞히면 10점을 얻게 된다고 했으므로 퀴즈 프로그램임을 짐작할 수 있다.

Q2: 퀴즈 문제의 정답은?

유리병에 들어 있고 꽃이나 과일 향이 난다고 했으며 화장품 가게에서 살 수 있다고 했으므로 정답은 '향수'임을 알 수 있다.

B [1-2]

W: Danny, I had a fight with my boyfriend.

M: Why?

W: He was acting too nice to other girls. I didn't like that.

M: But he's just a kind person, isn't he? Everybody knows that he only loves you.

W: That's true. Maybe I made a mistake.

M: Why don't you say sorry to him with a little present?

W: What kind of present?

M: How about a comic book? He really likes those.

W: Well, that's not romantic enough.

M: Then... how about a photo album with pictures of you both?

W: Good idea!

여: Danny, 나 남자 친구랑 싸웠어.

남: 왜?

여: 그가 다른 여자애들한테 너무 친절하게 행동해서. 난 그게 싫었어.

남: 하지만 그는 그냥 친절한 사람이잖아, 그렇지 않아? 그가 너만 사랑한다는 건 모두가 다 알아.

여: 그건 맞아. 내가 실수한 것 같아.

남: 작은 선물과 함께 그에게 미안하다고 하는 게 어때?

여: 어떤 선물?

남: 만화책은 어때? 그는 그것들을 아주 좋아하잖아.

여: 글쎄, 그건 별로 낭만적이지 않은데.

남: 그럼… 너희 두 사람의 사진이 들어 있는 사진 앨범은 어때?

여: 좋은 생각이야!

어휘

act[ækt] 동 행동하다   **other**[ʌ́ðər] 혱 다른   **comic book** 만화책   **romantic**[rouméntik] 혱 낭만적인
photo album 사진 앨범   [문제] **lie**[lai] 몡 거짓말
keep a promise 약속을 지키다   **friendly**[fréndli] 혱
정다운, 친절한   **wallet**[wɑ́lit] 몡 지갑

문제 해설

Q1: 여자가 남자 친구와 싸운 이유는?

① 그는 그녀에게 거짓말을 했다.

② 그는 다른 여자 친구가 있다.

③ 그는 약속을 지키지 않았다.

④ 그가 다른 여자애들에게 다정하게 대했다.

여자는 남자 친구가 다른 여자들에게 너무 친절하게 행동하는 게 마음에 들지 않았다고 했다.

Q2: 여자가 남자 친구에게 줄 것은?

두 사람의 사진이 들어있는 사진 앨범을 주려고 한다.

Critical ★ Thinking   p. 73

1 ③   2 ①

W: Jeff, I'm going to have dinner with Jason tomorrow.

M: Again? Why do you see him so often?

W: Last Saturday was his birthday. And I haven't given him a present yet.

M: Amy, I can't take it anymore. I don't like you seeing him.

W: What? He's my best friend.

M: In my opinion, boys and girls can't be just friends.

W: We've been friends for ten years. He's just like my own brother.

M: But nobody knows what will happen between you and him.

W: I can't believe it! Don't you trust me?

여: Jeff, 난 내일 Jason이랑 저녁 먹을 거야.

남: 또? 너 그를 왜 그렇게 자주 만나니?

여: 지난 토요일이 그의 생일이었어. 그리고 아직 그에게 선물을 못 줬거든.

남: Amy, 난 더 이상 참을 수가 없어. 난 네가 그를 만나는 게 마음에 안 들어.

여: 뭐라구? 그는 나랑 가장 친한 친구잖아.

남: 내 생각엔 남자랑 여자는 그냥 친구가 될 수 없어.

여: 우린 10년 동안 친구로 지냈어. 그는 그냥 내 남동생 같아.

남: 하지만 너랑 그 애 사이에 무슨 일이 일어날지 아무도 몰라.

여: 말도 안돼! 넌 날 못 믿겠니?

어휘

not ~ anymore 더 이상 ~ 않다　in my opinion 내 생각에는　happen[hǽpən] 동 일어나다　between A and B A와 B 사이에　trust[trʌst] 동 믿다; 명 신뢰 [문제] argue[áːrgjuː] 동 논쟁하다　friendship[fréndʃip] 명 우정

문제 해설

Q1: 두 사람은 무엇에 대해 논쟁하고 있는가?

① 진정한 우정은 무엇인가?

② 남자애들이 여자애들에게 원하는 것이 무엇인가?

③ 남자애들과 여자애들이 단순히 친구가 될 수 있는가?

④ 신뢰가 연인에게 왜 중요한가?

여자는 자신과 Jason이 친구 사이라고 생각하지만 남자는 남녀가 친구가 될 수 없다고 생각한다.

Q2: Amy가 내일 Jason을 만나고자 하는 이유는?

① 그에게 생일 선물을 주려고

② 그녀의 남자 친구에 관해 조언을 얻으려고

③ 그를 더 이상 만나지 않겠다고 말하려고

④ 함께 생일 파티를 위한 물건들을 사려고

아직 생일 선물을 못 줬다고 했으므로 생일 선물을 주기 위해 만나려는 것임을 알 수 있다.

UNIT 12 Jobs

Getting ★ Ready　p. 74

A 1 ⓓ　2 ⓐ　3 ⓔ　4 ⓑ　5 ⓒ

B 1 ⓔ　2 ⓐ　3 ⓒ

B 1 여: 넌 장래에 무엇을 하고 싶니?

남: 난 뉴스 리포터가 되고 싶어.

2 여: 당신은 무슨 일을 하시나요?

남: 저는 비행기 승무원입니다.

3 여: 넌 왜 수의사가 되었니?

남: 동물들을 도울 수 있는 걸 하고 싶었어.

Listening ★ Start　p. 75

1 ② / works at, choose the correct wine, good wines

2 ④ / Long time no see, What do you do, work as

1

M: Do you know what a sommelier does? A sommelier works at a restaurant. He or she knows a lot about wine. He or she helps customers choose the correct wine for their food. He or she also chooses and buys good wines for the restaurant.

남: 소믈리에가 하는 일이 뭔지 아세요? 소믈리에는 음식점에서 일해요. 소믈리에는 와인에 대해서 많이 알고 있죠. 소믈리에는 손님들이 그들의 음식에 맞는 와인을 선택하도록 도와줍니다. 소믈리에는 그 음식점을 위해 좋은 와인을 선택해서 구매하기도 해요.

어휘

sommelier[sàməljéi] 명 소믈리에, 포도주 담당 웨이터　wine[wain] 명 와인, 포도주　customer[kʌ́stəmər] 명 고객　choose[tʃuːz] 동 선택하다 (choose–chose–chosen)

문제 해설

Q: 남자가 소개하고 있는 직업을 고르시오.

소믈리에는 레스토랑에서 와인을 담당하는 직원이다.

2

W: Harry! Long time no see.

M: Lisa! It's great to see you again.

W: Do you still work at the fire station in Chicago?

M: Yes. What do you do? I heard that you work at a bank.

W: I did. But I changed my job. Now I work as a travel writer.

M: That's nice.

여: Harry! 오랜만이야.

남: Lisa! 다시 만나서 반가워.

여: 너 아직 시카고에 있는 소방서에서 일해?

남: 응. 넌 무슨 일을 해? 네가 은행에서 일한다고 들었는데.

여: 그랬지. 근데 직업을 바꿨어. 지금은 여행 작가로 일해.

남: 멋지구나.

어휘

Long time no see. 오랜만이야. fire station 소방서
bank[bæŋk] 몡 은행 writer[ráitər] 몡 작가 [문제]
firefighter[fáiərfàitər] 몡 소방관 police officer 경
찰관 bank clerk 은행원

문제 해설

Q: 여자의 직업은?

여자는 현재 여행 작가로 일한다고 했다.

Listening ★ Practice p. 76

1 (1) ⓐ (2) ⓒ (3) ⓑ 2 ③ 3 ③ 4 ②
5 (1) ⓐ, ⓓ (2) ⓒ 6 ① 7 ④ 8 ⓓ → ⓒ → ⓑ

1

W1: I'm Nancy. I help couples prepare their wedding day. I give them information about wedding halls, dress shops, and photographers.

W2: I'm Rebecca. I look after people on a plane. I serve them food and drinks.

W3: I'm Maria. I write songs. I feel happy when people love my songs.

여1: 나는 Nancy야. 나는 연인들이 결혼식을 준비하는 걸 도와. 나는 그들에게 결혼식장과 드레스 가게와 사진 작가에 대한 정보를 줘.

여2: 나는 Rebecca야. 나는 비행기에서 사람들을 돌보지. 나는 그들에게 음식과 음료를 제공해.

여3: 나는 Maria야. 나는 작곡을 해. 나는 사람들이 나의 노래를 좋아하면 행복해.

어휘

prepare[pripέər] 동 준비하다 information
[ìnfərméiʃən] 몡 정보 photographer[fətágrəfər] 몡
사진작가 look after ~ ~을 돌보다 serve[səːrv] 동
제공하다

문제 해설

Q: 각 인물의 직업을 고르시오.

(1) Nancy는 결혼식 준비를 도와준다고 했다.

(2) Rebecca는 비행기에서 사람들을 돌본다고 했다.

(3) Maria는 작곡을 한다고 했다.

2

M: What would you like to do in the future?

W: I'd like to open my own restaurant.

M: Your own restaurant? Why? Are you interested in cooking?

W: Yes, but that's not the main reason.

M: Then, what is it?

W: I think that most restaurant owners have a lot of free time.

남: 넌 장래에 뭘 하고 싶니?

여: 난 나의 음식점을 열고 싶어.

남: 네 소유의 음식점? 왜? 너 요리에 관심 있니?

여: 응. 하지만 그게 주된 이유는 아니야.

남: 그럼 그게 뭔데?

여: 내 생각에 대부분의 음식점 주인은 여가 시간이 많은 것 같아서.

어휘

open[óupən] 동 열다 own[oun] 형 자기 자신의
be interested in ~에 관심이 있다 main[mein] 형
주된 owner[óunər] 몡 주인, 소유주 [문제] run[rʌn]
동 달리다; *운영하다

문제 해설

Q: 여자가 음식점을 열고 싶어 하는 주된 이유는?

① 그녀는 요리하는 걸 좋아한다.

② 그녀는 돈을 많이 벌고 싶어 한다.

③ 그녀는 여가 시간을 많이 갖길 원한다.

④ 그녀의 부모님이 아주 유명한 음식점을 운영한다.

여자는 대부분의 음식점 주인이 여가 시간이 많은 것 같아서 음식점을 차리고 싶어 한다.

3

M: What do you want to be in the future?

W: I want to become a singer. But I don't think I can.

M: Why not? You're good at singing.

W: I'm very shy. I can't sing in front of lots of people.

M: Practice singing in front of people whenever you can. Then you won't feel shy anymore.

W: Okay, I'll try it.

65

남: 넌 장래에 뭐가 되고 싶니?

여: 난 가수가 되고 싶어. 하지만 될 수 있을 것 같지 않아.

남: 왜? 너 노래 잘 하잖아.

여: 난 수줍음이 아주 많아. 난 많은 사람 앞에서 노래를 못 하겠어.

남: 가능할 때마다 사람들 앞에서 노래하는 걸 연습해봐. 그럼 더 이상 부끄럽지 않게 될 거야.

여: 알았어, 그렇게 해 볼게.

어휘

be good at ~를 잘하다   shy[ʃai] 혱 수줍은   in front of ~ ~의 앞에서   practice[præktis] 동 연습하다   whenever[hwenévər] 접 ~할 때마다   anymore [ènimɔ́ːr] 부 더 이상   [문제] experience[ikspí(:)əriəns] 명 경험

문제 해설

Q: 남자의 조언은?

　① 노래 동호회에 가입해라.

　② 노래하는 데 시간을 더 많이 써라.

　③ 사람들 앞에서 노래를 자주 해라.

　④ 다양한 경험을 많이 해라.

사람들 앞에서 노래 연습을 자주 해 보라고 했다.

4

(Telephone rings.)

W: Hello, this is the Beijing Garden Restaurant.

M: Hello. I heard you're looking for a cook.

W: Oh, yes. Do you have any experience?

M: Well, I worked at a Chinese restaurant for six months.

W: Is that all?

M: Well, I took Chinese cooking classes for a year.

W: Um, I'm sorry. I'm afraid we want a cook with more experience than that.

M: Okay, I understand.

(전화벨이 울린다.)

여: 여보세요. Beijing Garden 음식점입니다.

남: 여보세요. 거기서 요리사를 구하고 있다고 들었는데요.

여: 아, 네. 경험은 있나요?

남: 음, 중국 음식점에서 6개월 동안 일했어요.

여: 그게 다인가요?

남: 저, 중국 요리 수업을 일 년 동안 들었어요.

여: 음, 죄송해요. 유감이지만 저희는 그것보다 경험이 더 많은 요리사를 원해요.

남: 네, 잘 알겠어요.

어휘

Chinese[tʃainíːz] 혱 중국의   I'm afraid (that) 유감이지만   [문제] order[ɔ́ːrdər] 동 주문하다   sign up for ~에 등록하다   make a reservation 예약하다

문제 해설

Q: 남자가 여자에게 전화한 이유는?

　① 중국 음식을 주문하려고

　② 음식점에서 일을 구하려고

　③ 요리 수업에 등록하려고

　④ 저녁 식사 예약을 하려고

남자는 음식점에서 요리사를 구한다는 말을 듣고 전화했다.

5

M: I'm a barista. I make drinks at a coffeehouse. It's a very cool job because I can taste many kinds of coffee. Also, it's fun and interesting to meet new people. But it's a hard job because I have to stand up all day long.

남: 나는 바리스타야. 나는 커피숍에서 음료를 만들어. 많은 종류의 커피를 맛볼 수 있기 때문에 아주 멋진 직업이지. 게다가 새로운 사람들을 만나는 것은 재미있고 흥미로워. 하지만 하루 종일 서 있어야 하기 때문에 힘든 일이야.

어휘

barista[bərístə] 명 바리스타   coffeehouse [kɔ́(ː)fihàus] 명 커피숍   cool[kuːl] 혱 멋진   taste[teist] 동 맛보다   hard[hɑːrd] 혱 힘든   all day long 하루 종일   [문제] various[vɛ́(ː)əriəs] 혱 다양한   headache [hédèik] 명 두통   strong[strɔ(ː)ŋ] 혱 강한

문제 해설

Q: 자신의 직업에 대한 남자의 의견을 고르시오.

　ⓐ 다양한 종류의 커피를 마실 수 있다.

　ⓑ 돈을 많이 번다.

　ⓒ 서서 많은 시간을 보낸다.

　ⓓ 다양한 사람을 많이 만난다.

　ⓔ 강한 냄새 때문에 두통이 생긴다.

다양한 커피를 맛볼 수 있고 새로운 사람들을 만날 수 있다는 점은 좋지만 종일 서 있어야 하는 점은 힘들다고 했다.

6

W: Joe, why did you become an animal doctor?

M: I love animals so much. I wanted to do something to help them.

W: Wow. You found the perfect job, then.

M: You're right. But I'm not always happy with my job.

W: Really? When are you unhappy with it?

M: Sometimes, when animals are too old or sick, I cannot help them. That makes me feel sad.

여: Joe, 넌 왜 수의사가 됐니?

남: 난 동물을 아주 사랑하거든. 난 동물들을 도울 수 있는 걸 하고 싶었어.

여: 우와. 넌 그럼 완벽한 일을 찾은 거네.

남: 맞아. 하지만 나의 직업이 항상 만족스러운 건 아니야.

여: 정말? 언제 불만족스러운데?

남: 때로는 동물들이 너무 나이가 들었거나 아파서 내가 그들을 도와줄 수가 없어. 그런 것 때문에 슬퍼.

어휘

animal[ǽnəməl] 똉 동물   perfect[pə́:rfikt] 쭹 완벽한
sometimes[sʌ́mtàimz] 봄 때때로   [문제] cure[kjuər]
됭 치료하다   behave[bihéiv] 됭 행동하다   badly
[bǽdli] 봄 나쁘게   rude[ru:d] 쭹 무례한

문제 해설

Q: 언제 남자는 자신의 직업이 만족스럽지 않은가?
   ① 동물들을 치료할 수 없을 때
   ② 동물들이 나쁘게 행동할 때
   ③ 무례한 손님들을 만날 때
   ④ 오랜 시간 일을 해야 할 때
동물들이 아파도 도와줄 수 없을 때 슬프다고 했다.

7

W: To become a bungee jumpmaster, you should have certain qualities. Bungee jumping is a dangerous sport. To help people do it safely, you must get enough training. Also, you must be brave, because you will work in very high places. And you should be very friendly to the bungee jumpers.

여: 번지점프 마스터가 되기 위해서는 특정한 자질을 갖추어야 해요. 번지점프는 위험한 스포츠죠. 사람들이 그것을 안전하게 하도록 도우려면 여러분은 충분한 훈련을 받아야 합니다. 또한, 매우 높은 곳에서 일하게 되므로 용감해

야 해요. 그리고 번지점프를 하는 사람들에게 아주 친절해야 하죠.

어휘

bungee jumpmaster 번지점프 마스터   certain
[sə́:rtən] 쭹 확실한; *특정한   quality[kwɑ́ləti] 똉 자질
bungee jumping 번지점프   dangerous[déindʒərəs]
쭹 위험한   safely[séifli] 봄 안전하게   training[tréiniŋ]
똉 훈련   brave[breiv] 쭹 용감한   [문제]
bungee-jump[bʌ́ndʒi:dʒʌ̀mp] 됭 번지점프하다
difficulty[dífəkʌ̀lti] 똉 어려움

문제 해설

Q: 여자는 주로 무엇에 대해 이야기하고 있는가?
   ① 번지점프를 안전하게 하는 방법
   ② 번지점프 마스터가 하는 일
   ③ 번지점프 마스터로서의 어려움
   ④ 번지점프 마스터에게 필요한 자질들
여자는 번지점프 마스터가 되기 위해 갖추어야 할 자질들에 대해 이야기하고 있다.

8

M: I used to be a basketball player. But I got hurt, so I stopped playing basketball. I started selling shoes at a store instead. One day, I met a movie director in the store. We became friends, and, with his help, I got an audition and became an actor.

남: 나는 농구 선수였어. 하지만 나는 다쳐서 농구를 그만두었어. 대신에 가게에서 신발을 팔기 시작했어. 어느 날, 나는 가게에서 영화 감독을 만났어. 우리는 친구가 되었고, 그의 도움으로 나는 오디션을 보고 배우가 되었어.

어휘

used to-v 이전에는 ~이었다   basketball[bǽskitbɔ̀:l]
똉 농구   player[pléiər] 똉 선수   movie director 영
화 감독   audition[ɔ:díʃən] 똉 오디션   [문제] sales
clerk 판매원

문제 해설

Q: 남자가 가졌던 직업을 순서대로 고르시오.
   남자는 농구 선수로 활동하다가 다쳐서 신발 가게 점원으로 일했고, 이후 배우가 되었다.

Listening ★ Challenge   p. 78

A 1 ② 2 ③   B 1 ② 2 ①

A [1-2]

W: Hello, Mr. Wilson. I'm Anna from *No.1 Magazine.*

M: Nice to meet you, Anna.

W: Let's talk about this fashion show. Where did you get the ideas for your new designs?

M: I got my ideas from the letters of Asian languages.

W: Letters?

M: Yes, I used Chinese, Korean, and Japanese letters.

W: Wow, you tried something new. I'm sure that wasn't easy.

M: No, it wasn't. It was difficult for me to learn Asian letters.

W: I guess so. They are very different from English.

여: 안녕하세요, Wilson 씨. 저는 〈No.1 Magazine〉의 Anna 입니다.

남: 만나서 반가워요, Anna 씨.

여: 이 패션쇼에 대해서 얘기해 봅시다. 새로운 디자인에 대한 아이디어를 어디서 얻었나요?

남: 저는 아시아 언어들의 글자들에서 아이디어를 얻었어요.

여: 글자요?

남: 네, 저는 중국어와 한국어, 일본어의 글자를 사용했어요.

여: 우와, 당신은 뭔가 새로운 것을 시도했군요. 분명 쉽지 않았을 것 같은데요.

남: 네, 쉽지 않았죠. 제가 아시아 언어의 글자들을 배우는 건 힘들었어요.

여: 그럴 것 같아요. 영어와 아주 다르니까요.

어휘

magazine[mǽɡəziːn] 명 잡지 design[dizáin] 명 디자인 letter[létər] 명 글자 Asian[éiʒən] 형 아시아의 language[lǽŋgwidʒ] 명 언어 Japanese[dʒæpəníːz] 형 일본의 learn[ləːrn] 동 배우다 [문제] reporter [ripɔ́ːrtər] 명 기자 photographer[fətágrəfər] 명 사진작가 condition[kəndíʃən] 명 (건강) 상태 alphabet [ǽlfəbèt] 명 알파벳

문제 해설

Q1: 화자 간의 관계는?

잡지사에서 온 여기자가 패션 디자이너인 남자를 인터뷰하는 상황이다.

Q2: 남자가 자신의 작품을 준비하는 게 힘들었던 이유는?

① 그는 몸 상태가 좋지 않았다.

② 그는 돈이 충분히 없었다.

③ 그는 아시아 언어의 글자들을 쉽게 배울 수 없었다.

④ 그는 세계 각지에서 온 사람들과 일했다.

남자는 아시아 언어들의 글자를 배우는 일이 힘들었다고 했다.

B [1-2]

W: Do you want to become a home shopping host? Our new project, "Dream with Us" will be a good chance. In this project, we'll ask you to do various tasks for one month. The winner will get a chance to work at Victory Home Shopping. Any woman under 40 can apply. Please send us an email before March 12th.

여: 홈쇼핑 진행자가 되고 싶나요? 저희의 새로운 프로젝트인 'Dream with Us'가 좋은 기회가 될 것입니다. 이번 프로젝트에서 저희는 한 달 동안 여러분이 여러 과제를 하도록 할 것입니다. 우승자는 Victory 홈쇼핑에서 일할 기회를 얻게 될 것입니다. 40세 미만의 여성은 누구든지 지원하실 수 있습니다. 3월 12일 전까지 저희에게 이메일을 보내주세요.

어휘

home shopping 홈쇼핑 host[houst] 명 진행자, 사회자 project[prádʒekt] 명 기획, 프로젝트 chance [tʃæns] 명 기회 task[tæsk] 명 과제 winner[wínər] 명 우승자 apply[əplái] 동 지원하다 [문제] advertisement[ædvərtáizmənt] 명 광고

문제 해설

Q1: 이 광고에 적합한 사람은?

① Julie: 저는 새로운 TV 프로그램에 대한 아이디어가 있어요!

② Helen: 저는 홈쇼핑 진행자가 되고 싶어요!

③ Marie: 저는 홈쇼핑 회사에서 일해요!

④ Sally: 저는 Victory 홈쇼핑에서 물건을 샀어요!

광고에서 소개하는 프로젝트에서 우승한 사람은 홈쇼핑 진행자가 될 수 있는 기회를 얻게 될 것이므로 홈쇼핑 진행자가 되길 원하는 사람에게 적합하다.

Q2: 이 광고에 의하면, 사실이 아닌 것은?

① 우승자는 많은 돈을 탈 것이다.

② 여성만 지원할 수 있다.

③ 40세 미만인 사람만 지원할 수 있다.

④ 이메일은 3월 12일 전에 보내야 한다.

우승한 사람은 홈쇼핑 회사에서 일할 기회를 얻게 될 것이라고 했다.

Critical ★ Thinking　p. 79

1 (1) T (2) F (3) T　2 ①, ④

M: I want to be a famous singer. I practice singing and dancing every day with my friends. If I'm lucky, I'll become a star like my favorite singer, Justin Timberlake. The lives of stars are really nice. They earn a lot of money easily. So, they have amazing houses, cars and clothes. Also, they meet many other stars and become friends with them. How wonderful!

남: 나는 유명한 가수가 되고 싶어. 나는 매일 친구들과 노래와 춤 연습을 해. 만일 운이 좋다면 나는 내가 가장 좋아하는 가수인 Justin Timberlake와 같은 스타가 될 거야. 스타들의 삶은 아주 멋져. 그들은 돈도 쉽게 많이 벌어. 그래서 그들은 멋진 집과 차와 옷을 가지고 있어. 게다가 그들은 다른 스타들도 많이 만나고 그들과 친구가 되지. 얼마나 멋져!

어휘
lucky[lʌ́ki] 형 운이 좋은　star[stɑːr] 명 별; *인기 스타
earn[əːrn] 동 벌다　amazing[əméiziŋ] 형 놀라운, 멋진　wonderful[wʌ́ndərfəl] 형 멋진　[문제] for free 무료로

문제 해설
Q1: 사실이면 T, 사실이 아니면 F에 √표 하시오.
　(1) 그는 매일 춤 연습을 한다.
　(2) 그의 친구들 중 한 명은 유명한 가수가 되었다.
　(3) 그는 Justin Timberlake를 가장 좋아한다.
Q2: 스타에 대한 남자의 두 가지 의견을 고르시오.
　① 그들은 돈을 쉽게 번다.
　② 그들은 세계 곳곳을 여행할 수 있다.
　③ 그들은 비싼 옷을 무료로 얻을 수 있다.
　④ 그들은 유명한 친구들이 많다.
　남자는 스타가 돈도 쉽게 많이 벌고, 다른 스타들과도 친구가 된다고 생각한다.

JUNIOR
LISTENING EXPERT

Level 1